Lift Up Your Hearts

Homilies and Reflections
for the "C" Cycle

James A. Wallace, CSsR
Robert P. Waznak, SS
Guerric DeBona, OSB

Paulist Press
New York/Mahwah, N.J.

Cover design by Sharyn Banks
Book design by Lynn Else

Library of Congress Cataloging-in-Publication Data

Wallace, James A., 1944-
  Lift up your hearts : homilies for the "C" cycle / James A. Wallace, Robert P. Wanak, and Guerric DeBona.
    p. cm.
  ISBN 0-8091-4410-7 (alk. paper)
    1. Church year sermons. 2. Catholic Church—Sermons. 3. Sermons, American.
1. Waznak, Robert P. II. DeBona, Guerric, 1955–. III. Title.
  BX1756.A2W35 2004
  252'.6—dc22

                                                        2004011443

Published by Paulist Press
997 Macarthur Boulevard
Mahwah, New Jersey 07430

www.paulistpress.com

Printed and bound in the
United States of America

Contents

Introduction vii

ADVENT

You're Going to Make It: First Sunday of Advent...............................3

God's a Comin': Today as Well as Yesterday, Now as Well as
    Tomorrow: Second Sunday of Advent 8

'Tis the Season to Be Schizophrenic: Third Sunday of Advent............12

Not Angels but People—of God: Fourth Sunday of Advent..............16

CHRISTMAS

Wanted: Shepherds and Angels: Christmas, Mass at Midnight...........23

God's Family: The Nativity of the Lord (Mass at Day).....................29

It Takes a Family... The Holy Family of Jesus, Mary, and Joseph 34

The Voice That Is Great Within Us: The Solemnity of the
    Blessed Virgin Mary, Mother of God....................................42

Could *That* Be an Epiphany?: The Epiphany of the Lord 47

Beloved and Well-Pleasing to God: The Baptism of the Lord............53

LENT

Lent, Season of Love: First Sunday of Lent 63

Transforming Word: Second Sunday of Lent.....................................68

Our Lenten Hope: Third Sunday of Lent 72

'Til by Turning, Turning, We Come Round Right:
    Fourth Sunday of Lent...76

Keeping Score: Fifth Sunday of Lent 82

Meeting Jesus in Luke's Passion: Palm Sunday of the
    Lord's Passion..87

EASTER

The First Easter Parade: Easter Sunday 95

From Fear to Faith: Second Sunday of Easter 101

An Easter Witness Speaks: Third Sunday of Easter 105

His Master's Voice: Fourth Sunday of Easter 111

How to Be More Than Nice on Mother's Day:
    Fifth Sunday of Easter 116

Do We Really Need More Lawyers in the Church?:
    Sixth Sunday of Easter..120

Depth, Not Distance: The Ascension of the Lord...........................124

First Steps: Seventh Sunday of Easter.....................................129

A New Pentecost: Pentecost Sunday..133

ORDINARY TIME

[See Beloved and Well-Pleasing to God: The Baptism of the Lord]:
    First Sunday in Ordinary Time 53

Little Resolutions and Big Changes: Second Sunday in
    Ordinary Time...141

A Light in the Darkness: Third Sunday in Ordinary Time 145

Not Following Sensitivity Guidelines: Fourth Sunday in
    Ordinary Time...150

When the "B Team" Is the Better Team: Fifth Sunday in
    Ordinary Time...155

Blessed Are You Whose Hearts Are Loving: Sixth Sunday in
    Ordinary Time...162

The Logic of Redemption: Seventh Sunday in Ordinary Time 168

Heart Storage: Eighth Sunday in Ordinary Time............................175

Faith Seeking Healing: Ninth Sunday in Ordinary Time 180

I'll Meet You at the Gate: Tenth Sunday in Ordinary Time.............186

Tears in the House of Love: Eleventh Sunday in Ordinary Time......190

Nomination Brings Obligation: Twelfth Sunday in
    Ordinary Time...195

What Freedom Do We Celebrate This Fourth of July?:
    Thirteenth Sunday in Ordinary Time..............................200

On Not Glossing Over the Healing: Fourteenth Sunday in
    Ordinary Time...205

Graced Hospitality: Fifteenth Sunday in Ordinary Time 210

Setting the Record Straight: Sixteenth Sunday in Ordinary Time 215

It All Depends on Friendship: Seventeenth Sunday in
    Ordinary Time 221
The Clock's Ticking: Eighteenth Sunday in Ordinary Time 226
Watchwords: Nineteenth Sunday in Ordinary Time 232
A Faith on Fire: Twentieth Sunday in Ordinary Time 237
On Saying Goodbye: Twenty-First Sunday in Ordinary Time 242
What God Means by Humility: Twenty-Second Sunday in
    Ordinary Time 246
True Discipleship: Twenty-Third Sunday in Ordinary Time 250
No "Idol-ing," Please: Twenty-Fourth Sunday in Ordinary Time 255
WWJS?: Twenty-Fifth Sunday in Ordinary Time 261
Mind the Gap: Twenty-Sixth Sunday in Ordinary Time..................268
Rethinking Faith: Twenty-Seventh Sunday in Ordinary Time..........274
After 9/11: Are the Clouds Really White?: Twenty-Eighth
    Sunday in Ordinary Time 279
Our Lady of Consistency: Twenty-Ninth Sunday in
    Ordinary Time 285
The Problem with Religion: Thirtieth Sunday in Ordinary Time 290
A Graceful Descent: Thirty-First Sunday in Ordinary Time 295
This Side of the Grave: Thirty-Second Sunday in Ordinary Time.....301
The Bottom Line: Thirty-Third Sunday in Ordinary Time 305

FEASTS
    It's Raining, It's Pouring: The Solemnity of the Most Holy Trinity ..313
    The Sign of the Kingdom: The Solemnity of the Most Holy Body
        and Blood of Christ 319
    God Does the Heavy Lifting: The Assumption of the
        Blessed Virgin Mary 324
    In the Gutter Gazing at the Stars: The Solemnity of All Saints.........329
    The Lady of the Harbor: The Immaculate Conception 333
    Christ Alone Is King: The Solemnity of Our Lord
        Jesus Christ the King 337

*To our preaching students, past, present, and future
and to the parishioners of Holy Trinity Parish,
Georgetown, Washington, DC*

Introduction

A homily is not meant to stick around. By its nature it is a sound experience, something carried by the human voice to the ears of listeners only for the moment. It is the ultimate disposable commodity, present only in the hearing, then gone, like the early morning fog that burns off so quickly under the sun's heat—a comparison that might have more similarities with preaching than most preachers would like to admit. However, when a homily achieves its purpose, it manages to make the journey from the mind and heart of one person to the minds and hearts of those who have surrendered themselves to the profoundly human act of attentive listening. More important, when it has met its goal, it has managed to give expression to the faith of the community in such a way that this community is moved to celebrate the Eucharist.

To put homilies into a book is to freeze-dry them. The sound of a living person speaking is not there; neither are the face, gestures, passion, conviction, emotional changes, and all those other hard-to-define characteristics and qualities that make up an experience of listening to a preacher. Even so, our hope is that something of the life with which these homilies were first spoken has lingered, caught in the interstices of words, punctuation, and silence. We hope that these homilies may still bring a message that may speak to a listener, whether that person is a preacher or not. And so, we offer the third and final cycle of homilies for the "C" Cycle in the Sunday Lectionary.

The homilies contained in this book, like those contained in the previous two volumes for the "A" and "B" cycles, are rooted in a particular understanding of the homily. This understanding is found expressed in a document published almost twenty-five years ago. *Fulfilled in Your Hearing: The Homily in the Sunday Assembly* states that the homily is to be "a scriptural interpretation of human existence that enables a community to recognize God's active presence, to respond to that presence in faith through liturgical word and gesture and through a life lived in conformity with the gospel."* The homily, then, is to offer a scriptural understanding of some aspect of human existence that touches the life of the community of faith, moving its members both to an awareness of the living God, active and present in our world, and to a response to this God who was fully revealed in Jesus Christ. This response is intended to be twofold, finding expression in both liturgy and life; that is, expressed in giving praise and thanks within the setting of a particular act of worship, and then embodied and enfleshed in some way when the community leaves this holy place of worship to return more firmly committed to living out the life of a disciple of Jesus, our crucified and risen Lord.

We hope that these homilies for the "C" Cycle prove helpful not only to preachers but also to listeners. They are not intended as a substitute for any preacher's personal preparation but as a complement to the efforts of preachers and as a supplement to listeners still hungry for further understanding of the Sunday readings and how these might relate to life. These homilies are the efforts of three men who are both preachers and teachers of preaching and who hope that their work reflects the spirit and understanding of the homily found in the liturgical documents of Vatican II and thereafter, especially in the document already mentioned, *Fulfilled In Your Hearing*, which is a unique contribution of Catholic scholarship to preaching in the United States. We hold this particular document in great regard for its theological, liturgical, and especially its pastoral understanding of what the homily is and what it can do for a worshiping community.

At the heart of the "C" Cycle is the Gospel of Luke, probably written between 80 and 85 by a gifted storyteller. For Luke, Jesus is the Lord, the prophet like Moses, God's embodied message/messenger of mercy and costly love, and especially the savior sent to redeem all humankind. Luke's unique perspective on Jesus, the prophet who is impelled by the Spirit of God from the Jordan to the desert to the land of Galilee and finally to death and resurrection in Jerusalem, provides the final perspective on Jesus from the Synoptic tradition.

---

* Bishop's Committee on Priestly Life and Ministry, National Conference of Catholic Bishops, *Fulfilled in Your Hearing: The Homily in the Sunday Assembly* (Washington, DC: USCCB, 1982), 29.

In Luke's Gospel, Jesus is the one who finds his identity in the words of Isaiah the prophet: "The Spirit of the Lord is upon me, because he has anointed me to bring glad tidings to the poor. He has sent me to proclaim liberty to captives and recovery of sight to the blind, to let the oppressed go free, and to proclaim a year acceptable to the Lord" (cf. Luke 4:16ff.). Luke's Jesus draws our attention to the plight of the poor, to prayer, and to the power of the Spirit of God at work. For Luke, the work of Jesus began in Galilee, moved on to Jerusalem, then spread from there to the ends of the earth through his disciples, bringing about a universal church dedicated to carrying out the ministry of this Jesus, now recognized as risen Lord and Savior of the world. You must, of course, read both Luke and Acts of the Apostles to get the full story.

During this cycle we hear stories and parables found only in the third Gospel. Luke gives us such unique and memorable stories as the raising of the son of the widow of Nain (Tenth Sunday), the good Samaritan (Fifteenth Sunday), Martha and Mary (Sixteenth Sunday), the rich man and his barns (Eighteenth Sunday), the prodigal son (Twenty-Fourth Sunday), the rich man and Lazarus (Twenty-Sixth Sunday), the ten lepers (Twenty-Eighth Sunday), the widow and the judge (Twenty-Ninth Sunday), the Pharisee and the tax collector who went up to pray (Thirtieth Sunday), Zacchaeus the tax collector (Thirty-First Sunday), and the good thief (Christ the King). He also gives us two unique Easter stories, but they are not heard during this cycle: the disciples on the road to Emmaus (Third Sunday of Easter, "A" Cycle) and the story of Jesus providing a post-resurrection morning fish fry (Third Sunday of Easter, "B" Cycle).

Luke was writing well after the time of the historical Jesus, and so the early Christian community found itself facing issues not unlike our own. Indeed, we can trace our cultural contours in the face of the good Samaritan to find the charity that must be extended to all people in a pluralistic society. We can see the invitation to live simply in the modern world without the need for material goods in Jesus' invitation to the little rich man, Zacchaeus, to dine with him. And we can know the forgiveness that must reach fractured families in our day in the parable of the prodigal son. Luke's Gospel is as contemporary as it ever was because God's Word is ever new and ever present.

With this volume we come to an end to what can be simply described as a labor of love. Contained here are the final examples of the preaching of the late Robert P. Waznak, SS, a gifted teacher of preaching at the Washington Theological Union in Washington, DC, and superb homilist, who died of cancer in 2002. Bob and I began to think about doing a book of our homilies in 2000. Due to his untimely death in December 2002, the project was put on hold. Fortunately, Benedictine preacher and homiletic scholar Guerric DeBona was willing to join me in this project so we could bring it to completion. Without him, there would not have been three volumes of *Lift Up Your Hearts*. I remain greatly indebted to his generous spirit.

A word of gratitude also must be expressed to Ms. Margaret Costello, who has provided the stimulating "Questions for Reflection" and offered perceptive "Other Directions for Preaching" for the homilies of Robert Waznak. Margaret earned a M.Div. at the Washington Theological Union while serving as the director of liturgy at Holy Trinity parish in Georgetown, Washington, DC. She has also been a co-presenter at summer preaching workshops offered at the Washington Theological Union. Finally, a word of appreciation to the editorial staff at Paulist Press, especially Paul McMahon, who has graciously presided over this project from its inception, and Nancy de Flon, whose collaborative spirit, generous support, and sense of humor have been a cherished part of preparing this final volume.

The work of preaching the Gospel is never finished. The ways of giving expression to the gospel message will never be exhausted. All of our efforts, in retrospect, seem like so much straw, to be blown away by the wind of new experiences and new challenges to bringing God's Word to coming generations. Yet we must continue to make this effort, confident in the ongoing help of the Spirit, because from the beginning God called men and women to be heralds of the Good News. It is both burden and joy, and it is to be done with fidelity and humility. We hope our efforts here might be of some little help in this ongoing work that combines divine grace with human effort to speak a word that renews and redeems.

James A. Wallace, CSsR
September 13, 2005

ADVENT

You're Going to Make It
FIRST SUNDAY OF ADVENT

READINGS:
Jeremiah 33:14–16; 1 Thessalonians 3:12—4:2;
Luke 21:25–28, 34–36

When Ed Koch was the mayor of New York City

he used to say that the most spiritual experience he had was when he

attended the Catholic funerals of city policemen and firemen.

When a reporter asked him why that was so, he said,

"It was that hymn they always sang that lifted my spirits:

'Be Not Afraid.'"

Throughout the Scriptures, God is telling us over and over again:

"Be not afraid."

Scholars call this special form of speech in the Bible a "salvation oracle."

In other words, into the midst of desperate and fearful situations,

God's presence springs abruptly.

God's "Fear not" is an amazing announcement that the situation is not

what we thought it was because God is present where we thought

God would never be.

"Fear not!" God tells Abraham. "I am your shield" (Gen 15:1).

"Fear not," God tells Isaiah. "I have called you by name: you are mine"

(Isa 43:1).

"Do not be afraid," the angels tell the shepherds. "For today in the city of
     David a savior has been born for you who is Messiah and Lord"
     (Luke 2:10–11).
"Do not be afraid!" the Easter angel proclaims,
     "I know that you are seeking Jesus the crucified.
     He is not here, for he has been raised just as he said" (Matt 28:5–6).

On this First Sunday of Advent, Jesus knows his disciples are afraid.
In Luke's Gospel Jesus speaks these words of the end time just before his
     own end time, which was to take place in a fearful place indeed, the
     place of the skull, Golgotha.
And so Jesus knows something about the fear and dread that grip our souls.
Of the four evangelists, Luke wrote the best Greek because he probably was
     a Greek.
The Greek word he uses for the fear that people will have is imaginative.
It means that it will literally cause some people to die.
That's what fear can do to you, if you allow it.

Today we begin Advent, the church's lovely season of quiet and peace
     that precedes the coming of Jesus the Christ at Christmas
     and the coming of the King of kings at the end of the world.
But as all of us know, there are many people, events, and things that will
     rob us of our Advent waiting,
     that will fuel our anxieties and fears,
     that will bloat us with indulgence, drunkenness, and worldly cares.
The church calls it Advent.
But we know it as the Christmas rush.
The Catholic theologian and storyteller John Shea captures the reality of
     what most people feel at this time of year, in his wonderful book
     Starlight: Beholding the Christmas Miracle All Year Long, in a story
     about a parking lot encounter:
It was in the parking lot of the Jewel Food Store three days before Christmas.
A woman was moving bags of groceries out of a cart and into the trunk of
     her car.

She was muttering over and over to herself,
> "I'm not going to make it. I'm not going to make it."

As John passed her, he smiled and said, "You're going to make it. You're
> going to make it."

The woman's head came out of the trunk, along with a look that said,
> "What the hell do you know, fella," and she firmly repeated, "I'm not
> going to make it."

Taking the correction, John trudged into the store.
The "Under Ten" check-out line had twenty people in it.
He wondered if he was going to make it.*

What is the "it" we are afraid of as we begin this charming yet dangerous
> season?

It can mean getting everything done.
It can mean just surviving the season, the office party, the demanding
> relative, church officials, avoiding a breakdown, or the most modest
> ambition of not yelling at fellow motorists, salespeople, postal
> workers, and, most impossible of all, your own children.

"I'm not going to make it" might mean we fear that we will never get into
> the Christmas spirit; that somehow, Christmas is going to happen, but
> it's not going to happen to us.

Today's Gospel does not deny the fears of our lives, including our Advent
> fears; it simply tells us how to deal with them.

Jesus tells us to watch, to pray, and not to allow the season's cares
> to entrap us.

Somehow, in the midst of trying to make it, each of us has to learn to be
> imaginative
> in how we watch, how we pray, how we not overindulge.

There was a clip on CBS evening news the other night about the nine
> high-tech toys that are the rage this Christmas.

---

*John Shea, *Starlight: Beholding the Christmas Miracle All Year Long* (New York: Crossroad, 1992), 19.

The toys do just about everything because of the marvels of computers.
A reporter asked the toy manufacturer, "But doesn't this take away the
     imagination that kids are supposed to have when they play?"
"Oh, no," came the response. "They actually stimulate imagination."
I sat there and thought, "What a crock of cranberries."
Imagination is not something someone can manufacture for us
     but something we ourselves must find.

I remember walking down a street in a very poor neighborhood in São
     Paulo, Brazil.
Out of nowhere, a little boy appeared with his head sticking through a large
     cardboard box.
But to him, this was not a cardboard box bumping down a smelly dirt street.
It was a jet plane soaring through the clouds with great power and glory.
I will never forget his transfixed face.
In fact, whenever I hear or read the word *imagination,* I always think of him.

Yes, we all need to take the words of Jesus to heart this Advent:
     to watch, to pray, not to overindulge.
But we must do all this in new ways, in more imaginative ways
     so that we can turn this season of fear into a season of hope.
The Lord is coming indeed, in ways we could never imagine.
We are going to make it.

RPW

Questions for Reflection

1. As followers of Jesus, the "just shoot" of David, what could it mean for us "to do what is right and just in the land"?

2. How is doing what is right and just connected to being safe and dwelling in security?

3. What are the "signs of the times" saying to us this Advent? What nations are in anguish?

Other Directions for Preaching

1. This is the time when we begin to think about sending out Christmas cards, extending our wishes for Christmas blessings to those we love. In his letter to the Thessalonians, Paul is extending his wishes for them—that their hearts may be strengthened in holiness.

2. Apocalyptic readings alert us to God breaking into human history. Today's Gospel alerts us that our salvation is close at hand. If we are living as just and righteous people, we can stand with our heads held high in anticipation of "the great day."

God's a Comin':
Today as Well as Yesterday,
Now as Well as Tomorrow
SECOND SUNDAY OF ADVENT

READINGS:
Baruch 5:1–9; Philippians 1:4–6, 8–11; Luke 3:1–6

Advent gives us images that help us move into the celebration of Christmas.
The season begins by reminding us that Jesus, the risen Lord, is coming back
    and we wait on him with patient endurance.
This is the emphasis as we begin every Advent; the focus on what happened
    the first Christmas only comes at the end of Advent.
We are called to live in hope of Jesus' return because he told us so,
    and he is trustworthy.

During these middle Sundays of the season John the Baptist emerges as the
    primary figure, with his call to turn to God, to repent, for the
    kingdom is at hand.
These Sundays remind us that Christ continues to come, even now.
He comes to us in the everyday events of life.
He comes today as well as yesterday, now as well as tomorrow.

The Book of Baruch was written for a people who had grown tired of
    waiting on God's coming to save them.
They were a people who had been taken into exile, uprooted from their
    land.

This passage from the book speaks a message of consolation and hope.

A voice calls to Mother Jerusalem, weeping over her children,
  children snatched from her arms, some killed, others taken off to a
  foreign land.

The voice rings out: Change your clothes! Take off the robes of mourning
  and misery. Put on the cloak of justice; wear the crown that shows the
  glory of God's name. Watch, for your children are coming home. Look
  to the east. God is bringing them back.

The author of this book was giving his listeners, a people scattered far from
  home, a word to carry them into the future.

Luke, writing for a community of Gentile Christians, is also giving hope.

At a time when Rome held all power, when Rome's heel was on Israel's
  neck, God's Word came bellowing forth from the desolate wilderness.

John was God's trumpet blast, calling the people to be washed in the waters
  of repentance, turning to God for the forgiveness of their sins.

John was the embodiment of one of whom the prophet Isaiah had spoken:
  the voice proclaiming that God was coming, that all flesh would see
  God's salvation.

God not only came in the past, and is not only to come in the future—God
  was coming now.

Advent gives us images to remind us that such has been and continues
  to be the case.

Our God continues to come to us in ways that are mysterious.

God comes to us, brings us together, even in conditions of great sorrow,
  and sometimes in most unexpected ways.

A few weeks ago I heard an interview on National Public Radio with a man
  who had been held in a Nazi concentration camp.

The interviewer asked, "Were there ever any happy times there?"

There was a long pause, then the man said,
  "Not happy times...but there were some beautiful moments."

He paused again, then said, "This will sound very strange to you, but these
   happened at some of the worst moments. There were those dreadful
   times when a woman would lose a child, and the other women would
   gather around and sing the songs of their land.
We men would hear the singing and know that a child had died,
   but there was a deep beauty in the singing, in that effort to comfort.
And during those days when I was there, I was only sixteen,
   and I was so cold.
Often the clothes we wore became mere strips of cloth, barely holding
   together.
An older man noticed me shivering one day, and he said,
   'Don't worry. We will warm you.'
And he and others put their bodies around me and held me gently,
   enfolding me in the warmth of their own nakedness."

In the midst of great horror and sadness, the presence of God comes,
   moving people toward one another.
The movement of those women toward a grieving mother,
   and the movement of the men toward a shivering boy—
   both were movements of life, nurturing life in the moment.
And in those moments God moved among the people,
   bringing them together in grief and sorrow, in need and desperation,
   in a communion of the helpless, through each other, God was
   embracing them.

God moves among us these days, bringing to completion the work begun at
   baptism.
In the midst of the horrors of our time—the wars, the fatal accidents, the
   out-of-season illnesses, the famines, the bombings, the unnecessary
   deaths—we can still find the presence of the Spirit of God,
   moving through the actions of those reaching out in compassion
   and care.

Today we came to this holy place to see God move.
The Spirit of God moves among us,
>turning print on the page into the living Word of God,
>changing bread and wine into the Body and Blood of Christ,
>transforming us into the Body of Christ sent out into the world.

JAW

Questions for Reflection

1. Have you known that movement of God in your life that has brought people together, returning them "home" in some way?

2. What events happening in our world today speak of the God who comes to us unexpectedly? What speaks of our need for God to come?

3. What do you most hope for? Is that part of your prayer?

Other Directions for Preaching

1. Both Baruch and Luke have taken from Isaiah the theme of God leading the people back home. God commands us to level the road, fill in the gaps, make a path for God to travel. Consider what needs to be filled in, what needs to be straightened, so others will know God is with us.

2. Paul's joyful praise of his beloved Philippians for their collaboration with him invites us to consider how leaders and people presently work "in partnership for the gospel." Paul's prayer is our prayer: complete the good work that has begun in Christ and increase our love in knowledge and insight so as to "discern what is of value."

'Tis the Season
to Be Schizophrenic
THIRD SUNDAY OF ADVENT

READINGS:
Zephaniah 3:14–18a; Philippians 4:4–7; Luke 3:10–18

Even though 'tis the season to be jolly,
> physicians tell us there are more cases of depression and cardiac arrest
> now than any other time of the year.

Many speculate on the reasons for this startling statistic:
> anxiety, the added burdens of shopping and preparation,
> the excessive drinking of "Christmas cheer."

But I wonder if there's another reason.

Maybe it's the clashing of moods that causes people
> to drink, eat, and worry too much.

'Tis the season to be schizophrenic.

The clashing images tend to confuse us: commercials of happy families
> enjoying lots of gifts and holiday goodies—but then we're confronted
> with the hollowed, ancient faces of starving children in Africa.

The season bids us to lighten up and go to the mall to buy gifts—
> but the sagging economy tells us to hold back and be somber and
> serious about choices.

The season centers on the joys of being with family—
> but many people have lost loved ones this past year; many live alone
> or are estranged from families that have caused more pain than joy.

I wonder if somehow these clashing moods of Advent eventually wear us
    down and cause us to wonder in our hearts, what exactly is going on?

Even when we come to church this time of year we still can't escape the
    clashing of moods.
Today's Scriptures seem to tell us to be both joyful *and* serious.
There's a reason for this apparent schizophrenia in our Advent liturgy.
It has to do with its complex history.

The first place in the world where Advent was celebrated was in fifth-
    century Gaul.
The folks in that part of the world celebrated Advent as a time of
    repentance and change
      in preparation for the great feast of Christmas.
But not everyone in the world celebrated Advent in that serious and
    penitential way.
For the church in Rome at that time, Advent was a festive and joyful time
    of preparation for the feast of Christmas.
There were no purple colors and grim moods,
    no long days of fasting and calls for repentance.

After a few centuries of debate
    the church finally combined both the tradition of joy
    and the tradition of repentance into the celebration of Advent.
That's why the candle we lit on our Advent wreath today is rose in color.
It's a souvenir of the joyful old Roman tradition of Advent
    amid the purple tradition of penance of the church in Gaul.
In the midst of a serious season for a change of heart
    we celebrate *Gaudete* or Joyful Sunday.

But the central character of today's Gospel, John the Baptist,
    is anything but joyful.
At least that's the way preachers and teachers have traditionally
    portrayed him.

We have in our minds the image of a wild man,
   an overly serious religious crusader who preached fire and brimstone
   every time, and struck fear even into the hearts of tax collectors and
   soldiers.
We have the image of a man whose face never lit up with joy.

It's true that John had a serious message to preach:
   people had to change their ways because they had forgotten
 · who they were and what God expected of them.
People like the tax collectors who lined their pockets by taxing the poor
   above and beyond what was demanded by the law;
People like the soldiers who were the bodyguards of the tax collectors
   who used brute force to bully and threaten the people.
John the Baptist said to these and to all who flocked to hear him,
   "Enough is enough.
   "It's time to change your lives and the way you relate to one another."

But, somehow, I believe there was another side to John.
Yes, it's true that it was his lot in life to have people
   face the pitiful facts of their lives and world.
But remember, he was the same John who danced with joy
   in his mother Elizabeth's womb at the visit of the mother of Jesus.
And I simply cannot image a grim John
   the day he spotted the one mightier than he
   walking toward him along the banks of the river Jordan.
When he yelled out, "Behold, the Lamb of God who takes away the sins of
   the world," I bet you his craggy old desert face burst forth with a
   stupendous smile of joy.

The two sides of John the Baptist, repentance and joy,
   remind us that there is a cure to the schizophrenia of this season.
It lies in our ability to make some real changes in our lives
   in the way we relate to people,
   in the way we do our work and relax our bodies,

in the way we share our possessions,
in the way we trust in God.

John the Baptist shouts out to us today,
  "The cure to the schizophrenia of your Advent season is how you face
  up to the needed changes in your lives before you find your joy in the
  Lord."

RPW

Questions for Reflection

1. How does John the Baptist speak to your life this Advent?
2. Can you think of one aspect of your life where change would lead to
a deeper joy?
3. What specific steps can you take to bring about this change?

Other Directions for Preaching

1. Zephaniah's words proclaim the God of Israel as one who is "in your
midst, a mighty savior." The prophet places the cause of our joy in God who
renews us "in his love"; God is indeed Emmanuel.

2. Paul's words to the Philippians remind us that our joy is not a matter
of our own efforts. Anxiety can lose its power when we turn to God in prayer
and petition, making our requests known to God. "Then the peace of God
that surpasses all understanding will guard your hearts and minds in Christ
Jesus."

3. John expected the one coming to "gather the wheat into his barn, but
the chaff he will burn with unquenchable fire." How does this compare with
the One who did come?

Not Angels but People—
of God
FOURTH SUNDAY OF ADVENT

READINGS:
Micah 5:1–4a; Hebrews 10:5–10; Luke 1:39–45

This lovely season of the year is made for stories:
> stories that move the heart and help us know what we are waiting for
> this Christmas.

Of course, not all the stories of the season capture the mystery of the
> Incarnation.

Some are just downright dumb.

The holiday television season began last month with a ditsy story of a dead
> woman training for angel wings by helping a young family cope with
> the loss of their mother.

The woman in training was Dolly Parton.

The show ended with her singing Handel's "Hallelujah Chorus,"
> fluttering her new wings, along with a heavenly choir.

The problem with such stories is that they seem to rob their characters of
> their humanity.

They are so heavenly, so unlike us that they seem as unreal as an artificial
> Christmas tree.

The stories of the Bible that we have been hearing this Advent are not TV
> schmaltz.

They *are* wondrous stories, but the principal characters in them never lose
     their humanity.
They are in many ways like us: wondering, anticipating, fearful, hoping.
The great prophet who leaped in his mother's womb in the presence of Jesus
     is human, like us.
John preached somber justice and pictured God as a mean thresher of grain
     or someone
     who threw into the fire every tree that wasn't perfect.
But when the Messiah did come, he preached a forgiving and loving God
     as a host of a marvelous party or a father who can't bring himself to
     throw his children out even when they dishonor and abandon him.
Jesus called John the greatest of all the prophets, but even John wasn't
     perfect in his vision of God and the world.
He was human like us.

We must not miss the divine images and message in today's Advent Gospel,
     but we must also not miss the human.
There is Zechariah, Elizabeth's husband, who says nothing in today's story.
That's because he was struck dumb when he found it hard to accept the
     angel's message that his elderly, barren wife would soon conceive.
I know that it comes as a great shock to the Catholics who are actively
     protesting the TV series *Nothing Sacred,* but read my lips:
     Priests are human.
Maybe if both priests and people accepted that fact,
     God would be able to work more miracles through their humanity.

Next is Elizabeth, who, because of her speechless husband,
     takes on the traditional male role as the greeter of the visitor Mary.
She was barren for so many years,
     you would have thought that hope was no longer in her vocabulary.
Luke tells us that when she became pregnant she withdrew privately for five
     months.
In those days an old woman who became pregnant
     was the hot topic of gossip in the neighborhood.

Despite the embarrassment, the many years of trying to conceive,
   new life dances within her and she boldly proclaims that Mary is
   blessed and the mother of her Lord.

And our last great Advent figure: Mary.

She is a young pregnant girl of fifteen or sixteen who leaves familiar
   surroundings and heads toward Judah with haste, to the countryside
   where her son would one day be crucified.

She leaves behind the exotic experience of an angel's appearance to search
   for an intimate sense of communion with her elderly cousin who
   needed her joy, her youth, her faith.

Thomas Merton once wrote that Mary is "in the highest sense a person."

By that he meant that she didn't "obscure God's light in her being."

One of my favorite storytellers is Katherine Paterson, author of many
   children's stories.

Her young characters are not perfect.

They are unlike the make-believe goody-two-shoes of William Bennett's
   books of virtue.

Paterson's characters are human like us.

Her story "The Handmaid of the Lord" captures the essence of who the
   real biblical Mary was and what she can teach us.*

It is about Rachel Thompson, a minister's daughter, who, when she was
   five, had the part of an angel in the church nativity play.

But since Rachel was allergic to the stiff gauzy stuff that the angels dressed
   in, she scratched all the way through the heavenly host's chorus.

Mrs. MacLaughlin, who ran the pageant, yelled at her in front of
   everybody: "Rachel Thompson! Angels are spiritual beings! They do
   not scratch themselves when they sing!"

---

* Katherine Paterson, *A Midnight Clear: Stories for the Christmas Season* (New
York: Lodestar Books, 1995), 178–93.

When Rachel reached the right age, she was convinced that she would get
   the part of Mary.
But Mrs. MacLaughlin still didn't trust her and so picked Carrie Wilson.
Rachel was sick to her stomach with the thought of Carrie Wilson with her
   blond curls all the way down her back and that fake smile.
Carrie Wilson looked more like a department-store dummy than the real
   Mary.
Rachel was told that since she was so smart, she would be the understudy.
She would prepare for all the parts in case any of the actors became ill.

But nobody became ill.
Rachel Thompson sat in the front pew as the nativity play unfolded.
But suddenly a miracle occurred.
Baby Jesus began to cry.
Not just cry, SCREAM.
Carrie Wilson forgot about being Mary; she panicked.
She looked at Joseph. "Do something!" she whispered.
Joseph's face went bright red but he didn't move a muscle.

Rachel jumped up in haste from her pew and dashed to the nativity scene.
She was panting when she got to the manger.
Rachel poked around under the baby until she located the pacifier.
She jammed it into the baby's mouth.
He clamped down on it at once.
First Presbyterian Church was silent except for his noisy sucking.
Rachel smiled down at him.
He was a lovely Jesus.

"Who do you think you are?" Carrie Wilson hissed through her teeth.
But the whisper was almost loud enough to be heard in the back row.
"Behold." Rachel straightened up and stared sternly in the direction of the
   offender.
There was no doubt that the people in the last pew could hear her.
"I am the handmaid of the Lord."

This children's story echoes today's Gospel of Luke.
Mary's extraordinary mission in life was lived by ordinary action for others.
We are not called to be God, not called to be angels,
    not even called to be saints.
We are called to be human, fully human and to hold on to the message of
    the angel to Mary: "Nothing is impossible with God."

RPW

Questions for Reflection

1. How often do the most important leaders come from small, out-of-the-way places?

2. As we prepare to celebrate Christmas, are we truly aware that the joy of this feast springs from the realization of God's presence in our midst?

3. Why *does* Mary go to visit Elizabeth?

Other Directions for Preaching

1. In today's Gospel we have two women, each of whom trusted that the Lord's words to her would be fulfilled. Each one trusted in the face of considerable odds: Elizabeth was well beyond the expected time of child-bearing; Mary was young, betrothed, but not yet married. They trusted in God's call to them, even though their calls flew in the face of the cultural and religious norms of their time.

2. As the Eucharistic Prayer indicates, this is a season for active (as opposed to passive) remembering. We remember the coming of Christ, not only as a historic event, but as a continuing event in human history, a present event in our individual and communal lives.

CHRISTMAS

Wanted: Shepherds and Angels
CHRISTMAS, MASS AT MIDNIGHT

READINGS:
Isaiah 9:1–6; Titus 2:11–14; Luke 2:1–14

In the spirit of Caesar Augustus I would like to take up a little census this
   evening.
Don't groan—I am aware you are standing ten deep in the back—it's only
   two questions:
   1. How many of you have ever taken part in a Christmas pageant?
   2. Who were you?
How many of you were Jesus? (Started at the top, huh?)
How many were Mary? Joseph? The Wise Men?
Now, how about the shepherds? And the angels?

These last two roles have always struck me as great "catch-all" categories.
There's only room for one Jesus, one Mary, one Joseph, three wise men,
   but you can have dozens of shepherds and angels.
There's no mention of how many shepherds were out in that field.
And while one of the angels gets a nice little speech,
   a multitude of the heavenly host leaves room for...well, a multitude.

In the past I must confess to not giving too much thought to the shepherds
   and the angels
      except as a backdrop for the main action—necessary but not all
   that interesting.
But recently I have begun to reassess their importance.

As a matter of fact, I would propose that, if God were putting an ad these
  days in the *Washington Post*'s Help Wanted section,
    or the *City Paper*'s "In Search Of" column,
      it might very well be for shepherds and angels.

Consider the shepherds.
They are described as "living in the fields and keeping the night watch over
  their flock."
The phrase "living in the fields" struck me.
"Keeping night watch" tells us they were doing their job, making sure none
  of the sheep was sick or had wandered off and that a wolf didn't get
  into the sheepfold.
The work of shepherds was to give full attention to the care of the sheep.
And the image of the shepherd was used for the king, going back to David,
  the shepherd-king.
The prophet Ezekiel used the image of a shepherd first to castigate the
  leaders of Israel for their failure to care for the people,
    then spoke of God as taking up the shepherding of his people (see
    Ezek 34).
And one of the most beloved of all psalms begins with the words:
  "The Lord is my shepherd..."

God still needs shepherds, good pastors (pastor is the Latin word meaning
  "shepherd") to care for God's people, and especially to care for the
  least: the poor, the weak, the defenseless.
The pastoral staff in most parishes today includes both clergy and
  laypeople.
Leaders are needed to minister to God's people, to serve their needs.
Dedicated priests and laypeople in ministry are needed
    to help lead the community of faith more deeply into the mystery of
    Jesus Christ,
    to help the community recognize that "the grace of God has truly
    appeared, saving all" (Titus 2:11).

Prophetic voices are in demand to continue the work of "training us to
    reject godless ways and worldly desires and to live temperately, justly,
    and devoutly in this age."
We need the voice of shepherds who know their sheep, who call them by
    name, who lead them to green pastures and guide them along the right
    path.
So the first need for shepherds has to do with the care of God's people,
    a project no longer limited to the clergy and the religious, as in
    the past.

The first shepherds also served another purpose—as receivers of the
    message.
At the heart of the Christmas story is a message:
    "Behold, I proclaim to you good news of great joy that will be for all
    the people.
    For today in the city of David
    a savior has been born for you who is Christ and Lord" (Luke
    2:10–11).
The shepherds heard the message and took it to heart.
Their response to the message was immediate: "Let us go, then, to
    Bethlehem to see this thing that has taken place, which the Lord has
    made known to us" (Luke 2:15).
Without shepherds, there is no response to the message.
And without shepherds, no spread of it either.

God also continues to need angels—
    those who proclaim this Good News to people needing to hear it,
    and those who celebrate the Good News in a liturgy of praise.
Sometimes it is a lone voice that proclaims the Good News about Jesus.
It can take great courage and commitment to do this.
At other times, it is the work of the community to sing God's praises in a
    way that will draw others into it.
Both messenger angels and a multitude of the heavenly host were needed
    that first Christmas—and still are.

These can be discouraging times—a lot of sadness in our world this
    Christmas.
There are people whose loved ones are dying in Iraq,
        people who are losing their jobs,
        people who find it hard to get a decent job,
        more people than ever living below the poverty line in our country,
        and growing numbers throughout our world who do not have basic
        needs met.
We need angels who will speak this message of hope again and again.
We need angels who remind us that God loves this world and all who are
    in it.
        And that God's will is for "peace to those on whom his favor rests"
        (Luke 2:14).

The Christmas story is meant to challenge and change us, not just make us
    feel good.
It does more than direct our attention to the lovely manger scene that we set
    under the Christmas tree or on top of the TV set.
The Christmas story contains a call to action and a challenge to change.

One of my favorite Christmas stories is Barbara Robinson's *The Best
    Christmas Pageant Ever?*
It is the story of the Herdman children—Ralph and Imogene, Claude, Ollie,
    and Gladys.
They are described as "the worst kids in the school."
The heart of the story is about what happens the year the Herdman children
    volunteer to be the main characters for the Christmas pageant.
At first they want to change the story, deciding the three kings should lynch
    old Herod and that Joseph might burn down the inn that refuses him
    and Mary entry.
Gladys, as the head angel, goes around shouting and bopping shepherds on
    the head to get their attention,
        and Imogene as Mary won't let anyone come near the child,
        even Ralph, who is Joseph.

But when the night arrives to perform before the school,
> the "horrendous" Herdmans are transformed—by the story.

Rather than their changing the characters, the characters change them.

Ralph and Imogene really look awed by the parts they are playing.

Ollie and Claude come in bringing the Christmas ham as their gift to
> the babe.

Gladys, with a conviction never before heard from the Christmas angel, shouts:
> "Hey, unto you a child is born!"

They have become transformed by the mystery of God become human.

And all those watching are also caught up in this so familiar story and what
> it has done to the Herdmans,
> declaring it to be "the best Christmas pageant ever!"

The Christmas story is a story that can change the world if we let it in.

It is about the God who continues to make new our world,
> who continues to love the world into new life.

That infant born and laid in an animal feeder continues to nourish the
> world with his Body and Blood.

And the power of the Holy Spirit continues to work its way into the matter
> of our world,
> starting with bread and wine, water and oil,
> and going on to the hearts of men and women.

So, I humbly suggest tonight: Wanted: Shepherds and Angels.
> Wanted: men and women who allow their lives to be interrupted by
> this child, who hear the news of his birth, and take the time to go and
> be with him.

Wanted: proclaimers and receivers of the Good News
> that a Savior has come and continues to come.

Wanted: people willing to join in that first birthday song of celebration:
> "Glory to God in the highest
> and on earth peace to those on whom [God's] favor rests."

JAW

Questions for Reflection

1. What role in the Christmas story is God calling you to play this Christmas season?

2. How might that role change your life?

3. What role do you see your parish community playing in the world? How does this role call your community to speak and act in the world?

Other Directions for Preaching

1. Consider the titles found in the reading from the prophet Isaiah: Wonder-Counselor, God-Hero, Father-Forever, Prince of Peace. How do they help us to understand Jesus and his role "for our salvation"?

2. What forms does the darkness take at this time in our world, and where does the light shine?

3. What is the "lawlessness" that the birth of Christ delivers us from, and to what good does it direct us?

God's Family
THE NATIVITY OF THE LORD
(MASS AT DAY)

READINGS:
Isaiah 52:7–10; Hebrews 1:1–6; John 1:1–18

When I was a young seminarian I worked one summer in a large county
    hospital in Texas.
If I was on the night shift as the chaplain, I'd have to negotiate some
    suspicious territory in the parking garage.
Once in the hospital, there were the faces in the waiting rooms filled with
    trauma and anxiety, looking for the least sign of hope in the air.
Nighttime was like that in the hospital—tainted with a humid, damp air
    of fear.

But there was an exception, I soon learned, to the usual territory of human
    anguish and brokenness.
One day I was assigned to the sister hospital across town that was
    exclusively used as a maternity center.
The exhilaration and vitality of new life were palpable as soon as I walked
    in the door.
New life has that effect on us.
Maybe it was a couple that was longing to conceive and finally did.
Perhaps there was a family waiting to receive another child into their care.
Then, suddenly, shouts of joy for a new beginning!
Those lively infants sounded like a chorus from ancient Israel,

announcing that a bright future had finally come after a long,
bleak advent.
The endless night was over forever.

The birth of Christ was like no other.
As the Letter to the Hebrews reminds us, God's communication to us in the
past had been only partial and various.
Things were going to be different now.
That cry in the night was the Word made flesh.
That Word was present from the dawn of creation and its very instrument.
The Herald of new life was the bringer of light to dispel our darkness,
even as it made chaos into creation and parted day from night.

In the end, we know that sin, like the night it loves, will always keep us in
the dark.
The tragedy of the human race is the blindness that accompanies action in
the hands of the powerful.
Violence and war have been perpetrated over the centuries because of one
thing: the darkness of sin.
Racism and bigotry continue to exist in this country and throughout the
world because of the blindness that comes from systemic evil.
The quest for domination and control arises from the scar of sin that clouds
the eyes of even the best of us in our places of work, the country, and
the church.
Sin is the bareness of the human story that was transformed by God's entry
into history.
The human race now has a new lease on life.
"Break out together in song, O ruins of Jerusalem!" (Isa 52:9).
Christ is the firstborn of those who would no longer be bound to the
darkness of sin.
We celebrate this Christmas morning with the whole human family that
God's Son has become our brother and he has brought down the reign
of sin and death.

And yet our joy cannot end with recognition of new life alone.
We must take the child, our brother, into our arms and back home to
    embrace him and nourish him.
Now that we acknowledge that God has done something utterly new to
        break the sterility of sin on us, now that the people who have walked
        in darkness have seen a great light, it must make a difference that
        there is a new member of our family.
Imagine if the parents who gave birth to a child at the hospital, who were
        overjoyed to see their new gift, then left the baby there.
Imagine a mother who left her child to the care of nurses
        or a father who figured the doctors would raise the kid.
Unthinkable, right?

True parents, like baptized Christians, nurture and protect the child
        that has been entrusted to their care.
God's Son is about to move home with us.
How will we care for him?
Our faith is nothing less than embracing and feeding and loving
        the Christ who has been born to us this day.
Our brother, Jesus, must have a home.
The Word must be enthroned in our temple.
What kind of room will there be for him there?

When Saint Teresa of Avila described the world of prayer in
            The Interior Castle, she used the image of rooms
            in a great mansion to describe the place
            where God makes his dwelling,
            echoing Jesus' own statement that "in my Father's house
            there are many dwelling places" (John 14:2).
God is going to take up residence in our homes.
This morning we move God from this church to our hearts.
If we leave him here, he will be well taken care of by the church,
        but he will not take up a dwelling in our hearts, where he belongs.
The heart is where the Word lives and thrives and longs to be spoken.

The opportunity to bring home the Word exists for us not only on this
    feast, but in this sacrament.
The Eucharist is our encounter with the Christ, who comes into our hearts.
We bring him back to our homes to live, to change us and to change the
    world around us.
The holy meal that we will receive grants us a participation in the family of
    God, through God's Son who gave himself once, but continues to do
    so in this Eternal Banquet.
The Eucharist brings us light where there was once darkness and challenges
    us to ignite the world with God's peaceful presence on the earth.

When this Mass is ended we go forth in peace to love and serve the Lord.
We are children of God because of the child that has been born to us
    this day.
God has spoken to us for all time in this Word made visible,
    this God made a child,
    this Jesus our brother.
The people who walked in darkness have seen a great light.
That brightness shines in our homes, our hearts, and our lives so that all the
    ends of the earth shall see the salvation of our God.

GD

Questions for Reflection

1. Where is the darkness in my life that needs to be illuminated by the light of Christ? in my family? in American society?

2. In Christ we are slaves no longer but children of God. Is my relationship with God a familial one? If not, why not?

3. One of the most powerful expressions in all of Scripture is "the Word became flesh." How do you experience this truth as a reality in your life? Is the Word "dwelling among us"?

Other Directions for Preaching

1. The Word of God came once and for all in Christ, but it now lives in our action and our proclamation of the Good News.

2. The mystery of the Incarnation expresses the mystery of the Trinity: the Son of God, present at the foundation of the world with the Father of all creation, now becomes one of us through the power of the Holy Spirit.

3. We must bring and prophesy news of salvation to those poor who are near and far, even if it costs us our time, our jobs—our very lives.

It Takes a Family...
THE HOLY FAMILY OF JESUS, MARY, AND JOSEPH

READINGS:
Sirach 3:2–7, 12–14; 1 John 3:1–2, 21–24; Luke 2:41–52

Years ago, I remember a mother who said to me one Mother's Day as she
was going into church before the Mass began,
"I hope you are not going to preach about Mary today.
She makes us all feel so guilty."
Perhaps the same reaction was there when it was announced that today is
Holy Family Sunday, the focus for the Sunday after Christmas.
Some of you might be thinking, "Oh, no, a homily about the Holy Family!
Who can compare with a foster father who was often visited by angels,
a mother who conceived by the Holy Spirit,
and a child who was the son of God?"
And perhaps your thought might have taken you as far as: "And I have
to listen to someone go on about family life who doesn't even have
a family!"

Let me address the second thought first.
I stand before you quite humbly on this day.
True, I do not know what it is to *have* a family as far as being married and
raising children.
But I did come *from* a family, and the memories do linger of the ups and
downs of family life.

The arguments and discussions, angers and joys, sorrows and celebrations
  that marked my experience of family have stayed with me
  over the years.
And I also have three brothers who, with their wives, are still raising their
  children, and this continues to educate me about the tenderness and
  tensions that bind and bend families today.

I know that being a family takes work.
Our society and culture isn't always supportive of family life.
There seem to be a lot more broken, or at least fractured, families in our
  world today.
My friend the Dominican preacher Jude Siciliano recently recalled on his
  website for preachers, *First Impressions,* his encounter with a teenage
  boy who spoke of his "real father" and then went on to speak of his
  stepfather, who had been like a real father to him.
Noticing the use of the past tense, Jude asked him about his stepfather.
The boy replied that his mother had just divorced him.
Then, too, families are often separated by geography as the children
  grow older
  and spatial distance can easily result in emotional distance,
  unless efforts are made to bridge the gap.

All the more reason to celebrate this feast today,
   not as a potential guilt trip, but as a call to us to reflect on
   what it means to be family in light of the mystery
   of the Incarnation of God's son into the human family.
The celebration of Christmas is meant to be Good News for families as well
  as individuals.
I like to think of the feasts that follow on Christmas as an ongoing
  celebration of the mystery of the Incarnation, which literally means the
  en-flesh-ment of God,
  the eternal Word of God taking on a human body and soul.
Christmas Day focuses on the mystery of the Incarnation as an event
  in history—

God came to us in human flesh to save us,
a once-and-for-all event.
The grace of God, manifested to us in Christ Jesus, entered into the world
as an infant born of a Jewish woman, Mary, and entrusted to a Jewish
man, Joseph.
This event occurred once and for all over two thousand years ago,
in a backwater town called Nazareth in the Galilee section of Israel,
a land occupied by a foreign power.
And this grace of Incarnation continues to manifest itself to us, in us, and
through us today.
As the mystic Meister Eckhardt wrote: "The incarnation is always
happening, but what good is it, if it does not happen in me?"

The days following Christmas invite us to ponder how the grace of the
Incarnation flows into our world and touches the lives of individual
families (today's feast), the family that is the church (the feast of Mary,
Mother of God and Mother of the Church), and the family of all the
nations of the world (the feast of the Epiphany).
The feast of the Holy Family is a celebration of God's call to be a
holy family, not an occasion for feeling guilty or sheepish
or battered or bashed.
To help in this, the family of Joseph and Mary and Jesus is set before us.

It is good to remember that Jesus came out of a family, a human family.
And like all other families, this family must have had moments of
disagreement, tension, and disappointment in each other.
And we shouldn't be surprised.
A family is something that either develops and grows over the years,
or weakens and disintegrates.
That's why I love this story of Jesus as a teen or "tween," to be exact,
since he was only twelve.
This is the only time in Scripture we hear anything about Jesus as a boy.
And at the heart of it is a moment of tension between the parents
and their child.

In Luke's account, the family had gone up to Jerusalem from Nazareth,
    a journey of three days at that time, to celebrate Passover.
After the days were over, indeed, after they had already gone back a day,
    his parents realized that Jesus was not with either their relatives or
    acquaintances.
Most in the village would have gone to Jerusalem for Passover,
    and a young boy would be likely to be with his cousins or his friends
    as they traveled.
After looking for him among family and friends, Mary and Joseph
    discovered he was with none of the travelers from Nazareth.

For any good parent to discover their child is lost is an occasion of worry,
    fear, anger, blame, and heartbreak.
In the story, this worry and fear must have accompanied them every step of
    the day's journey returning to Jerusalem,
    and then another two days searching for him.
But there he was, chatting with the teachers in the Temple about matters of
    the law.
And when they tell him how worried he made them, there's no word of
    apology, just the equivalent of "what's the fuss?"
    and then the puzzling, if not flippant,
    "Did you not know I *must* be in my Father's house?"
You wonder if they were more tempted to hug him in relief or give him a
    swat for his impertinence, given the reverence parents expected their
    children to show them, as Sirach reminded us today.
They did not understand his words, Luke simply tells us.

Nor do we, as far as having any certainty on the meaning of his reply.
Biblical scholar Luke Timothy Johnson translates this response as:
    "I must involve myself in my father's affairs."
What is clear is that Jesus felt some kind of necessity to be where he was,
    a necessity that overrode his duty to his parents.

Jesus is presented as engaging in dialogue with the teachers, listening to
them and asking them questions and astounding all who heard him
with his understanding and his answers.
He is teaching the teachers, as he will do later in the Gospel when he comes
to Jerusalem
and responds to the questions of the Sadducees, scribes, and Pharisees.
Luke explicitly refers to this later occasion as teaching in the Temple [see
Luke 20–21].

Being involved in "my father's affairs" would continue to puzzle all who
followed Jesus during his ministry and through the centuries.
Today's story ends happily by noting:
"[Jesus] went down with them...and was obedient to them;
and his mother kept all these things in her heart.
And Jesus advanced in wisdom and age and favor before God
and man."
No word on Joseph, who probably went off to his carpenter shop,
possibly muttering how it was much easier to build a house than raise
a son.
Growing in wisdom, age, and favor is a process that all God's children have
to undergo.

We call them the *holy* family.
They were a family who lived in faithful relationship to the God of Israel,
going to synagogue, keeping the commandments and the celebrations
of their faith.
Jesus was brought up in the customs and traditions of Judaism.
And we see the result of his upbringing in the man he became,
one who was open to the outpouring of the Spirit again and again.
His parents helped to lay the foundation that brought him to maturity
and to that wisdom that marked him as a prophet, as Luke's
Gospel witnesses.

The picture of the Holy Family we get today reminds us that the business of
    being family was not always an easy road even for them.
Along with moments of joy come those of anxiety and surprise,
    especially when their child began to move toward being an adult.
But it is more than this reminder about the original holy family and its
    growing pains.
Hearing the story of Jesus in the Temple at Christmastime reminds us that
    while Christmas is a time for family, it doesn't make being family
    any easier.
Families don't change for the holidays.
Still, Christmas reminds us that the potential for being a holy family is there
    for all of us. Holiness has to do with handing on the means of holiness
    by example and instruction, and with an ongoing dedication to loving
    each other unselfishly and respectfully.
Holiness at times means suffering each other as we grow in wisdom, age,
    and favor before God and others—
    just as God suffers us as we grow up, maturing in Christ.
There was a line in a little movie about family called *Junebug*.
At one moment, a young about-to-be-mother says to her brooding, always
    angry husband, "God loves you just as you are but too much to let
    you stay that way."
God suffers what is often a prolonged adolescence in his children.

The feast of the Holy Family invites us to examine how
    we are doing as family.
This includes the families we belong to by birth and by baptism.
How are we doing as parents and as children called to honor our parents?
How are we doing as children of God in a world that often beckons us to
    ignore, if not actively renounce, that parentage?
How are we doing as members of the human family, called to look out for
    the least among us, the poor and the struggling across the world and
    in our own country?
As the Letter of John says: We are God's children *now*;
    what we shall be has not yet been revealed.

We do know that when it is revealed we shall be like God,
    for we shall see God as God is.
That's the plan—to be activated sooner, rather than later.

Getting there as family is the challenge.
The same Spirit that guided Jesus continues to guide us,
    through all our bumbling, faltering steps,
        inviting us to ponder the mystery that we have entered by baptism,
        in which we became brothers and sisters in Christ, sent out to witness
        to the world.
Out of that mystery, we pray today when we call on God as our Father,
    and into that mystery we grow when we are united in celebrating the
    dying and rising of Jesus,
        Son of Mary and Son of God.

JAW

Questions for Reflection

1. What has your experience of family been—as child and as adult?

2. How do you see your family's role in preparing you to be part of God's family?

3. How does your parish family draw you into being about your "father's affairs"?

Other Directions for Preaching

1. An alternative reading for today's feast during Cycle "C" is 1 Samuel 1:20–22, 24–28. In an age in which people talk about letting children decide for themselves regarding the role of religion in their lives, we have the example of Hannah and Elkanah and Mary and Joseph, who saw first their responsibility to God in bringing their sons to know the Lord God of Israel through their fidelity to the Law of the Lord.

2. Our attention is drawn in 1 John to the basic requirements of being part of God's family in Christ: to believe in the name of God's Son, Jesus Christ, and to love one another as Jesus commanded us.

3. The Temple was central to the identity and life of the families of Israel. What is the appropriate role of the local church in the lives of families today?

The Voice
That Is Great Within Us
THE SOLEMNITY OF THE BLESSED
VIRGIN MARY, MOTHER OF GOD

READINGS:
Numbers 6:22–27; Galatians 4:4–7; Luke 2:16–21

My sister, Noreen, has her hands full showing the three children
    the right time to kneel during the liturgy.
Small legs don't always want to bend for worship.
It is always edifying to see parents teaching their children how to pray.
At Sunday Eucharist you can watch Mom or Dad help the little ones
    genuflect when they come into church or help them make the sign of
    the cross.
All for the good.

These practices are necessary teachings and important foundations for
    learning to be a thoughtful, religious person in God's house.
Similarly, in Paul's time the Law functioned a bit like a dutiful parent,
    raising children in the faith.
And keeping them there for a lifetime.
You keep the Law, and the Law will keep you.
The instructions given to Israel provided a vital code for human living.
The Law showed people how to act both externally and interiorly, how to
    live a good life.
The Law was a moral armature that ensured good behavior.

And the Law was comprehensive.
It covered every possible human activity, from ritual behavior to
marital relations.

All the more reason for a shock to the system, that something new has
replaced the Law: the coming of God in the flesh.
Paul tells the Galatians that it is time for Israel to grow up because the
Christ event has changed years of dealing with the Law.
In Christ we are set free from the parental restrictions of the Law.
In Christ humanity has been redeemed.
In Christ we have been justified.
And ultimately it comes down to this:
if we have been justified according to the Law alone,
then Christ died needlessly.

Being justified would become a crucial theological expression for Paul,
not only in Galatians but also in the Letter to the Romans.
For the Galatians, to be justified means that those who have been baptized
have no need for any Law to make them whole—
particularly the law of circumcision.
Instead, the Spirit fulfills all we need.
We have to do nothing because it has already been done by Christ himself.
And if Jesus' saving blood cried out and redeemed us from the cross, that
Spirit still intercedes for us in words too deep for any of us:
"Abba, Father!"
Those are words of the Son praying to the Father that we repeat in this
Eucharist as we lift up our hearts through Christ our Lord.
The Law is replaced by the Spirit.

That is what makes Mary so extraordinary in the role of salvation history.
Together with Joseph, she took Jesus to be circumcised under the Law.
Under the Law!
The very one who was to free us from the constraint of such practices
was submitted to its yoke.

But that would be only the beginning of how he gave himself to our
humanity, ending on the cross.
When we see how the unfolding of these events took place we can only
stand awestruck at God's humility in Christ.
God would be born into our history, into our time, and submit to our laws
and our condemnation in order to free us from
what the Law demands of us: death.
Freed from slavery by one we enchained.
Do we have words for this?

We can only find ourselves like Mary herself—pondering all these things in
our heart.
And it was Mary's unique role, precisely as mother of God,
to allow divine humility to come about in the first place.
If the annunciation carried the mysterious weight of a *fiat*—God's will
be done—this presentation in the Temple would only underline
that submission.

In my homiletic classes at Saint Meinrad Seminary, I continually remind
the students that there should be an underlying call to mission in
every homily.
I call this the pastoral imperative.
The preacher is also a shepherd in the call to worship.
How does what I have just preached make a difference in the lives of the
baptized Christian assembly?
Luke's Gospel might ask the question like this: What now must I do?

That does not necessarily mean action.
For in this great Solemnity of the mother of God our real mission is to
stand in silence at the God of all creation who became one of us
and the woman who made it possible.
The festivities and shouts of Christmas give way to an Octave that is
wrapped in silence.

This day is for pondering deeply in our hearts, the way Mary considered
 those mysteries that were beyond all telling.
We take that silence into the New Year.

Mary's silent intercession in history is ongoing, even as she petitions for us
 as individuals and for the whole church.
The alternative Opening Prayer for today's liturgy puts it well:
"May her prayer, the gift of a mother's love, be your people's joy through
 all ages.
May her response, born of a humble heart, draw your Spirit to rest on your
 people."
Thanks be to God that we have been given the incomparable gift of the
 Eucharist, celebrating this day that accomplishes more than we can
 possibly know.
For the moment, we can just stand in ecstatic wonder before the Madonna
 and her Child
 and let the Spirit cry out, "Abba, Father!"
That is the voice that is great within us.

GD

Questions for Reflection

1. Do I rely too much on externals in my religious practices and fail to interiorize deeper observances?

2. How will this feast of Mary, the mother of God, change the New Year for me? Will I be different at the end of the year?

3. What might our world learn from a celebration of this feast?

Other Directions in Preaching

1. Although we live in a time of violence, peace will come to our world when we are able to transcend the written law and attend to the covenant of love that binds all people together.

2. A respect for unborn life and the work of motherhood honors God's creative power to renew the year and the earth.

3. Human laws change. Only love survives even during difficult times. Mary's obedience to God is a model for all time.

Could *That* Be an Epiphany?
THE EPIPHANY OF THE LORD

READINGS:
Isaiah 60:1–6; Ephesians 3:2–3a, 5–6; Matthew 2:1–12

Is there anyone who has not felt overwhelmed this week by the images of
   the tsunami and its legacy of death and destruction?
It has been a week of death on a scale that is barely comprehensible,
   too much for us to grasp: one hundred and twenty thousand
   dead so far.
Today's feast seems to be from a totally different world where nature, in the
   form of a star, leads a small group called the Magi into the heart of
   the mystery of God's love enfleshed in a child.
How do we reconcile the God of this story with the God so many see
   behind the horrors of this past week?

The Epiphany celebrates the birth of Jesus over two thousand years ago,
   but we also celebrate it as calling us to recognize God's ongoing
   manifestation in our world and in our lives as
   Emmanuel, God-with-us.
However, in light of recent days, some might be tempted to question this
   assertion: "Really? God with us? God with whom?
   Where was God-with-us as the tsunami slammed into the countries of
   some of the poorest people in our world?
   Where was God-with-us as men, women, and children were carried off
   by the water?
   Where is God-with-us for the survivors?"

47

This horrible event has led many to question where God is in all this.

"Is this a punishment of Allah or a test?" asked Islam online.

Others were willing to give an answer to this question:

"This is an expression of God's great anger with the world," said Israel's
Sephardic chief rabbi.

Another religious leader said, "The world is being punished for
wrongdoing, for people's hatred of each other, their lack of charity,
and moral turpitude."

A Hindu leader also agreed with this line of thought: "The tsunami is divine
retribution."

Not a little unsettling was the response of a Christian leader who, pointing
to Sri Lanka, India, and Indonesia, found it significant that there was
such a miraculous survival of a great many Christians in countries
where Christianity is greatly persecuted.

The wisdom of theologian and historian Martin Marty brought some
needed balance.

Marty stated with eloquent simplicity: "People are asking for trouble
when they are precise in knowing God's will."

Discretion and humility would be more welcome in many of the comments
by religious leaders at this tragic time.

Speaking on God's behalf should be less in evidence, acting on God's behalf
more so.

Why such events happen cannot be answered by any person with assured
authority.

Pointing to the fact that this world has been marked by natural disasters for
millions of years seems at least to have a scientific base for credibility.

Giving consideration to what we human beings and the societies we have
created are doing to our environment, how our so-called advances in
first world countries have helped contribute to global warming—these
factors would also seem to reflect a willingness to look to our own
responsibility for what is occurring in our world.

I don't think God needs an attorney, but can we reconcile a God who loved
the world so much that he sent his only son for our salvation;
can we really reconcile this God with one who stirs up tsunamis or
earthquakes or hurricanes or floods or any other such disasters to
punish people?
If the Christmas season proclaims anything, it is that God is irrevocably for
us, hence the name Emmanuel, which translates as God-with-us, even
now, in our suffering.
And that God is at work with us in the generosity of people doing all they
can to bring aid in various forms, directly and indirectly.

Today's story reminds us that God is a God of the journey,
sending people forth to discover new life,
and that God accompanies them on the journey.
This has been so from the beginning of God's dealings with humankind.
God chose a man called Abram and told him: "Go forth from the land of
your kinsfolk and from your father's house to a land that I will show
you" (Gen 12:1).
And God went with Abram.
And God also went with his grandson Jacob when he set off, fleeing his
brother's murderous threats.
And God was with Joseph when his brothers threw him into the pit,
and when he was taken down into Egypt and became great in
Pharaoh's kingdom.
And most of all, God was with Moses and the people as they set out from
their land of slavery to find a place where they could live and prosper,
and worship the God who had shown himself to them in great signs
and wonders.

The story of the Magi witnesses again to God's getting people to set off in a
direction leading deeper into the mystery of God and a deeper sharing
in communion with God.
In the end it is a story of discovery of who God is
and how God helps us arrive at the place where we finally find God.

Matthew's astrologers got to the right place by being attentive to the world
    around them.
The lesson to be learned might be that God is with us, reaching out through
    the occurrences of our lives, the events that befall us, the joys and
    sorrows we experience.
Natural disasters can make this hard to believe, especially in the face of
    such suffering.
But it is the story of Epiphany that reminds us of something to be spoken in
    the face of any and all suffering,
        whether on a personal scale or a cosmic one.
God will not let suffering and death have the final word.

The Epiphany tells us God in Christ has come to scatter the darkness.
The light God has set before us in Christ is one that comes from a vision
    given by faith.
This vision allows us to continue to "rise up in splendor," even in the
    darkest hours,
        and to reflect on the light that has shone on us,
        the glory of the Lord that is the grace of Jesus Christ within us.

We often lose sight of that light.
Indeed, we often are the cause of deep darkness, but not always.
I saw the movie *Hotel Rwanda* last night.
It dramatizes what one man did in the face of great darkness that
    overwhelmed the nation of Rwanda when the Hutu militia went on a
    murderous rampage of revenge against the Tutsi people.
Paul Rusesabagina, a hotel manager in Kilgali, managed to save hundreds of
    Tutsis from being slaughtered in the genocidal wave of terror
    unleashed.
In this story of deep sadness, 800,000 people were slaughtered over an
    eight-month period.
And the world watched and did nothing—including our country.
But one man did, and lives were saved through the Spirit at work in him.

As horrible as this tsunami has been for all those it touched,
    the response of people around the world has been its own sign
    of hope.
This time we have recognized that we are bound together by a common
    humanity.
While we continue to walk, often through our own darkness in both our
    personal and communal lives, we can bring light to places where
    people have been overwhelmed
    by the tragedies and sorrows of life.
The journey of the Magi continues in our world until all arrive at the place
    where God dwells.

The journey of the Magi is one we take every week when we journey here.
Like the Magi, who arrived in Jerusalem where the words of the prophets
    were consulted,
    we come here to hear the words of prophets, apostles, and evangelists.
Like the Magi, we finally arrive at the place where the Lord is to be
    found—
    in the sacrament of his Body and Blood.
And like the Magi, we return home a little more transformed as we continue
    to grow into being the Body of Christ.

God continues to draw us onto the road, offering guidance and sustenance
    so we might reach our destiny.
May we walk the path, through the times of darkness and times of light,
    with hearts of faith, hope, and love for all who are
    on the road with us.
May we be attentive to the signs set before us,
    those above our heads and those placed within our hearts.
And may we finally come to the place where we can offer our own gifts,
    especially the one God cherishes most of all—an adoring heart.

JAW

Questions for Reflection

1. Can you think of times when a "star" appeared to guide you out of the darkness?

2. Who are some of those who are making the journey with you? How do you help one another keep going?

3. Do you recognize the light that comes from seeing all people as family, recognizing God's ongoing Epiphany in the various peoples of our world?

Other Directions for Preaching

1. The great diversity in our world and in our nation today calls us to ponder the many ways God continues to be a "light for the nations."

2. The "stewardship of God's grace given for (our) benefit" leads us to ask how the Spirit is at work today revealing ways of deepening our communion.

3. The movement of Christmas is the movement of God's grace, drawing us more deeply into the mystery of the Incarnation and sending us out into the world to lead others to it.

Beloved and Well-Pleasing to God
THE BAPTISM OF THE LORD

READINGS:
Isaiah 42:1–4, 6–7; Acts 10:34–38; Luke 3:15–16, 21–22

At the Evening Prayer of the Liturgy of the Hours for the feast of the Epiphany, the following antiphon is recited before and after the Canticle of Mary:

> "Three mysteries mark this holy day: today the star leads the Magi to the infant Christ; today water is changed into wine for the wedding feast; today Christ wills to be baptized by John in the river Jordan to bring us salvation."

The Epiphany is not limited to the story of the Magi, but embraces a number of the early stories of Jesus in which he was revealed as being more than the carpenter from Nazareth, son of Mary.
Three events are considered under the title of Epiphany.

Each occasion is highly symbolic; each announces a particular manifestation of Jesus: the Magi signify God's self-manifestation in Jesus Christ to the Gentile world; the changing of water into wine at Cana manifests Jesus to his family and friends.
But what about the baptism of Jesus?
Whom is Jesus being manifested to there?
Some might say the baptism reveals Jesus to the larger Jewish community.

53

And Matthew's account of the baptism would bear this out.
But there is another way of thinking about this that we can consider,
    this one rooted in Luke's account.

Without a doubt his baptism was one of the key moments in the life
    of Jesus.
Luke does two significant things in his presentation of this event.
First, he gets John the Baptist out of the picture as quickly as possible.
Luke allows John to say,
    "I am baptizing you with water, but one mightier than I is coming.
    I am not worthy to loosen the thongs of his sandals."
This points out clearly that John was the forerunner, the overture to the
    main event.
Then his final words: "He will baptize you with the Holy Spirit and fire."
Exit John.

The second thing Luke does—and this is surprising—is to ignore the actual
    moment of Jesus being baptized.
Luke doesn't say anything about the baptism.
What is important happens *after* it is over, when Jesus is praying.
Then, the heavens open.
Then, the Holy Spirit comes "in bodily form like a dove."
And it is *then* that the voice speaks—while Jesus is praying.
Luke wants us to focus on the words spoken, so he has set them apart from
    the baptism.
"You are my beloved Son; with you I am well pleased."

Now, notice that God speaks directly to Jesus here.
In Matthew's account the voice speaks to those standing around, saying:
    "This is my beloved Son, with whom I am well pleased."
God sounds like a proud father, introducing his son.
But in Luke, and in Mark, the voice is addressed to Jesus:
    "*You* are my beloved Son; with *you* I am well pleased."
Is it possible that the Epiphany here is to Jesus?

Is this the event when Jesus was manifested *to himself?*
Listen to those beautiful, tender words.
   "You are my beloved Son; with you I am well pleased."

Years ago I read a book called *Understanding the Human Jesus* by
   Andrew Canale.*
The author, a psychologist, was not writing as a biblical scholar or as a
   theologian,
      but as a human being, trying to understand the completeness of
      Jesus' humanity.
One of the events he considers is the baptism of Jesus.
Canale suggested that something must have been going on in Jesus for some
   time, some inner stirrings that made him leave his family,
      that made him unsatisfied with his daily life and sent him off, down to
      Judea, out into the desert,
         to hear this prophet that was preaching repentance.
He must have wrestled with himself: he was only a carpenter from Nazareth,
   his family was depending on him for its well-being,
      and yet he felt a need to move on, that he was being called to
      something....
Then he heard John's voice, a voice in the wilderness calling others to live
   in readiness, to undergo a change of heart,
      that someone was coming who would baptize with the Spirit.

And Jesus found himself moving toward the water.
What did he have to repent of?
Canale suggests the English word *repent* is linked to the Latin word for
   pain, and speculates that Jesus would know his decision to leave his
   family would cause pain, and this would be cause for repentance.
All we know is that he was there, listening to John, and he went down into
   the water, and then something happened that helped shape the rest of
   his life.

---

   * Andrew Canale, *Understanding the Human Jesus* (New York: Paulist Press, 1985),
33–34.

He heard a voice:
> "You are my beloved Son; with you I am well pleased."

These words are heavy with meaning.
They refer back to the Hebrew Scriptures, to one of the psalms and
    to Isaiah.
Psalm 2 was used when a king was anointed in Israel;
    there God calls the king "my son":
    "You are my son, today I am your father" (Ps 2:7).
And the words "with you I am well pleased" come from a nameless prophet
    of the exile whom we call Deutero-Isaiah or Second Isaiah,
    not to be confused with an earlier prophet Isaiah.
Jesus knew the book of Isaiah and those portions we call the Servant Songs.
These are poems in which God speaks about his servant and says:
    "Here is my servant whom I uphold, my chosen one with whom I am
    pleased" (Isa 42:1).
This servant was the one sent to bring justice to the nations.
He was marked by compassion, and would not break a bruised reed
    or quench a smoldering wick.
This servant was the one sent as a covenant of the people, a light for the
    nations, to open the eyes of the blind and bring freedom to captives.

Jesus heard a voice speaking to him and a road opened before him.
He knew it was the truth, God's truth.
And in this truth was his calling.
That's the meaning of the word *vocation*—a calling.
And the Spirit who came in bodily form was the spirit of truth, God's truth.

This feast of the Baptism of Jesus invites us to think of our own baptism,
    that event which first told us who we are and what
    we are to do in life.
Sometimes we forget, or lose awareness of its meaning, or even ignore it.
But God called to us at our baptism: "You are my beloved; with you I am
    well pleased."

Our calling is to live as *beloved,* as one who pleases God.
This call is not due to anything we've done; we have not earned it;
      it is pure gift.
We are sons and daughters in the beloved Jesus.
We have been baptized in the name of the Father, and of the Son, and of the
      Holy Spirit.
We are the body of Christ in the world,
      sent to bring justice and compassion, to be a light in our world,
      salt that gives savor, and bread for the hungry.

Sometimes you hear it said that the church is no longer capturing the hearts
      of its own people.
Perhaps you even feel this on occasion yourself.
Could that be because it is not speaking the truth often enough,
      not repeating the message that each person needs to hear again and
      again: "You are God's beloved; with you God is well pleased"?

As a child, I remember thinking of baptism mainly as washing away the
      stain of original sin.
This is certainly part of our tradition.
And who would deny the reality of sin and its continuing power in the
      world—the newspaper constantly reminds us of the reality of sin,
      original and ongoing.
But the heart of baptism is not a corrective action, but an embracing,
      empowering one.
We are to know we are and always will be God's beloved,
      swept up into the mystery of the dying and rising of Jesus,
      and the new life possible in the Holy Spirit.
We are called to continue the journey, together, as a community,
      in his name.
This journey is not an ego trip, not about "getting it all together."
In the end, it is about laying down one's life, about self-emptying.

Coming out of the water and listening to the voice that calls is
    a lifelong task.
Like Jesus, we need to listen again and again for the voice of God.
And we will need to make decisions.
Notice that Luke's Jesus is constantly going off to pray.

So, the Epiphany was not a onetime event—not for Jesus, not for us.
It was not restricted to the Magi or the people at the Jordan or those
    at Cana.
Epiphany is God calling to us and showing us to ourselves again and again
    and this showing calls for a going out into the world, taking on
    God's mission:
    not to snap the rigid or crush the wavering,
    but to embrace the weak and protect the hopeless,
    to be light, savory salt, fresh bread, and rich wine,
    beloved sons and daughters in whom God forever delights.

JAW

Questions for Further Reflection

1. Do you think of your baptism as an epiphany?

2. What is your response to the words God spoke at the baptism of Jesus? Can you see them as also being spoken to you?

3. Jesus' baptism sent him out into the wilderness to confront Satan, and then into his special ministry of preaching and healing. Where does your baptism drive you?

Other Directions for Preaching

1. God calls to his servant to bring justice to the nations, but how is this to be carried out today, and what are the implications for our parish, our country, our church?

2. Peter's message to Cornelius and his household about the impartiality of God toward all peoples who fear him and act uprightly challenges any proprietary approach to God.

3. Consider the responsibility of baptizing children into your parish community and what that means for the adult members.

LENT

Lent, Season of Love
FIRST SUNDAY OF LENT

READINGS:
Deuteronomy 26:4–10; Romans 10:8–13; Luke 4:1–13

Have you ever thought of Lent as the season of love?
This might be unlikely since it begins on such a somber note,
    and is marked by such a somber color, one several shades from
    Valentine red.
If I were to ask you what comes to mind when I say "Lent," what would
    you say?
Some likely responses might be "penance," or "a time to give things up,"
    or "the season for going to confession."
Ashes do seem to be a good symbol for Lent, reminding us of the passing
    nature of our lives,
    and calling us to reflect on how we are managing our dwindling days.
But I would propose a living, beating, healthy, loving heart as the symbol
    of Lent.
Lent is the season of awakening our hearts.
"Rend your hearts, not your garments," cries the prophet Joel on
    Ash Wednesday.
And today's readings reinforce this cry.

Each year Lent begins with the story of the temptations in the desert.
Jesus, led into the desert by the Spirit, is being tested by Satan.
The devil could be seen as the active one, doing the tempting; Jesus reacts.
Action, reaction.

But it really comes across as a duel of wits.

To every temptation that Satan throws out, Jesus has an answer.

For every trap Satan sets, Jesus finds an escape.

Taken together, the three temptations lure Jesus to take control of his
destiny, according to Satan's master plan.

At issue is what will control the heart of Jesus.

For what controls Jesus' heart will decide his actions.

The first temptation has to do with control over things.

Satan says, "You're hungry. Use your power. Change these rocks into bread."

The second temptation is to control people.

Satan whispers, "I will give you power over all the kingdoms of the world,
just worship me."

And the third temptation is to control God, forcing God's intervention.

"Leap off the Temple," Satan coaxes. "God will take care of you."

To all three snares, Jesus responds by quoting the book of Deuteronomy,
the great book of the Pentateuch that calls Israel to be a people of the
covenant, to give their hearts to God,
to trust that the God who led them out of slavery would continue to
take care of them.

Israel in the desert again and again fails the tests that come.

The people complain about the lack of food, complain about Moses,
and at one point even complain that God brought them out to the
desert to let them die.

But Jesus in the desert is the ideal Israel, refusing to turn from trusting God.

He says in short order:

My real food is the bread of God's Word.

The only one I worship is God.

I do not test God.

Jesus neither seizes control for himself nor yields it to Satan.

It is the Father that remains in control.

Jesus only yields to the will of his Father.

To quote the words of an old song: his heart belongs to Daddy.

Scholars say this event is shorthand for the temptations Jesus had to deal
    with all through his ministry:
To use his powers for his own benefit—whether to nourish his body or
    his ego.
To use his powers to win the crowd for himself.
To ask the Father to do things according to what Jesus saw as best.
There is no more dramatic example of this yielding of control than
    at Gethsemane,
        when he prays, "Father, if it is your will, take this cup from me;
        yet not my will but yours be done."

Lent begins by reminding us that Jesus made the decision over and over
    again to seek the will of God and to do that will.
His heart was firmly rooted in the will of the Father.
We see him making a profession of faith in God, his Father.

This same note of professing faith in God is sounded in the other
    two readings.
Moses is telling the people that on the day they offer the fruits of the
    harvest, when they give their offerings to the priest who, in turn, will
    set them before the altar,
    on that day the people are to profess their faith before God.
They are to declare before God their story of how God saved them from the
    oppression of Egypt, and delivered them with strong hand and
    outstretched arm, and gave them a land flowing with milk and honey.
God is to be trusted, and they are to profess publicly their trust.

In his Letter to the Romans, Paul writes,
    "If you confess with your mouth that Jesus is Lord
    and believe in your heart that God raised him from the dead,
    you will be saved."
Again, a call to the Christians at Rome to acknowledge publicly where they
    place their hearts, to whom they dedicate them.
And God's response? The gift of salvation.

Lent is a time to ready our hearts to make a profession of faith.
We will do this on Easter.
In an age when so often we are not sure whom to believe,
> or who tells the truth, or whether the truth can be found,
> we are called to be individuals and a people who tell the truth,
> both to God and to one another.

For this reason every Easter we renew our baptismal promises, which
> declare that we believe in God,
> who is Father, Son, and Holy Spirit,
> and that we will live as children of God.

Every Easter we renounce Satan and all his promises and all his works.
For the next forty days we prepare our hearts to do this.
"Rend your hearts," cries Joel.
> Peel away the tough rind that can surround our heart.
> Peel away the rind of indifference, the tough skin that hardens our
> heart, created by holding on to resentment, anger, cynicism, and all
> those attitudes that weaken our ability to love God and our neighbor.

So, today let us resolve to turn to the Lord with all our heart, our mind,
> and our soul.
Every Eucharist is a pledge of God's love and loyalty to us.
Jesus does not abandon us but draws near to feed and nourish us.
May this Lent be truly a season of a heart renewed,
> of falling in love once again with our God.

JAW

Questions for Reflection

1. To whom do I give my heart?
2. How can I best prepare to make my profession of faith this Lent?
3. Where does the heart of our community reveal itself?

Other Directions for Preaching

1. What are some of the ways the church continues to be tempted?

2. The Eucharist is where we bring the fruits of our labors and offer them to God. How does this action declare our Christian story of liberation from slavery?

3. Paul's Letter to the Romans allows us to address how we are justified by faith and that in our confession of faith we are saved.

Transforming Word
SECOND SUNDAY OF LENT

READINGS:
Genesis 15:5–12, 17–18; Philippians 3:17—4:1;
Luke 9:28b–36

The readings during Lent continue to draw us ever deeper into the
paschal mystery.
Last week we traveled with Jesus into the desert, where he was tempted for
forty days and forty nights.
This Second Sunday finds our Lord on top of a high mountain praying in
the company of his disciples.
The wilderness becomes a preparation for the theophany on Mount Tabor.
Hunger and temptation make way for dazzling robes and mystical revelation.
The contrast between the desert and the mountain sets the tone for this
remarkable transfigured moment itself.

While radiant and in glory, Jesus speaks to Moses and Elijah about his
suffering—about his exodus, which he was to accomplish in Jerusalem.
His exodus.
His passion.
Our liberation from bondage.
Here is the Lamb of God become the paschal victim, dazzling white with
the glory that foreshadows the blood that will accomplish his exodus.

Some folks might point out that this transfiguration of Jesus is literally a
peak experience.

All the great seers had one.
Moses.
Elijah.
Jesus is in good company.

The poet William Wordsworth, in his long poem *The Prelude,* spoke of such
    a visionary spot in time when he crossed the Alps.
God seems overwhelmingly present at a particular vantage point in nature.
A kind of rapture in a horizon beyond our knowing.
Many are hungry for such moments, since they are few and far between
    in our hectic world.
I recall being taken once by helicopter through Glacier National Park.
It was an encounter unlike anything I had experienced before.
There was a sense of being out of time, lifted from a present moment while
    circling the snow-covered mountains and lakes.
What one sees on such an expedition defies explanation.
I must have felt something of what Peter sensed on that trip up the
    mountain: "It is good to be here!"
Yes. Let's stay and never return.
There is nothing like the spectacle of nature to keep us engaged, wanting
    more and longing for separation from the nitty-gritty world.
But Tabor was different.
For Jesus, like Abraham before him, there was no captivating spectacle.
Our Lord is not like Wordsworth or a truth seeker, peering into nature.
He is the Truth.
After all, the Son of God witnessed the creation of the world before
    time began.
Nature holds no secrets from him.
Jesus is transfigured by the Father's promise, the eternal covenant,
    for our sake.

We might not think of the moment God appears to Abraham as a
    "transfiguration," but it was.
Abraham was not on a mountain.

Instead, God brought the wonders of promise to him in the dusty plains:
"'Look up at the sky and count the stars, if you can.
Just so,' he added, 'shall your descendants be.'"
Indeed, God was transfiguring the Word before Abraham's very eyes.
So God transformed Abraham, who, by faith, became dazzling with
righteousness.
Abraham was transfigured by a covenant.

The external manifestations of that covenant we witness in Genesis.
Splitting animals in half and laying them out in the desert may wound our
modern sensibility.
Yet Abraham sealed a promise with God that was something like being in
the midst of a life force.
Two halves that were once whole witness the power of the covenant.

That is what God's promise is like: a mysterious, eternal power of fidelity.
On Mount Tabor, Moses and Elijah become the representatives of God's
promise who speak to Jesus about the covenant he will ratify.
The Paschal Lamb will be torn in two when he accomplishes his exodus in
Jerusalem, leading us through the Red Sea,
a passage he has made possible by the price of his own blood.

And let's not pretend that we can have it any other way.
That is the witness of Tabor when the Word was transformed for
the disciples.
An anticipation of what would be.
Our culture may promise us the short route to happiness, or even spiritual
experiences.
But our grounding in all Being is made possible by the Blood of the Lamb.
Our salvation comes not from a vision but from the work of Christ.
That exodus he did accomplish once and for all.
That exodus brought us into new life.
That exodus is with us today—not on the mountain, but in the everyday
world of God's promise.

The transfigured Lord is a graced reminder that God's covenant is forever.
There are a lot of false promises out there today—
    everything from eternal youth to the right to die however and
    whenever we choose.
Imaginary spectacles that don't last.
And some of these, like movie stars, we will fall for.
But let's remember to come down the mountain with the Lord as he takes
    up his cross and goes to Jerusalem.
What better promise could we hope to have?

GD

Questions for Reflection

1. How is the season of Lent informing my own spirituality, my transformation by God's saving Word?

2. Paul says not to be occupied with "earthly" things. To the extent that it is possible in my particular calling in life, what do I have to do to keep my eyes fixed on the things of heaven?

3. How strongly in my prayer do I hear the Father's voice when he says, "This is my chosen Son; listen to him"?

Other Directions in Preaching

1. Imagine a monologue by Peter, James, or John (or all three) about his experience on Tabor.

2. Paul states that longing for the Lord is his joy and crown. That desire is at the heart of our relationship with God. Lent is our time to find both the joy and the crown waiting for us at Easter.

3. If I were a witness to the events of Mount Tabor, what would I see? How would this occasion change my relationship with Jesus?

Our Lenten Hope
THIRD SUNDAY OF LENT

READINGS:
Exodus 3:1–8a, 13–15; 1 Corinthians 10:1–6, 10–12; Luke 13:1–9

There are some priests who should never be priests.
There are some physicians who should never be physicians.
Many of these priests and physicians are certainly smart enough to do
their work.
They fail not because of lack of smarts.
They fail because of lack of hope.

A number of years ago I developed a high fever while on chemotherapy.
A very bright doctoral fellow examined me and, in a disdainful voice and
with a snobbish face, declared: "You're infected!"
I felt bad when I first came into the hospital, but now I felt rotten.
Then my personal physician, Craig Kessler, entered the room, examined me,
and declared in the most positive way possible:
"Fr. Waznak, I am truly impressed with the level of your toxicity."
Dr. Kessler is not only a brilliant oncologist/hematologist but a man with
great bedside manners, a man who gives hope to his patients.

When I told this story to a small group of priest friends, one of them asked:
"But are you sure he's not just giving you false hope?"
I replied, "At this stage of my life, I would rather have false hope than no
hope at all."

The former Archbishop of Canterbury, Donald Coggan, once wrote:

"Of St. Paul's trio—faith, hope, and love—the greatest, he affirms, is love. True; but the most neglected is hope. Yet, in the Bible it is a major theme."*

But who is it that neglects hope in our day?

Not just some priests and physicians but some politicians, parents, teachers, and others who find themselves serving others;

It is sad, but true, that these servants who lack hope should simply find another career.

Those of us who are waiting for our little fruitless fig tree to grow need voices of hope.

And down through the ages, there have been many voices who have never neglected
the virtue of hope.

Let us listen, you and I, to a few of them:

"The last thing that dies in a person is hope," says Diogenes.

"As long as man breathes, he should not lose hope," says the Talmud.

Emily Dickinson wrote: "Hope is a strange invention / A Patent of the Heart / In unremitting action / Yet never wearing out."**

"If it were not for hope, the heart would break," wrote Thomas Fuller, MD, in *Gnomologia*, in 1732.

"We must accept disappointment, but we must never lose infinite hope," said Martin Luther King, Jr.

"I cannot imagine that I should strive for something if I did not carry hope in me. I thank God for this gift. It is as big a gift as life itself," said Vaclav Havel, in one of his speeches.

---

*Donald Coggan, *God of Hope: A Bible Study and a Comment* (San Francisco: HarperCollins, 1991).

**The Complete Poems of Emily Dickinson,* ed. Thomas J. Johnson (Boston: Little, Brown and Co., 1960), 597.

And, finally, my favorite: "Hope is going to your mailbox on a Sunday
morning," says Joseph Gallagher, a priest of the Baltimore
archdiocese.

In Luke's parable today it is not a poet, a physician, or a priest who offers
hope, but a gardener.
It is the vocation of the gardener to give people hope, to have nothing to do
with despair.
People who plant learn to be people of hope, to wait for the harvest, to
know that even beneath the winter snow lies the seed that in the
springtime becomes the rose.
The owner of the fig tree has given up.
He is like my neighbor, Thelma, who has convinced herself that she doesn't
have a "green thumb."
I think the "green thumb" theory is nonsense, an utter myth.
Thelma doesn't need a green thumb but a gardener of hope.
I try to be that for her.

When I prayed over this parable, I noticed something wonderfully hopeful.
The gardener pleads for restraint and offers a prescription of hope:
    "Sir, leave it for this year also, and I shall cultivate the ground around
    it and fertilize it;
    it may bear fruit in the future."
And then the gardener says something quite startling:
    "If not, *you* can cut it down."
So even if the fig tree still does not bear fruit,
    the gardener will have nothing to do with destroying it.
This respectful gardener tells the owner to cut it down!
People of hope are like that.

Hope is not just a virtue for Advent but for Lent as well and all the seasons
of our lives.
We are preparing for the great Easter Pasch.

We know that passion, suffering, dying, and burial are to come for Jesus
and for us.
But we know that the resurrection is the goal of our Lenten journey.
This is the faith we profess and the reason we keep on hoping.

RPW

Questions for Reflection

1. All of our language about God is metaphorical. What does God's response to Moses tell us about God's self-identity?

2. Many people believe that bad things happen to them because they have sinned or failed to live up to God's expectations for them. How do we address this issue?

3. The owner of the vineyard was looking for timely results. Is reforming our lives a process that yields timely results? Does God expect us to at least make a start—perhaps this Lent?

Other Directions for Preaching

1. Where is the holy ground in our life? Perhaps we limit that answer to places that have a clear religious connection. What about our homes, our work places, our relationships? In order to reform our lives, we need to make of our entire lives holy ground.

2. We recognize that tragedy can occur suddenly and unexpectedly. The challenge is to live our lives so that we are always reconciled with God and with one another. Living in this way gives us peace and serenity in an uncertain world.

'Til by Turning, Turning, We Come Round Right
Fourth Sunday of Lent

READINGS:
Joshua 5:9a, 10–12; 2 Corinthians 5:17–21;
Luke 15:1–3, 11–32

Perhaps you remember the old name for this Sunday?
It was used in those days when the Mass was still in Latin.
Today was called Laetare Sunday, from the Latin word for "rejoice."
In the middle of Lent there was a Sunday given over to rejoicing,
    a day of reprieve from penance and fasting and even the color purple.
Since it was the mid-point of Lent, three weeks down and three to go, it
    reminded us that the joyful feast of Easter was drawing near.
To express joy, the priest would wear rose vestments—
    which not many clergy appreciated, since few looked particularly
    "pretty in pink."
But I can remember as a boy how, suddenly, radiant rose replaced
    somber purple.

But, even though we seldom see rose vestments anymore, the note of joy
    that marked this day is still recognized as belonging to Lent.
If the presider has been using the first Preface for Lent as the Eucharistic
    Prayer begins, you will have heard these words over the last few
    weeks: "Each year you give us this *joyful* season when we prepare to
    celebrate the paschal mystery with mind and heart renewed."

Lent is about conversion, and conversion is about turning toward God.
And turning toward God renews our hearts and minds, thereby
    bringing joy.
I think of the words of the beautiful Shaker hymn:

> 'Tis a gift to be simple, 'tis a gift to be free,
> 'Tis a gift to come down where we ought to be.
> And when we have arrived at the place just right,
> It will be in the valley of love and delight.
>
> When true simplicity is gained,
> To bend and to bow we shall not be ashamed,
> To turn, turn will be our delight
> 'Til by turning, turning, we come round right.*

In the turning we "come round right" and find joy.
So today, on Laetare Sunday, we hear one of the most beautiful stories in
    the Bible, a story that involves turning and in the end offers the
    hope of joy.
We call it the story of the prodigal son, but I can remember years ago the
    biblical scholar Barnabas Ahearn said we should call it the story of the
    prodigal father.
This father was lavish in his love; his heart was as loving as a human heart
    could be.
In this story, we have several turns.
There is the young son who turns away from his father, asking for his share
    of the family wealth—a great insult, since the family wealth was only
    divided when the father had died.
So the request for "my share" was equivalent to saying: "Drop dead, Dad!"
Furthermore, this dividing would mean a loss of the family fortune for all who
    remained, a threat to their security, endangering the family's well-being.
Even so, the father gives his youngest "his share" and the boy leaves.

---

* "Shaker Song No. 72."

Now, at first, everything is great for the young man: friends, fun, freedom.
But then the money runs out, and so do the friends and the fun and
    the freedom.
The boy finds himself in the worst possible position a Jewish boy
    could be in, working as a servant for Gentiles, far away from home,
    tending to the pigs, unclean animals that rendered all who touched
    them ritually unclean.
And this is where the first important turn comes in.

The boy turns inward and takes a good look at himself.
"Coming to his senses" is how the text puts it.
And when he sees what has happened, he says,
    What a mess! What am I doing here? The hired hands at home have it
    better! Well, I will have to eat crow, which is a lot better than eating
    this slop the pigs feed on. I will return to my Father and say, "I have
    sinned against God and you. Treat me as one of your hired workers."
Then he heads on home.

Some say the boy was being practical; others claim that his repentance
    was heartfelt.
I like to think he learned the lesson of the song:
    When true simplicity is gained, to bend and to bow we shall not be
    ashamed. To turn, turn will be our delight, till by turning, turning,
    we come round right.
The boy had come to see the simple truth: he had sinned against his father,
    been a self-serving little brother, focused only on the family fortune.
But now his heart had turned in the right direction; he had "come to
    his senses."

Then we come to the heart of the story.
The great ballet artist George Balanchine based one of his ballets on
    this story.
What I most remember was the return of the son.
When he reaches the father, the father stands there stonefaced.

The son ends up crawling up his body and curling himself up, holding onto
his father's neck.

But the father never reaches out to the son; he never takes the son in his arms.

The son holds himself up, clinging to his father, as the father moves off
stage with him.

I was shocked on seeing this cold homecoming.

This is not true to Luke's story.

The father sees him coming from a long way off.

The father turns from whatever he was doing and catches "sight of him."

And what does he do?

He runs toward this boy, sweeps him up in his arms, and kisses him.

This running is an important part of the story.

The father was running the gauntlet for his son.

Remember, the son had gone off with part of the family fortune, which
affected everyone—elder brother, other relatives living there, and
servants, and word would have spread to the neighbors about this
ungrateful son.

He would not have been welcomed back, and the first sight of him might
have evoked a violent response from any who regarded him as
someone needing a good beating.

That is why the father runs to his son before anyone else can get there.

The boy starts his speech, but the father will have none of it.

He turns—another turn!—to his servant, and, through his tears of joy, he
commands: Kill the calf. Bring my best robe. Put a ring on his finger.
Put shoes on his feet. My son has come home! He was dead to us but,
look, he's alive. He was lost, but, look, he's found.

And they all turned toward the house to have a party.

Of course, the story doesn't end there.

There is the second half: the return of the elder son from the field.

We know this older brother had stayed home, working the land—or did he?

He might have been "at hand" spatially, but his heart had also turned away
    from his father, tallying up all the days and hours he worked, resenting
    his returned younger brother, whom he refers to as "your son."
How else explain his refusal to celebrate his brother's return
    and his father's joy?
Now he turns away from his father, refusing to be at the party and to take
    his place at his father's right hand to welcome the guests.
By this action, he has insulted his father as much as his sibling.
And many a Middle Eastern father would have sent the servants to find him
    and take him to a place where punishment would be dispensed for
    dishonoring his father so publicly.
Not this father.

Again, the father goes out to his son, this time to beg him to come in.
In the face of this son's complaints, the father lovingly says:
    You are with me always; everything I have is yours.
    But we must celebrate your brother's return.
    Come back with me. Return to the house.

We don't know whether this son "came round right" or not.
Did he turn to his father and return to the party and embrace his brother?
I like to think that he, too, "came to his senses."

We hear this story on "Rejoice Sunday" to remind us that God waits for his
    children to return to him, and yearns to celebrate the return of any
    who have wandered off.
Lent calls us to turn inward, to look at ourselves, and,
    if anything separates us from God, "to come to our senses,"
    to turn "'til we come round right."
When we do this, we are assured, we will be greeted with great joy.

Sunday Eucharist offers us a place at that table which is a sign of the
    banquet we will one day sit down to, when the fullness of the

kingdom has come. In the meantime we eat the body and drink the
blood of the Son and are sent forth,
with the charge of Paul's words ringing in our ears.
God has entrusted "to us the message of reconciliation.
So we are ambassadors for Christ, as if God were appealing through us."
Our ongoing work is to help others return to the love of the Father.

JAW

Questions for Reflection

1. When you think about your life, can you remember any occasions on
which you turned away from God?
2. What helped you to turn back?
3. Have you said thank you for having things "turn round right"?

Other Directions for Preaching

1. The short excerpt from the book of Joshua paints a picture of the
Israelites entering the Promised Land from the desert and eating the food of
that land for the first time. God has been true to the promises made, a new
beginning is at hand, home has been reached.

2. Something radically new has happened in Christ and "whoever is in
Christ is a new creation." The reading from 2 Corinthians proclaims the
initiative of God "reconciling us to himself in Christ," and then giving us the
ministry of reconciliation.

3. Luke's parable is directed at those demanding strict requirements for
entering the kingdom. Jesus' response contrasts God's largess to our stinginess
when it comes to showing mercy and forgiveness.

Keeping Score
FIFTH SUNDAY OF LENT

READINGS:
Isaiah 43:16–21; Philippians 3:8–14; John 8:1–11

Most of us learn the value of a dollar from an early age.

One of my fondest childhood memories is going into the local bakery on
    Long Island with my father after Mass on Sunday.

While he stood on line for onion rolls and crumb buns, my dad would give
    me some change and send me next door to buy a copy of *The New
    York Times*.

My visits to the stationery store were a kind of initiation into the world of
    buying and selling, a way of letting a young child know that we live in
    a world of even exchanges.

You get what you pay for.

Nothing is free; the economy runs by the most obvious instincts of giving
    and receiving, an exchange of goods and services.

Even a little boy could figure out the tally sheet when he counted his
    change, while the familiar aroma of coffee and cinnamon breathed like
    a sacred song through the dampness of a Sunday morning.

I just did the math.

By contrast, Paul must not have much of a head for arithmetic.

"I consider everything as a loss because of the supreme good of knowing
    Christ Jesus my Lord," he tells the Philippians.

Paul would never make it on Wall Street.

There is no even exchange here, but rather a new economy.

A brand-new exchange of goods.

Like Paul, Christians are possessed by Christ in this economy of salvation,
    refashioned in the Savior's image.

Paul was imprisoned when he wrote this letter.

At the same time, he is ecstatic with peace and love of the Lord, to whom
    he has been united in suffering.

Early on in this letter Paul tells the Philippians that he is confident that he
    has become a witness to Christ's sufferings, a model of real
    proclamation of resurrection.

Even in the midst of profound suffering the Good News will be preached.

Even in chains Christ's message of salvation can be heard.

The Good News trumps even the darkest of corners.

Salvation has been bought by Christ, and those who share in that suffering
    inherit the "prize of God's upward calling, in Christ Jesus" (Phil 3:14).

This is the real order of things: that suffering wins a crown.

The most famous centerpiece for the Letter to the Philippians is the hymn
    that celebrates the Son of God, who emptied himself and became a
    slave for our sake.

Though he was in the form of God, Jesus did not grasp divinity but gave
    it away.

For us.

For me.

And so God exalted the name Jesus above all others.

Christ's passion and death bring everlasting life.

For free.

We live inside Christ's passion and death, as Paul did in prison.

God does not add or subtract in his new economy.

As the dying priest says at the end of George Bernanos's *The Diary of a
    Country Priest,* "All is grace."

It is hard to imagine that everything is gift, isn't it?

God is ever new, refashioning all creation into the image of the Son.

As Isaiah reminds us,

"Remember not the events of the past,

the things of long ago consider not;

see, I am doing something new!" (Isa 43:18–19).

We are being drawn into God's future by Christ himself, who has pulled us
into heaven.

We are like those who were adrift at sea, now hauled in through the life raft
of the saving wood of his cross.

The next time we are tempted to judge someone else, we might remember
that God is rewriting our future before our very eyes.

Judgment works like math, too.

I think I'll give this one a minus in my book, we say.

She does not really measure up to my standards.

Let's add up all the good things you've done for me.

As John portrays it, those who wish to throw stones at the woman outside
the Temple area just don't seem to get it until Jesus literally writes
them a note in the sand.

They would have the woman caught in adultery stoned according to the
Law of Moses.

They did not figure it out until Jesus confronted them with their own sin.

Only the one who was free from sin was capable of confronting
those who are filled with it.

Some commentators suggest that what Jesus was really writing in the sand
were the sins of those who were about to throw the stones.

I think Jesus was rewriting their future.

A kind of receipt, based on an economy of salvation.

Jesus was doing them a favor by freeing them from the Law.

He was etching a new law born not of false righteousness but of
compassion.

I might even say that those Pharisees and scribes were both shamed
and relieved.

Shamed because Jesus was writing their biographies on the earth.

After all, let's not imagine that any one of us is so virtuous
    that we'd not fall under the weight of God's justice.
And relief because we know that Christ has come to carve a new law into
    the sandy earth,
        the law of love and compassion and the forgiveness of sins.
The new Temple, Jesus himself, was doing something utterly new
    on that day.
He might have turned it into something dead.
An even exchange: death for sin.
But God in Christ has made condemnation into a story of salvation.
Jesus, God's new Temple, would be the house of love,
    not prescriptions of the Law of Moses.
Like God, charity is endlessly creative, and we will see it unfold in its
    fullness as we celebrate the paschal mystery in the upcoming Triduum.
We can start anew and bring forth life out of old ways of thinking
    about people.
We are co-creators with God when we love and stop keeping score.
Let's trade our stones for soft hearts at this Eucharist as we move
    toward Easter.
That is a gift given to us that lasts forever.

GD

Questions for Reflection

1. Have I been quick to judge someone I knew was wrong? Is it OK to condemn others even if they are wrong?

2. Mercy is hard to come by in our culture. When was the last time I was merciful toward another? toward myself?

3. What will be the quality of my Christian compassion by the end of the Lenten season?

Other Directions for Preaching

1. Imagine a monologue of the woman caught in adultery after the crowd leaves her and goes on its way.

2. Imagine a monologue spoken by one or two of those who were about to throw stones before Jesus confronted them.

3. Lent is a time for building up, not tearing down, so let us together take our collective stones and create a house made of mercy and forgiveness.

Meeting Jesus in Luke's Passion
PALM SUNDAY OF THE LORD'S PASSION

READINGS:
Luke 19:28–40; Isaiah 50:4–7; Philippians 2:6–11;
Luke 22:14—23:56

Palm Sunday of the Lord's passion is the name given to this day in the
liturgy books, but I doubt if it will catch on.
For most of us it will remain Palm Sunday.
No harm in that, I'm sure.
But it is important that we see the connection between that piece of palm
we take home and the passion we have just heard.
We don't want to separate the two "pieces of the liturgy"—
the blessing of the palms and the reading of the story of the passion
of Jesus.
A piece of palm is a slender thing, but we hold it as a way of signaling that
this day we greet Jesus as our Messiah, our Lord, the King who comes
in the name of the Lord.
In taking home this piece of palm we signal our willingness to follow
in his footsteps,
today and tomorrow and thereafter.

The Jesus found in the passion of Luke's Gospel is distinct from that of
Mark and Matthew's Gospels, on the one hand, and John's
on the other.

The Jesus we meet in both Mark's and Matthew's accounts of the passion
and death is one who suffers total abandonment.

The Jesus of John's passion is one in total control, very self-possessed.

Luke's presentation stands somewhere in the middle.

I would like to point to three qualities of Jesus in the passion we have
just heard that invite our reflection today and during the final days
of Lent.

First of all, the Jesus of Luke's passion is a tranquil Jesus.

Tranquility marks Jesus at the Last Supper when he calmly reminds the
disciples, "I have eagerly desired to eat this Passover with you before I
suffer, for, I tell you, I shall not eat it again until there is fulfillment in
the kingdom of God."

Tranquility also marks his farewell speech when he calls the Twelve to use
their authority to serve as he did.

He tells them:

"I confer a kingdom on you, just as my Father has conferred one on
me, that you may eat and drink at my table in my kingdom;
and you will sit on thrones judging the twelve tribes of Israel."

And it marks his words to Simon Peter, only found in Luke's passion:

"Simon, Simon, behold Satan has demanded to sift all of you like
wheat, but I have prayed that your own faith may not fail;
and once you have turned back, you must strengthen your brothers."

Jesus' tranquility as the servant of the Lord is to be theirs,
and his kingdom will be their kingdom.

This tranquility sustains him along the way of the cross.

We see it manifested as he comforts the women of Jerusalem,
as he comforts the thief on his right with the promise
that today he will be with him in paradise.

But Luke's Jesus is also a tested Jesus.

During the time of prayer in the garden, Luke presents him as an athlete,
with an angel coming to coach him; and the agony is portrayed as an

intense struggle, with Jesus sweating so fiercely it is like drops
of blood.
Jesus is tested by a trial led by religious leaders who twist his words after
taking him to Pilate.
And Jesus is tested before the Roman authorities; neither Pilate nor Herod
finds anything on which to convict him.
Three times Pilate says, "I find this man not guilty."
Since Jesus refuses to speak to him, Herod can only mock him and return
him to Pilate.
Jesus is tested in fulfillment of the Scriptures.
This is the hour of darkness, he says.
And it proves to be so when Pilate, after declaring Jesus' innocence three
times, then yields to the pressure of the crowd and hands him over to
be crucified.

Finally, the Jesus of Luke's passion is a trusting Jesus.
Throughout the Gospel Jesus urges his followers to put their trust not in
money, but in the Father who gives daily bread and delivers us from
the test.
And his last words are addressed to that same Father:
"Into your hands I commend my spirit" (Luke 24:46).

The Jesus of Luke's passion speaks to our own experience.
We know that life involves testing.
We know this from the many forms of violence that surround our
lives today.
Yesterday we remembered that thirty years ago, Martin Luther King was
shot to death.
This past week, two school children shot to death some of their classmates
and a teacher.
How many here this morning have had their lives touched in some way
by violence?
And it is not just physical violence, but verbal violence or violence done to
our spirits that tests us.

And how many have known the sadness that overwhelms a life
unexpectedly—a sickness, an accident, a sudden death, events that
change life irrevocably?
We all know testing before too long.

The promise of Luke's Jesus is that, even in the darkest trials, tranquility
can be found in God—if we trust.
There will be testing, but as he said to Simon:
"I have prayed that your own faith may not fail;
and once you have turned back, you must strengthen your brothers"
(Luke 22:32).
I would think Simon Peter would remember these words again and again in
future days.
These words remind us there is never cause for despair, no matter what
has happened.
The Lord who prayed for Simon continues to intercede for us.

There is even further reason to trust.
We have been baptized not just into faith in Christ, but into the faith *of*
Christ.
We do not only believe in Jesus but we are gifted with a participation in the
faith *of* Jesus.
That is why every year we renew our baptismal promises on Easter.
It makes us conscious again of the mystery in which we live,
and empowers us to live with the faith *of* Christ.
This faith that allowed Jesus to say at the last, "Into your hands I commend
my spirit."
His final words were a statement of trust, an act of entrusting his life
to his Father.

Such faith can lead us to tranquility.
Peace is the first gift of the risen Christ to his followers locked in by
their fears.

We will be tested, yes—but we are enabled to move through trust to
tranquility.

That is the promise of this day, the promise of the palms, and so we cry out
in faith: "Blessed is he who comes in the name of the Lord."

JAW

Questions for Reflection

1. How does the Jesus of Luke's passion—presented as one who is
tested, tranquil, and trusting—speak to your life?

2. Often we want to avoid testing and to dwell instead in a constant
state of tranquility. Is that really possible, or even truly desirable?

3. Do we witness as a parish community to being a people who trust
the Father?

Other Directions for Preaching

1. One commentator on the passion of Luke says that the portrait of
Jesus that emerges is that of an innocent martyr. How does martyrdom relate
to the role of the church in the world? How does it speak to our role as a
church in today's society?

2. Consider Holy Week as a time to put on the "mind of Christ."
Today's Second Reading is preceded by the words: "Let the same mind be in
you that was in Christ Jesus." It is followed by the great hymn to Christ's life
as self-emptying.

EASTER

The First Easter Parade
EASTER SUNDAY

READINGS:
Acts 10:34a, 37–43; Colossians 3:1–4; John 20:1–9

I found myself thinking about Irving Berlin the other day.
He wrote one of the few popular Easter songs:
    "In your Easter bonnet with all the frills upon it…"*
Fred Astaire sang it as he was walking Judy Garland down Fifth Avenue in
    the movie *Easter Parade.*
Of course, the song has nothing to do with the religious meaning of Easter;
    it is similar in spirit to "The Christmas Song:"
    "Chestnuts roasting on an open fire, Jack Frost nipping at your
    nose…"**—a pleasant song needing no theological commitment.

Even so, the Irving Berlin song reminded me that there was an Easter parade
    at the beginning.
A meager one, to be sure, but nonetheless, a steady procession to the
    tomb—at least, in the Gospel of John.
First Mary Magdalene, then the beloved disciple, then Simon—
    all marching off to the tomb.
Only the Gospel of John recounts the first Easter this way.
At first this account can seem disappointing—no angels in dazzling clothes,

---

    * Irving Berlin, "Easter Parade," in *Reading Lyrics,* ed. Robert Gottlieb and Robert Kimball (New York: Pantheon, 2000), 75.
    ** Robert Wells, "The Christmas Song," in Gottlieb and Kimball, *Reading Lyrics,* 639.

no resounding message that Jesus has risen, no appearance of the
Lord, just this parade to the place of the dead.

But the parade that began then continues now, with the same recognizable
route.
The story of Easter, then and now, moves from darkness to light—
from grieving to believing.
Mary Magdalene is everyone who has experienced the darkness of death.
Her darkness is more than the time of day, that period "while it is still dark."
It is the darkness of grief, pain, loss, and the finality of death.
Notice that in this Gospel there is no mention of going to anoint Jesus or
for any other reason; she goes simply to be there.
She goes to the tomb simply because there is nowhere else she wants to be.
She loved him, and she wants to be near what remains of him.

She speaks to us today about the darkness that surrounds our lives:
the darkness of war, hatred, sickness, broken relationships,
the darkness of pain, suffering, and death.
Was her world as much in love with death as ours seems to be?
Children told to strap on bombs and blow themselves up;
young women sent into restaurants to detonate themselves and
everyone else around them, no matter that this includes old men and
women, families, and little children.
Americans are at the top of the list for terrorists, according to ABC News
last week.
Then there is the darkness of civil war, famine, drugs, gang wars, any form
of violence that takes the lives of the innocent.
The deep darkness of the powers of evil and death is as real now as it
was then.

The Easter story begins in darkness.
But then comes something unexpected: the stone has been moved.
What was meant to seal Jesus in or keep Mary out is no longer there,
and she comes to the logical conclusion that the body has been taken.

That rolled-back stone is indeed the first clue that something has happened.
Mary doesn't even look into the tomb.
She immediately runs to tell Simon and the one Jesus loved:
"They have taken the Lord from the tomb...."
And this report sends them racing to the tomb.

Some curious details follow.
First it is noted that the beloved disciple gets there first but waits
for Simon.
Is this graveyard courtesy?
Or is it a subtle acknowledgment of Simon's restored place of honor in the
community by the time that John's Gospel was written?
In Mark's account of Easter morning the young man at the tomb tells the
women to tell the disciples *and Peter* that Jesus has risen, implying
that Peter was no longer counted a disciple since he had denied Jesus.
In Luke, Simon goes to the tomb but does not enter it.
But by the time of John's Gospel, Simon Peter is given entry to the tomb.
To enter into the tomb is to enter into the dying and rising of Christ.

Then there are those burial cloths.
Twice we are told about them.
First the beloved disciple notices them, then Simon.
Simon also sees that the cloth that had covered Jesus' head was rolled up in
a separate place.
Why all the attention to these cloths?
Well, thieves would not have taken this kind of care to strip the body and
fold the cloths.
Some suggest all this refers back to the raising of Lazarus.
Remember when Lazarus came out of the tomb, he was tied hand and foot
with burial cloths, and his face was wrapped in a cloth.
Lazarus comes out bound, with these cloths clinging to him, because he is
not really done with them.
He will need them when he dies once again.
But Jesus is finished with death; he leaves it and all its trappings behind.

John's Gospel also gives importance to the act of seeing.

We are told Peter *saw* the cloths; but only the beloved disciple sees and
believes.

Remember, the deepest kind of seeing in John's Gospel is to look with faith.

Only the beloved disciple comes to some kind of faith at this moment.

Only he enters into the dying *and rising* of Christ.

And that is the destiny of every beloved disciple.

Finally, the story concludes, "they did not yet understand the Scripture that
he had to rise from the dead."

Why "had to"?

This week's *Time* magazine had as its cover story an essay entitled "Why
Did He Die?"

Today we might ask, "Why did he *have to* rise from the dead?"

What does it mean to say that he rose again according to the Scriptures?

He had to rise because the God and Father of Jesus will not settle for death.

God will not allow death to be victorious.

God is not absent, even in the darkest of times.

And God will not allow death to have the last word.

He had to rise from the dead because this was why he came:

"And when I am lifted up from the earth, I will draw everyone to
myself" (John 12:32).

And, earlier in John's Gospel, he says:

"Just as Moses lifted up the serpent in the desert,

so must the Son of Man be lifted up,

so that everyone who believes in him

may have eternal life" (John 3:14–15).

In John's Gospel this lifting up refers to both the crucifixion and the
resurrection.

The crucifixion is the hour of glory (quite different from the Gospels of
Matthew and Mark—and Mel Gibson!—where the crucifixion is the
hour of suffering and abandonment).

In John the hour of glory is the hour of the cross, when Christ reveals the
      love of God for us and thus glorifies his Father.
The lifting up also refers to the resurrection, when the Father glorifies
      the Son.
He had to be lifted up so that all who see—all who look with faith on him
      and believe—
         will have eternal life.
The Son of Man came that we might have life and have it abundantly.

We have the next fifty days to ponder this mystery of the death and
      resurrection.
We have fifty days to absorb the words from the Letter to the Colossians:
      "Think of what is above, not of what is on earth.
      For you have died [in the sacrament of baptism],
      and your life is hidden with Christ in God.
      When Christ your life appears,
         then you too will appear with him in glory."
This is the mystery in which our lives are to be lived.

So, whenever darkness threatens to surround us,
         we are told to turn to the Scriptures to see who God is,
         to read the stories that testify to God,
         who created all life, and who entered into an eternal covenant
         with us through the Blood of Jesus.
Our God wants a family that honors and praises him and rejoices in the
      divine love Jesus revealed.

My brothers and sisters,
         we are part of that ongoing Easter parade of people who know that
         death is not our destiny.
Sometimes we are crawling, sometimes stumbling, sometimes running,
         but always we are moving toward the light of a new dawn.
We move forward into the light of the risen Lord, singing the song of Easter:
         Alleluia, alleluia, alleluia.

Praise God who is Father and Son and Holy Spirit.
Today is Easter. Amen! Alleluia!

JAW

Questions for Reflection

1. How have you known the light of Easter in your life?

2. How does your parish community witness to the power of the Resurrection in its liturgical and apostolic life as a community of faith?

3. Where is an experience of the risen Christ most needed in our world? Pray to God for that.

Other Directions for Preaching

1. Look to the alternative Pauline text offered for the feast: 1 Corinthians 5:6b–8 and its call to "Clear out the old yeast, so that you may become a fresh batch of dough." Connection with the Eucharist and with the renewal of baptismal vows can be made.

2. If you have been preaching the Gospel for Easter Sunday Mass year after year, consider using the Gospel for the Easter Vigil, making use of its unique images for proclaiming the Easter Gospel. Unique to Luke is the question of the two men in dazzling garments: "Why do you seek the living one among the dead?" This is followed by the Easter proclamation, "He is not here, but he has been raised," then by a call to "remember what he said to you while he was still in Galilee."

From Fear to Faith
SECOND SUNDAY OF EASTER

READINGS:
Acts 5:12–16; Revelation 1:9–11a, 12–13, 17–19;
John 20:19–31

The death of Pope John Paul II yesterday makes this a day of sadness
and sorrow.
The light of Christ present in John Paul, who so wisely guided the church
for more than a quarter of a century, is no longer with us.
And the world seems a little darker for his absence.
For the first time in over twenty-seven years, we will not hear his name
mentioned during the Eucharistic Prayer.
And until the cardinals gather to elect his successor, we will continue to feel
the loss of the one we call the holy father, the vicar of Christ, the head
of the Catholic Church.

Even in the face of this loss so keenly felt today, we are called to live in the
awareness of how our faith comforts us.
We gather as a community of believers to worship God whom we
call Father.
We recognize God as the Father of our Lord Jesus Christ, who raised him
from the dead.
The church considers Easter week as a day in the celebration of Easter.
Easter speaks to the darkness of death.
Indeed, in the Gospel of John, Easter begins in darkness.
Mary Magdalene goes to the tomb "while it was still dark."

Many of the other Easter stories begin in darkness of one sort or another.
There is the darkness of fear spoken of in this morning's Gospel,
>with the disciples gathered behind locked doors for fear of the Jews.
There is the darkness of doubt that leads Thomas to say,
>"Unless I see the mark of the nails in his hands and put my finger into
>the nail marks and put my hand into his side, I will not believe."
The two disciples walking down the road from Jerusalem to Emmaus find
>themselves enveloped in the darkness of hopelessness,
>>their hope that Jesus would be the one to redeem Israel having
>>been shattered.
The movement in all the Easter stories is from darkness to light,
>from death to new life, from doubt to hope, from fear to peace.
This movement is the movement of faith.

The author of Revelation addressed his hearers as one who "[shares] with
>you the distress, the kingdom, and the endurance we have in Jesus."
Through his words, we hear the risen One speak to our hearts and minds:
>"Do not be afraid. I am the first and the last, the one who lives.
>Once I was dead, but now I am alive forever and ever.
>I hold the keys to death and the netherworld."

I came across a poetic definition of faith the other day:
"Faith is the bird that feels the light and sings while the dawn is still dark"
>(Rabindranath Tagore).
Easter faith calls us to sing Alleluia in the face of darkness.
The paschal candle remains lit for fifty days, reminding us of the light that
>has come into the world with the resurrection of Christ.
Faith allows us to see in this candle the sign that darkness will not conquer.
Faith gives us Easter eyes.

Thomas is presented today as a figure who moves from doubt to faith.
We often call him Doubting Thomas, but that imprisons him in an early
>moment of this Easter story.
If you think about it, Thomas is no worse than the others.

Mark's women might have believed, but they do not even tell anyone
   because of their great fear [see Mark 16:8].
Luke's account says that when the women told the apostles, they did not
   believe them because the story "seemed like nonsense" (Luke 24:11).
While Thomas said he wouldn't believe until he put his fingers into Jesus'
   wounds and his hand into his side, even so, once the Lord was there,
   he forgot about that demand.
Indeed, he burst out with what has been called the strongest proclamation
   of faith in the Gospels:
   "My Lord and my God!"
Thomas gradually came to have Easter eyes.

To see with Easter eyes takes time.
In the end, it's not a matter of skill; it's a gift.
"Blessed are those who have not seen and have believed."
As we gather today let us thank God for all those people in our lives who
   did not see the risen Lord as Thomas did but yet have believed in him.
Let us give thanks for all those who have handed on the faith to us.

Today we thank God for the twenty-seven years that John Paul II shared his
   gifts of wisdom, strength, courage, and compassion.
Many fine statements have been spoken about him in the last
   twenty-four hours.
President Bush said, "The world has lost a champion of human freedom."
Reporters have commented on how the pope traveled the world to come to
   the people, and praised him for his efforts to mend fences between
   Catholics and Jews, Catholics and Muslims, and Catholics and both
   the Orthodox and the various Protestant branches of Christianity.
But, above all, he was a figure of faith and a herald of hope.
He was a living embodiment of the motto he chose for his papacy, "Do not
   be afraid," and a witness to the risen Christ in a world that rarely gets
   beyond what it can see.
He witnessed not only by his words but by his actions.
He taught us not only how to live in faith but also how to die in faith.

It was most appropriate that Pope John Paul's final word was "amen,"
    which is Aramaic, the language Jesus spoke, and is translated
    "so be it."
May the gift of faith that allows us to see the risen Lord in our world and
    in our lives allow us to live lives that ultimately say "amen."

JAW

Questions for Reflection

1. Can you recall times when you have been able to move from fear to faith?

2. Who are the people in your life that have helped you believe?

3. How do you experience the faith of your community? Where do you see it in action?

Other Directions for Preaching

1. The reading from Acts shows that the healing power Jesus embodied in his ministry has passed to Peter and the apostles. This healing power continues to be found in the presence of the believing community.

2. The theme of fear before the Son of Man is also found in the apocalyptic vision of the seer John in today's Second Reading. This figure is said to hold the keys to death and the netherworld. This vision is given for the sake of the church.

3. The first gift of the risen Lord is shalom (peace), a very rich Hebraic concept that goes beyond the absence of war.

An Easter Witness Speaks
Third Sunday of Easter

READINGS:
Acts 5:27–32, 40b–41; Revelation 5:11–14; John 21:1–19

Easter is a season of witnesses.
It begins with the witness of the women who went to the tomb
    and found it empty.
Their sorrow was swept away by the words:
    "Why do you seek the living one among the dead?
    He is not here, but he has been raised" (Luke 24: 5–6).
Last week we had the witness of the apostles in the upper room and
    of Thomas.
And today Peter witnesses to us, both in the First Reading and
    in the Gospel.
It is Peter who is set before us as the first public witness,
    from the day of Pentecost when he got up to preach before the crowds
    to this incident in Acts when he defied the Temple police.
Peter's voice is the first Easter voice, so I have decided today to yield the
    pulpit to him.
I ask you to use your imagination to see before you Simon Peter,
    son of John.

Good morning, my friends.
You know me as Peter, though in my village they called me Simon
    bar Jonah.
You just heard my favorite Resurrection story.

You might wonder what we were doing back in Galilee.

Perhaps you remember how he had come to us that Sunday night in
    Jerusalem and said, "Receive the Holy Spirit. Whose sins you forgive
    are forgiven them, and whose sins you retain are retained"
    (John 20:23).

Well, to be quite honest, we weren't sure where to go with all that.

So we went on home to Galilee and thought we would figure it out from
    there.

Only when we got home, things weren't much clearer.

There we were up in Galilee, sitting around, glum, uncertain,
    missing him.

Nothing was coming to any of us.

And if the Holy Spirit had any plans, it wasn't letting us in on them.

Finally, I said, "Enough of this—I'm going fishing!"
    and about six of the others got up and joined me.

Well, nothing came of that either.

All night we worked, but no fish were coming around.

Believe me, it is backbreaking work and not everyone knew what
    he was doing.

Not to mention any names, but the only net a certain tax collector knew
    was net profits.

Right before dawn we were all dozing and a voice came across the water:
    Any luck?

Nothing, Nathaniel yelled back.

Toss the nets off to the right, the voice said.

This time the voice sounded familiar.

There was nothing to lose, so we did.

And suddenly, the nets began to sink with the weight of the fish.

It was as if all the fish of the lake had suddenly found their way there.

Then someone yelled, "It is the Lord."

I know it sounds crazy, but I reached for my clothes and jumped in.

I had to get there first.
I still felt a shadow hanging between us.

There had been no time alone since the night before he died.
He had said to us that night,
> "Where I am going, you cannot follow me now, though you will
> follow later."

And I had said to him,
> "Master, why can't I follow you now?
> I will lay down my life for you."

And he looked at me sadly and said,
> "Will you lay down your life for me? Amen, amen, I say to you,
> the cock will not crow before you deny me three times"
> (John 13:33, 36–38).

You know what happened, of course.
Three times they asked me: Aren't you his disciple?
Three times I said: I am not.
And right after the third time, the cock crowed.

When I got to shore, there he was fixing breakfast for us.
The man loved to eat—both before and after those terrible days.
He loved to eat and talk and laugh.
After breakfast he nodded to me, signaling that we go off.
And we began to walk down the beach.

Is it really you, Lord? I asked, uncertain of what to say.
Yes, it is, Simon, he said.
Then, he asked, "Simon, son of John, do you love me more than these?"
"Yes, Lord, you know that I love you," I said, so forcefully it surprised me,
> like I had been waiting for that question all my life.

"Feed my lambs," he said.
We walked a little further and he asked again, "Simon, son of John, do you
> love me?"

I thought to myself: OK, he has a right to make sure.

I said again, "Yes, Lord, you know that I love you."

And he said, "Tend my sheep."

But after going a little further on he asked for a third time,

"Do you love me?"

Well, this was torture.

I spoke to him as if he was hard of hearing:

"Lord, you know everything; you know that I love you."

And his face burst into a smile and he said, "Feed my sheep."

I've thought a lot about why he asked me three times.

You might think it was tit for tat.

Three denials, three professions of love.

Or maybe he knew I had to say it three times to find peace, to be able to
    move on.

But, you know, he might have asked me three times because he needed to
    hear it three times.

Maybe it was for his benefit as much as mine.

But, with the passing years, I've come to think it might be something
    else again.

To love him means to love those he loves.

To love him means to care for those in the community who need tending.

And to love him means caring about what is happening both in and outside
    the fold.

It means going wherever there is need of any kind.

All this flows from being called to witness to the risen Lord.

Others will know him now through you.

Even in our day, we brought each other to him.

John the Baptist pointed him out to my brother Andrew, and Andrew
    brought me.

I told James, and he brought his younger brother John.

Philip brought Nathaniel, and the other James brought Simon.

And so forth and so on, right up to those good people you baptized here
    two weeks ago.

You never know where it will lead.

None of us finished life where we thought we would.

I ended my days in Rome, as you know.

Me, a fisherman from Galilee, in the city of the Caesars.

They came and took me and tied me fast and carried me off to die
    as he died.

John ended up on Patmos, writing his version of Jesus' story and some
    other strange piece.

James was stoned, literally, in Jerusalem; Andrew crucified in Greece.

Magdalene we're not too sure, though I love that picture an artist did of her
    standing before Caesar and denouncing Pilate—she would've, too.

Martha and Mary and Lazarus—well, some say they ended up in France,
    which makes sense; Martha was always a good cook.

The others scattered to the winds, and we're still not sure where they met
    their end, temporarily, of course.

You never know where the Spirit will take you, if you open your life to it.

We continued to meet the Lord in the breaking of the Bread.

And he continued to remind us in the same breaking of the Bread
    what our lives were all about: our bodies given for others,
    our blood poured out for others.

Now it is up to you to move it forward.

You never know when or how the Lord will come to you,
    or what he will ask.

I never expected that voice coming out of the mist across a lake after a
    frustrating night of fishing.

Sometimes it's the voice of a stranger asking for help, or a confused young
    person, not knowing what she wants, or someone sick or lonely or
    grieving or dying.

He continues to ask: Do you love me?

And then, in one way or another, to follow up with: "Feed my lambs. Tend
    my sheep."

So try to pay attention. There are lots of people who need caring
   for out there.
And he looks to this community here for some help.
Let Easter continue to be lived out in your lives!

JAW

Questions for Reflection

1. How do you answer the call to witness?

2. How do you answer the question, "Do you love me?"

3. Who are the lambs and sheep this community tends? What part do
you play?

Other Directions for Preaching

1. Does Peter's response to the Sanhedrin, "We must obey God rather
than men," continue to have relevance in our day?

2. Revelation invites us to reflect on the link between John's vision of
heavenly worship and our own celebration of the Eucharist.

3. The apostolic mission of the church is symbolized in the catch of fish.
We are now fishers of men and women. Our faith in the risen Lord directs us
to this.

His Master's Voice
FOURTH SUNDAY OF EASTER

READINGS:
Acts 13:14, 43–52; Revelation 7–9, 14b–17;
John 10:27–30

In 1898 a little-known depiction of a fox terrier would
revolutionize human perception.

The painting, by British artist Francis Barraud, showed a little white dog
mesmerized by a brass horn that was part of an invention known as a
gramophone.

The Victor Talking Machine Company picked up the painting as its
trademark, and when that agency was bought out by RCA in 1929,
the symbol of a small pooch bewitched by electronic sound would
dominate the recording industry worldwide.

Eventually, the tiny canine and his sound system were even turned into a
series of stained glass windows and are still enshrined today on the
waterfront in Camden, New Jersey.

The famous name given to Barraud's painting suggests just how much the
world of technology would eclipse—and even erase—the sacred
presence of the human subject.

That painting's title would eventually symbolize the dynamics of a gigantic
recording industry—and our relationship with the emerging world
of technology.

The painting was entitled *His Master's Voice.*

When Jesus tells the disciples that his sheep hear his voice, I wonder if he
knew just how difficult it would be to do that now,
in these early years of the third millennium.
Certainly the early Christians like Barnabas and Paul faced competing,
politicized voices in the marketplace of Antioch.
It was tough dealing with some of the Jewish folks who were still linked to
their own tradition and would hear nothing of the Good News.
Sad to say, preaching does not always take root;
it even finds counter-trends in the making that deafen God's Word.
The age of technology has radically altered the stakes of discipleship
and forged an environment of imitation.
The shepherd's voice is mimicked by a sound not his own.
We live in a perplexing society of wolves dressed as sheep,
of pseudo-values masked as good.
The compassionate Shepherd calls out to his flock,
but it is up to us to decide if that voice is real or on Memorex.

Nowhere is counterfeit culture more evidenced than in the relativization of
the *ordo bonorum,* that is, the hierarchy of goods.
The Christian community recognizes that the highest good belongs to
God alone.
To hear the voice of the Shepherd is our ultimate, relentless priority.
But the drive toward the Good stands on shaky ground in a nation of
choice, disguised as democracy, disguised as freedom, disguised as
personal preference.
The unwanted pregnancy, the dying old man, the boring marriage—
all become subject to my individual discretion.
It is harder and harder to catechize about one overwhelming and
absolute Good.
Is it any wonder we may find it hard to hear the sacred,
authentic Shepherd's voice in the night, especially
when that strain is more than occasionally wrapped in the
suffering and obedience of the cross, the only experience that
will not submit to personal choice?

Christianity is always going to be at odds with a secular culture.
The rite of baptism challenges us to resist not just evil but its glamour.

Yet I have a persistent vision.
It is not of presidents and kings, or being redeemed by politics or art,
      still less of a fox terrier staring all agog at what my grandmother,
      Mary O'Neill, used to call the Victrola.
It is of God's holy ones forming a vast multitude and standing before
      the Lamb.
That vision begins and ends here, of course, around the Lamb's high feast,
      the Eucharist where all of us stand with open hands, open hearts, and
      open ears, to receive the One who calls us each by name.
Our disposition toward everyday life should continually reflect the church
      at prayer, the church at Eucharist, because it is here that the sheep are
      found waiting and listening and yearning to be fed.
Even now we hear him call out to us, as he does in the Song of Songs:
      "Arise, my dove, my fair one, and come away,
      for now the winter is past, the rain is over and gone" (2:10–11).
That is the sound of the real master's voice, because it searches for
      the beloved.
We wait together because only in the community of love is the Good
      ordered and redirected in faith.
The Lord is disclosed as Shepherd not to one member of the flock but to all.
We hold our community precious because in our day-to-day, ordinary
      encounters, we find the voice of the Lord and we sharpen our ears to
      his singular song of songs.

No one knew the value of community better than the beloved disciple,
      the only faithful apostle at the foot of the cross, and the one to whom
      our Lord himself gave his mother, the symbol of the church.
John's fidelity was stretched even further, since all his fellow apostles were
      martyred one by one, leaving him in his old age as the lonely disciple
      on Patmos. Yet even there John and his community found the
      unmistakable voice of the Lord:

"The Lamb who is in the center of the throne will shepherd them
and lead them to springs of life-giving water,
and God will wipe away every tear from their eyes" (Rev 7:17).
The community of the beloved disciple found the gift of the presence of the
Shepherd's voice.
That legacy is found in the mystical Johannine monologues of Jesus.
"I am the good shepherd. A good shepherd lays down his life for the sheep"
(John 10:11).
"I am the vine, you are the branches" (John 15:5).
"I am the way and the truth and the life" (John 14:6).
Continual prayer over these texts can only increase our sensitivity to the
unique counterpoint of the Shepherd's voice in a dissonant culture.

A few years after Barraud's painting achieved international attention,
a small window of the Good Shepherd holding a sheep was crafted by
Emil Frei studios in St. Louis and set in a newly constructed Abbey
Church of Maria Einsiedeln here at St. Meinrad.
Nestled in an obscure portion of southern Indiana, the window sits there to
this day over the west doors, rather unpretentiously.
But unlike our little bemused fox terrier,
the lamb calmly rests on his master's shoulders, comforted on the
journey, and waiting to return to the flock.
We join Christ Jesus now around this altar, where he has gathered us in,
both as Shepherd and as spotless Lamb.
Here, we wait together until eternity splits in two.
It's unimaginably psychedelic: united, discovered, and loved into
endless freedom.

GD

Questions for Reflection

1. What are the competing voices in my life that take me away from the Shepherd's call?

2. Have I prayed to listen to the voice of the Lord more clearly in my life? What do I have to do to hear the Shepherd more attentively?

3. What does it mean for me to be obedient to God's will?

Other Directions in Preaching

1. The post-Resurrection world reaches out to all people, as Paul and Barnabas show us in the book of Acts. That outreach continues to our day.

2. The Eucharist we celebrate anticipates John's vision of the great multitude standing before the Lamb.

3. Preaching the Good News is not easy, especially in a land contrary to Gospel values. Like Paul and Barnabas, it is important for us to press on with our mission.

How to Be More Than Nice on Mother's Day
FIFTH SUNDAY OF EASTER

READINGS:
Acts 14:21–27; Revelation 21:1–5a; John 13:31a, 34–35

On this Mother's Day, like many of you, I remember Mama.
She has long since left this earth, but her spirit and her counsel
    are still with me.
Her name was Sophie, and she was very proud when her youngest son was
    ordained a priest.
From the earliest days after ordination in the '60s,
    she would always say to me before Mass,
    "Now don't forget to prepare a nice homily."
Nice was a word Sophie used a lot.
As kids, she would always tell us,
    "Go to the store and buy a nice chicken, or some nice ham, or some
    nice lettuce."
We slowly caught on.
Nice to Mom meant the best, the freshest, the most worthy to take home.

But what did Sophie mean by telling me to prepare a nice homily?
Did she mean something fresh like the chicken or the ham or the lettuce?
"No, that's not what I mean," she said.
She told me she knew I was passionate about the new insights emerging
    from the Second Vatican Council at that time.

She also knew I opposed the war in Vietnam and was an ardent supporter
   of the civil rights movement.
That's why she told me,
   "Bobby, don't say anything that will get you into trouble or
   upset anyone.
   People have a lot of troubles the way it is.
   They go to church to be encouraged."
In other words, be nice!

Except for ignoring the prophetic tradition of biblical preaching, my mother
   made a lot of sense.
After all, the presider says to the assembly, "Lift up your hearts."
That is one of the chief reasons for the homily, to lift up our hearts,
   to go to Eucharist and to go out into the world encouraged.

In many of our Easter stories, there are messengers of encouragement.
We find Paul and Barnabas retracing their missionary steps,
   going back to the cities where they first proclaimed the Gospel.
Because they knew that, despite their new faith, those Christians were
   undergoing trials in their lives and needed to be encouraged.

The name Barnabas, by the way, means "son of encouragement."
The disciples were originally afraid of Paul because, after all,
   he was once the treacherous Saul who was in charge of a Pharisee
   goon squad that rounded up Christians and killed them.
It was Barnabas, "son of encouragement," who stepped in and encouraged
   the disciples to accept Paul and to believe that he truly was a
   converted follower of Christ.
The early churches grew in faith and spread like wild flowers because there
   were people like Paul and Barnabas and countless other men and
   women who encouraged others constantly.

In our Second Reading today, John writes of his vision to the seven churches
   of Asia Minor who were suffering persecution because of their faith.

He encourages them by offering them the final vision of the heavenly
    Jerusalem where cruelty, pain, and opposition will all be
    banished forever.
On this Mother's Day we are offered a poignant image of our God who
    always encourages us.
Our God is like a mother who bends down to kiss away a child's bruise
    and wipes away all tears.
Remembering that Sophie told me to be nice and not to upset anyone,
    I point out to those who have a hard time imagining God as Mother,
    that Pope John Paul I once did so in a homily.

In today's Gospel Jesus is saying farewell to his friends at the Last Supper.
Even as he begins his own trial that will lead to the cross,
    he leaves his disciples with a word of encouragement:
    Love one another, as I have loved you.

Some have criticized this new commandment as found in John's Gospel
    because it seems to be restrictive.
It is about the mutual love of the Christian community as compared to
    the Sermon on the Mount, where the command to love includes
    our enemies.

But I'm not sure that criticism is justified.
For how can we love our enemies if we cannot show encouragement to one
    another in the Christian community?
How can we expect our children to know what love is
    if they first have not experienced it in their homes and in their parish?
In a sense, it is true that charity begins at home.

It begins with a husband's gentle word of encouragement to his wife, who
    must undergo her feared mammogram.
It begins with a mother's firm but gentle word of encouragement to
    her daughter,
    who fears that the new braces will end her social life.

It begins with this parish community of Holy Trinity, which rises above
    petty differences, competing personalities, and outside forces to build a
    community of faith like the early Christian community
    that caused people to remark, "Look how they love one another."

It begins with this family Eucharist, where we remember that Jesus not only
    encouraged us to love one another but laid down his life for us.
This Christian story gives new meaning to the word *nice*.
It is stronger than death itself.

RPW

Questions for Reflection

1. How do you suppose the new Christians responded to the instruction that they were going to have to experience suffering and trials in order to enter into the reign of God? How do we respond to that today?

2. What is it that we yearn to see made new in our lives and in our world?

3. How does Christ's love for us provide a template for our love for one another?

Other Directions for Preaching

1. A liberation theologian might speak a word of challenge here, saying that the combination of today's First Reading and Second Reading could be used to offer hope in the heavenly reign as a way to control or maintain subservience among those who endure the terrible human suffering that we humans inflict on one another (Sudan, northern Uganda, Colombia, Guantanamo).

2. As we have now passed the mid-point of the Easter Season, how is our world changed by the resurrection of Christ? Has the renewal of our journey to baptism made any real difference in us?

Do We Really Need More Lawyers in the Church?
SIXTH SUNDAY OF EASTER

READINGS:
*Acts 15:1–2, 22–29; Revelation 21:10–14, 22–23;
John 14:23–29*

Once in a while I go to Mass.

By that I mean, I go somewhere in the Archdiocese of Washington or
the Diocese of Arlington to get a sense of how liturgy is being
celebrated, how preaching is either lifting up people's hearts or
dragging them down.

These church experiences offer me a treasure trove from which to illustrate
in my preaching classes.

A few Sundays ago, just when the current sex-abuse scandal was breaking
in the media, I went to Mass where a permanent deacon preached.

The deacon's homily was certainly biblical, but when it came to some sort
of practical application to the people's lives, there was nothing but a
mouthful of generic platitudes and do's and don'ts.

It seemed like the preacher was most comfortable dealing with the abstract
rather than the nitty-gritty of our lives.

After Mass, I introduced myself to the deacon and asked him what was the
intention of his homily.

I told him that I heard him cajole and encourage us to do many things,
but I didn't hear him offer one specific example.

I thought the deacon would be taken aback and possibly defensive,
  but he wasn't.
He simply told me that in his homiletic training as a permanent deacon in
  the archdiocese, he was told never to get specific in his homilies.
"What?" I blurted out. "Have you never read the biblical prophets?"
How about Jeremiah, who was so specific in prophetic preaching that he
  told the people to circumcise "the foreskins of your hearts" (Jer 4:4)?
Speaking about sex scandals in the church necessarily leads us into a
  minefield, but we have no other choice.
Gerard Sloyan put it this way: "Christian people are starved for a gospel
  view of questions public and private on which they must make
  decisions daily." *

Usually, I give an assignment to my student preachers to tackle a specific
  social-justice problem in our society.
The students tell me that it is the most difficult assignment.
They don't find it too difficult talking about God, God's love,
  even the commandments, as long as they speak in generalities.
It's when they have to get specific about social-justice issues that the
  students begin to squirm.
Mostly, they tell me, because they don't want to offend anybody.

Getting specific about our faith, our lives, our families, our nation can
  certainly be a risky business!
In our Reading from Acts today we have a story of the early church
  struggling to be true to Christ but also struggling to come up with a
  specific solution to a human dilemma.
Some members of the church were causing a big stink
  because they insisted that Gentile converts to the cause of Christ had
  to be first circumcised like the Jewish converts to Christianity.
Here was a situation where Jesus left no specific advice.

---

* Gerard S. Sloyan, *Worshipful Preaching* (Philadelphia: Fortress Press, 1984), 28.

But in our Reading we do see how the early Christians followed the general
principles that Jesus left them.

They remembered how we had told them that where two or three were
gathered in his name, he would be with them.

They remembered how he told them there would be moments in their lives
when their peace would be disturbed;
when they would be fearful and stressed out.

But they also remembered that Jesus told them that they were not alone but
had his Spirit, his Holy Spirit to guide them in all their specific and
tough decisions.

In our Gospel today, Jesus describes the Holy Spirit as a Paraclete,
another word for counselor or advocate or lawyer.

Just as a lawyer defends us when we get in a pickle, so too would Christ's
Holy Spirit be our guide, our counselor, our defense.

And so the young church gathers together.

It solves its specific problems not in isolation but in community.

Its members listen to all sides of the argument.

And then, with the aid of the Holy Spirit, they make a decision not to add
burdens to the Gentile converts by demanding that they be
circumcised.

But the early community of believers also comes to a compromise decision.

They ask the Gentiles to observe the dietary laws and ritual codes of their
Jewish brothers and sisters so that they could be in peace with one
another around the table of the Lord.

There are two major lessons in the way the early church handled this
specific problem that was tearing it apart.

First, they made their decision by listening to one another; they were not
afraid to listen to all the thorny issues that disturbed them.

Second, they were convinced that they needed someone outside their tiny
selves to solve their specific problem.

They make their decision with the aid of Christ's Holy Spirit, who dwells
within them and their community.

The agonizing problems we face in our Catholic community today, such as
the sexual scandal of priests and the coverups of bishops, are not
going to go away by a magic wand, a sound bite concerning zero
tolerance, more lawyers, more treatment centers, more money, and
more secrets.
We're going to have to face our problems boldly and openly together,
without fear or hypocrisy.
And Jesus left us his lawyer, the Holy Spirit, to remind us that we can do it.

RPW

Questions for Reflection

1. As a community (family, church, civic), how can we accurately
distinguish between those who enjoy creating dissension and the truly
prophetic voices? (Perhaps look to history or the lives of the saints.)

2. What graces would enable our lives to resemble the magnificent city
described in Revelation?

3. "Do not be distressed or fearful." Easier said than done. How do we
let go of our fears?

Other Directions for Preaching

1. It is easy to be selective about which words of God, through Christ,
we believe to be the core of the Christian message. Are there certain
nonnegotiable words? unconditional love for all, peace, justice, forgiveness,
fidelity? How does the Spirit help us to discern the meaning of these words in
our individual and communal lives?

2. Peace is Christ's farewell gift to his followers. Yet, Christ tells us that
his peace is not the same as the world's definition of peace. Explore the
qualities of Christ's peace.

Depth, Not Distance
THE ASCENSION OF THE LORD

READINGS:
Acts 1:1–11; Ephesians 1:17–23; Luke 24:46–53

Last year I missed the Ascension in two ways.
First of all, I literally missed it because the Archdiocese of Washington
    celebrates the feast on Sunday.
I was not here that Sunday but preaching up in New Jersey.
However, up in New Jersey they celebrated the feast the previous Thursday.
With life being confusing enough these days, I wish the powers that be in
    the church in the United States would get their act together and agree
    on the same day for celebrating this mystery of our faith.

But I also missed the feast in a more personal way.
I find the older I get, the more this feast has to say to my life.
For years I thought of it as the risen Lord leaving this earth.
The image from various paintings of the Ascension lingers: Jesus going up
    into the clouds, the apostles staring at the bottoms of his feet.
I used to think he was probably happy to return to the Father,
    given how he had been treated at the end of his life.
His job was finished and now he could sit at the Father's right hand,
    as the creed says, until it is time for him to return to judge the living
    and the dead.

I used to have a great deal of sympathy for the disciples, and could
    understand their asking Jesus right before he leaves:
    "Lord, are you at this time going to restore the kingdom to Israel?"

I thought it was similar to that moment in *Fiddler on the Roof,* when the
villagers who have to leave their beloved town, Anetevka, ask their
rabbi, "Rabbi, wouldn't this be a good time for the Messiah to come?"
But he answers, "It certainly is, but it looks like we will have to wait
someplace else."
The two men in white who suddenly are on the scene have a similar
response: "Men of Galilee, why are you standing there looking at the
sky?" (Acts 1:11).
In other words: Time to move on. He's gone. Other things to be done!

But it is not only that Jesus has left the apostles and us on our own to do
what we can do.
Remember, he sits at the right hand of the Father, interceding for us.
Remember, he said that he had to go to the Father in order for the Spirit
to come.
The Ascension does not end the story of Jesus;
Pentecost completes his work with the coming of the Holy Spirit.
Not that that totally completes the story either.
The story of salvation goes on until the end of time,
for we are now his Body in the world.
And the Ascension has relevance for us as the Body of Christ.
The feast of the Ascension is about depth, not distance.
The depth of God's commitment to us is signaled by the presence of the Son
at the Father's right hand in heaven.
This same Father
"put all things beneath his feet
and gave him as head over all things to the church,
which is his body,
the fullness of the one who fills all things in every way."
With the Ascension we are brought closer to the presence of God through
the One who intercedes for us, enabling us to enter more deeply into
the life of the Trinity.

This feast gives us a clue as to how the church has survived all these
centuries.

And also about how it will continue to survive.

Despite the fractious communities that have always been part of the church,
even from the very beginning—in places like Corinth, and Galatia,
and even Jerusalem,

Despite the violence its members have suffered, being beaten, beheaded,
battered, sworn at, stoned, and swallowed by wild beasts,

Despite the arrogance and exclusivity that has marked both leaders
and members,

Despite the sinfulness that remains in individuals and in communities, the
church has survived and will continue to survive.

For Jesus declared to his disciples,

"Behold I am sending the promise of my Father upon you."

We have a God who is not just a promise maker, but a promise keeper.

The feast of the Ascension leaves us with what can be called the Ascension
agenda.

Item one: always live as a community who waits on the Holy Spirit.

In Luke's Gospel today Jesus tells his disciples to stay in the city "until you
are clothed with power from on high."

This Spirit will come upon you and empower you to witness to Jesus.

This Spirit will enlighten you and give you words to speak.

And this Spirit comes as the spirit of peace and reconciliation.

The work of the Spirit is to bring about the kingdom of God.

So continue to wait on this Spirit, knowing I am interceding for you.

Item two: always witness to Jesus Christ in whatever way possible.

Both the Reading from Acts and Luke's Gospel tell the disciples they are to
be witnesses.

"You will be my witnesses in Jerusalem, throughout Judea and Samaria, and
to the ends of the earth," Jesus says in Acts,
reminding them of the extent of the work to be done.

In the Gospel, Jesus tells them they are witnesses of these things: that the
Christ would suffer and rise from the dead on the third day,

and that repentance, for the forgiveness of sin, would be preached in
   his name to all the nations, beginning from Jerusalem.
Here we have the basic message: Christ's saving death and resurrection have
   won for us repentance and forgiveness.

There is important work to be done.
The agenda set up by the bishops last September in their statement *Faithful
   Citizenship: A Catholic Call to Political Responsibility* is an
   imposing one.
The bishops gave priority to the protection of human life against the
   dangers of abortion, euthanasia, preemptive or preventive use of
   military force, and our nation's increasing reliance on the
   death penalty.
The bishops urged national concern for the promotion of the human family,
   the pursuit of social justice, and the practice of global solidarity.
This agenda is worthy of a national conversation, to say nothing of our
   wholehearted commitment.

The last gesture the Scriptures record Jesus making as he was ascending into
   heaven was one of blessing.
He raised his hands and he blessed them.
It wasn't a farewell wave but a raised hand
      calling for God's protection on these disciples and all who would
   follow them.
May we rejoice in the mystery we celebrate today, knowing we are not
   alone with a world full of insurmountable problems; rather, we live in
   the Spirit of the One who was raised from the dead, ascended to the
   Father, and intercedes for us throughout the ages.

JAW

Questions for Reflection

1. What does the image of Jesus ascending into the heavens say to you?

2. The image of Jesus seated at the Father's right hand is not meant to be a passive image but an active one. How do you ask Jesus today to intercede for our church? for our world?

3. How does this feast offer consolation to the church?

Other Directions for Preaching

1. Compare the two accounts of the Ascension, in Acts and in the Gospel of Luke. What is different? What is the same?

2. The role of Easter angels is interesting as an example of job diversification. They go from simple proclamation at the time of the Resurrection to coaching the apostles here in Acts 1, providing direction (see Acts 8:26 and 10:23ff.), offering assurance (Acts 27:23), striking down corrupt kings (Acts 12:23), and, most interesting, arranging jail breaks (Acts 5:19 and 12:7ff.).

3. An alternative Second Reading for today is Hebrews 9:24–28; 10:19–23, which emphasizes the unrepeatable sacrifice of Christ, which enables us to enter into the presence of our God, approaching "with a sincere heart and in absolute trust."

First Steps
SEVENTH SUNDAY OF EASTER

READINGS:
Acts 7:55–60; Revelation 22:12–14, 16–17, 20;
John 17:20–26

Few parents ever forget that magic moment when their child takes his or her
first steps.
It is really the most poignant of moments.
Little Jimmy is caught between the exhilaration of independence and the
need to hold on.
After a little help, there are a couple of awkward steps.
"Come on!" the family shouts.
Gleefully, the child's arms go up as he stumbles toward his dad.
Claire reaches out and plunges ahead to her adoring sisters,
beyond the world of infancy and into a life that will never be
the same.
Those few steps are a march into the unknown, a reach of the soul to the
future that only God has figured out.

The church is on the edge of walking on this middling, transitional Seventh
Sunday of Easter.
We are moving between the place from which Jesus ascended to the Father
in heaven, and the upper room where the Spirit will come as fire to
empower us forever.
There is some baffling space between the Ascension and Pentecost.
But we are not the first to be confused.

Remember the two men dressed in dazzling white who asked the Galileans
why they were standing looking up at the sky?

This scene captures for us the immobility of the disciples longing for the
future, waiting for new life to unfold before them like an English
garden in late spring.

The ascension of the Lord finds us in a state of longing, even loneliness, for
the risen Lord, whom we came to know so intimately beside the sea of
Galilee, at Emmaus, even behind locked doors.

At the same instant, we extend our hands, reach out with our hearts,
confident in the Lord's promise,
taking those few steps into God's future.

Waiting to be caught up by the power of the Spirit that Jesus has promised.

The Spirit that will capture us and hold us enthralled like never before.

The infancy of discipleship would be transformed into church.

This Sunday finds us searching for God in a unique way.

That longing for the Spirit appears before us like an icon in Acts with the
martyrdom of Saint Stephen.

Stephen reminds us that the early church was born of witness, martyrs to
Christ's presence in blood.

And it is that very longing that gives strength to the early church:
"Blessed are they who wash their robes so as to have the right to the
tree of life and enter the city through its gates" (Rev 22:14).

It is the spirit of desire that haunts the early church.

The martyrs fill us with inspiration.

Stephen was just the beginning.

Perpetua, Agnes, Cecilia...

That spirit of longing is not only captured by Stephen and the martyrs, but
will also be the church's prayer for endless ages as that vigil is kept for
the Bridegroom.

And the Spirit and the Bride say, "Come."

That is a mystical wedding to which we are all invited.

Surely that magnificent moment when we take our first steps is repeated for
many when they walk down the aisle on the day of their wedding.

This time it not a shaky step but a confident one that guides the lover to
  the beloved.
It is a wonderful thing to see a groom walk proudly toward the bride on the
  day of their wedding.
And the Spirit and the Bride say, "Come."

And perhaps that is all the longing the church can do on this strangest of
  Sundays: "Come, Lord Jesus."
These are virtually the last words of the Bible.
They invite us into vigil, to wait and to listen.
We are the church waiting in faith for the Word to be completed at
  our ears.
The Word rushes toward us like a lover, ever fresh, ever green.
We keep vigil for the Spirit, waiting to be completed at Pentecost.
It is not necessary to project ourselves back into time.
We will celebrate the Spirit's descent on the church next Sunday,
  but that will only be the beginning.
The Bringer of Gifts will unfold before us in ways we cannot possibly
  imagine.
No wonder our yearning is so great!
There is no end to the promise.
That Spirit is about to come down on us now,
  when we hear the Word of God and keep it.
That Spirit is about to come down upon us, even as we open ourselves up
  to receive the Lord in his Body and Blood.
That Spirit is about to come down upon us as we receive one another as
  brother and sister in this assembly.
We your people, Lord, cry out to you in love.
We your people, Lord, ask you to send forth your Spirit and make us
  one in you.
We your people, Lord, have only one prayer this day:
"Come, Lord Jesus!"

GD

Questions for Reflection

1. What does it mean for me really to long for the living God? Will I take that to Pentecost?

2. Have I invited God into my life when I pray? What would happen if I did?

3. Stephen's proclamation becomes also the occasion for his martyrdom. What did he say that was so offensive to those who killed him?

Other Directions in Preaching

1. Giving testimony to the risen Lord is a necessity to those who call themselves Christians; it will cost everything.

2. Imagine a monologue of Saul speaking before his conversion as he stands before the crowd and orchestrates the death of Stephen. Then show Saul as Paul in light of his transformation.

3. Jesus thanks the Father for the gift of his disciples to witness his glory. His promise for Pentecost comes when he asks that where he is they also may be. Growth in true holiness depends on companionship with the Spirit of Jesus.

A New Pentecost
PENTECOST SUNDAY

READINGS:
Acts 2:1–11; 1 Corinthians 12:3b–7, 12–13;
John 20:19–23

Just how does a parish celebrate Pentecost?
Christmas is the easiest feast to celebrate since we all want to receive and
give gifts.
Even the mystery of Easter is bolstered by lilies and the newness of baptism.
But Pentecost?

In central Europe people used to drop pieces of burning wick or straw from
a hole in the ceiling of the church to represent the flaming tongues.
But this practice was eventually stopped because it tended to put the people
on fire externally instead of internally as the Holy Spirit had done in
Jerusalem.

In thirteenth-century France real pigeons were released in the cathedrals on
Pentecost Sunday during the singing of "Come, Holy Spirit."
But this practice too was discontinued because the people complained that
something other than the Holy Spirit was dropping from the rafters.

Now we know that our liturgists here at Holy Trinity are practical people:
no burning wicks or pigeons for us today, thank God!
What we have decided to do at all the Masses today is to proclaim to the
entire parish community the fact that many of our members have
decided to answer the call to ministry.

And as we heard Saint Paul tell us a short while ago,
>their many kinds of service in the Body of Christ come from the same
>Spirit, the same Lord, the same God.

We may not be aware of it, but right here at Holy Trinity some have left
>high-paying jobs; some have decided to answer the call at the time of
>their retirement from lifelong work.
They've traded their golf bags for theological books; they've gone from
>sitting behind an executive's desk to standing at a hospital bed or a
>prison cell.

Others, still young, are defying parents, culture, and the advice of their
>mentors and have decided to enter theological schools and seminaries
>to prepare for ministry in the church.
At the end of this homily, we will invite a few such parishioners to
>introduce themselves and witness to their call to ministry.

Pentecost is a marvelous feast to have such a witness to ministry.
It offers a portrait of the disciples gathered in Jerusalem waiting for
>something to happen.
Life was not the same for them.
Jesus, as they had come to know him and love him, was gone.
Yes, there was that promise that he would send his Holy Spirit to them, but
>when? How?
And what did that mean?

The disciples had experienced the death of Jesus.
They had been told not to cling to him, to let him go back to the Father in
>Ascension.
And now they experienced Pentecost, the coming of the Holy Spirit that
>broke down their closed doors of fear and anxiety, that made them
>bold enough to proclaim the Good News to the whole world.
Now they knew that they weren't just breathing their own breath but that
>very breath of Christ: the Holy Spirit.

What follows this story of Pentecost in Acts is the sermon of Peter, who told
      the people that the disciples weren't drunk, since it was only 9 o'clock
      in the morning.
No, Peter said, they were filled with the promised Spirit of Jesus Christ.
At the end of this sermon, we are told, three thousand people stepped
      forward for baptism.
When some of our most scholarly theologians today search for a
      proof for the gift of God's church, they say that despite enormous
      political, social, and religious obstacles, the church spread
      not because it made sense, not because it offered pie in the sky,
      but because of the power of the winds of Christ's
      Holy Spirit.
Despite the best efforts, even of religious people, you cannot stop
      God's Spirit.

Two weeks ago 155 cardinals gathered in Rome with Pope John Paul II to
      discuss the future of the church in the third millennium.
Like the disciples in Jerusalem they were gathered behind closed doors.
There were media briefings, but the Vatican press office never produced a
      list of the cardinals in attendance and after the first day stopped telling
      reporters who had spoken that day.

But, despite the closed doors, many of the cardinals released their speeches
      to the press.
And many of them were saying bold and wonderful new things.
High on the list was that their structures must change, that there must be
      more time and room for dialogue and less interference by the
      bureaucratic climbers in the curial offices.
Cardinal Lorscheider of Brazil announced:
"All of us suffer from a faraway bureaucracy that seems ever more deaf."
You cannot hold back the Holy Spirit's power in the church and world.
Despite all obstacles, the Holy Spirit moves where she wills in delicious and
      surprising ways.

Pentecost is not a time of completion, of clinging to the same old ways,
but of moving forward into new ways, new structures, new ministries
that proclaim the age-old Gospel of Jesus Christ.

Some think we have a vocation crisis in the church today.

I do not.

I believe we have a vocation opportunity, a new and marvelous way to
respond to God's call.

Now in some biblical events, like the Transfiguration, only a few select
followers are called to be witnesses to the work of God's Spirit.

But at Pentecost the tongues of fire rested upon *each* of the disciples because
each one had been touched by God's Holy Spirit.

The disciples spoke in every language then known in the world.

No one was excluded.

There are some leaders of the church today who wring their hands in
despair, like the disciples before Pentecost, who were fearful of the
new time they were in.

Thank God for other leaders of the church today, who are beginning to
break out of pre-Pentecost fear and speak with tongues of fire.

They are followers of Blessed John XXIII, who condemned prophets of
gloom and proclaimed not just to the church but to the world that we
are in a new Pentecost!

They know that men and women, young and old, rich and poor, straight
and gay, married and single, lay and clerical, and so-called ex-priests
and religious are being prompted by the Holy Spirit to get on board.

They are slowly learning that once you realize that you have the Holy
Spirit, the logical thing is to give her away!

RPW

Questions for Reflection

1. How open are we today to being utterly amazed by the Spirit and the ways in which she works in our lives and in our world?

2. How do we embrace diversity as the work of the Spirit in our parishes, communities, and our world?

3. Where are the places in our lives where we have locked ourselves in because of fear?

Other Directions for Preaching

1. The gifts of the Spirit can be recognized by the fact that they are always given for the common good. Is the common good determined by each one of us deciding what is good for him or her and then putting all of these "goods" together? Or does Catholic social teaching point us toward some other criteria for determining the common good?

2. The Sequence for Pentecost (both the prose and poetic texts) contains many comforting images. Explore some of these images in a contemporary context. Look to the lives of the assembly, current events, and your own life for this contemporary setting.

ORDINARY TIME

Little Resolutions and Big Changes
Second Sunday in Ordinary Time

READINGS:
Isaiah 62:1–5; 1 Corinthians 12:4–11; John 2:1–12

The story of Cana has always had a special place in Catholic piety.
We were told in parochial school and CCD classes that the very presence of
    Jesus at the wedding feast in Cana
    was a sign that Jesus blessed marriage as a sacrament.
Catholic piety also viewed Mary's actions and words in this Gospel
    as a sign of her power,
    as one who interceded with the Lord.
And, of course, when Jesus changed the water into wine
    that was a sure sign that he was more than a man.

In recent years biblical scholars have not so much dismissed these
    interpretations as told us that there is yet more to this story than we
    first suspected.
There are deeper signs in the story that call out for our attention.

We are told that when this story was first told
    it was preached by missionaries
    in order to convert Greek-speaking Jews to Christianity.
Such stories as the miracle at Cana worked.

Many Greek-speaking Jews became Christians,
    but they also still clung to their old spiritual traditions;
    they still prayed in the synagogues.

But by the time the evangelist wrote his Gospel
    a new crisis had occurred for those Jewish Christians.
They were being thrown out of the synagogues because of their belief in
    Jesus as the Messiah.
These Jewish Christians were in a bind.
Some of them were beginning to hide the fact that they were Christians
    in order to keep their seats in the synagogue.

And so the evangelist retold the miracle of Cana in order to move his
    listeners to make a decision.
The very word *crisis* means decision, implying that a decision has to be made.
The evangelist was asking his listeners to make a decision
    between light and darkness,
    between life and death,
    between old ways and God's new way.
Just as Jesus had changed the water into wine,
    they were encouraged to change from being timid disciples
    to courageous followers of the Messiah.

Change is never easy.
Often the depression that can overwhelm us in life comes from the fact that
    there is a part of us that knows that we need to change.
Yet, we also know that deep down in our hearts we'd like to stay just the
    way we are.

I'm not talking about the little changes that made up our New Year's
    resolutions two-and-a-half weeks ago:
    losing weight, cutting out booze or cigarettes,
    getting more exercise, spending more time at homework.
Not that these little changes are insignificant.

But notice how New Year's resolutions are usually about our own lives.
They rarely are about the changes we need to make in how we relate to our
    loved ones and how we relate to the ones who are difficult to love.
New Year's resolutions are rarely about how we relate
        to what is outside our tiny selves:
        how we relate to our community,
        our world, our God.

In many ways we are like those people for whom the evangelist first told
    this story of the wedding feast.
Just as they had one foot in their old religion and one foot in the kingdom
    Jesus preached about,
        we often find ourselves divided in our loyalties between making it in
        this tough world, which makes so many demands on us,
        and remaining loyal to the Christ of our convictions.
This division in our hearts, this refusal to take the next step of change,
    saps us of so much energy and joy.

It's not an accident that wine is so central to today's Gospel story.
For the ancient Jews wine was a symbol of joy.
The rabbis would often say,
    "Without wine there is no joy."
And so when Mary ran to Jesus and told him, "They have no more wine,"
    she was really saying, "They have no more joy."
The real miracle of Cana was that this story brought back the joy the
    people had been drained of because they were caught in a bind
    between loyalty to their old ways and loyalty to the new ways of God
    that Jesus had come to bring them.

New Year's Day is the hour to decide to make small changes in our lives.
The story of the miracle at Cana reminds us that now is the hour to make
    that big change in our lives.

RPW

Questions for Reflection

1. In this time when half of all marriages end in divorce, is the spousal imagery in the First Reading helpful in envisioning the relationship between God and God's people? (On the other hand, half of all married people are still married, and it may be helpful to them.)

2. Do we value the diversity of gifts, or are we suspicious of them?

3. What does it mean to say that the signs that Jesus performed always pointed to a more profound reality than was obvious at first?

Other Directions for Preaching

1. Though the gifts of the Spirit need to be discerned within the context of community, there must be a genuine sense of respect for the many different ways in which the Spirit works in and through each member. If we give ourselves over to true discernment, there is no room for jealousy, petty criticism, and unfounded presumptions about the motives of another. Instead, we must celebrate the abundance and diversity of gifts given by the Spirit.

2. The extravagance of God is apparent in all of these readings. God does not parsimoniously parcel out joy, gifts, or even the wine served at the feast. God's extravagance is without limit because God and God's reign are beyond our wildest imaginings.

A Light in the Darkness
THIRD SUNDAY IN ORDINARY TIME

READINGS:
Nehemiah 8:2–4a, 5–6, 8–10; 1 Corinthians 12:12–30;
Luke 1:1–4; 4:14–21

If I were to ask you, "What do you listen to?"
    how would you answer?
Perhaps you would answer in terms of radio programming:
    "I listen to 'All Things Considered,'" or "I listen to the classical
    music station."
Or perhaps in terms of technology:
    "I listen to my iPod," or "I love to listen to my new
    Bose radio-CD player."
Would it occur to you to say, "I listen to the Word of God"?
Today's readings reveal the important role the Scriptures played in the lives
    of God's people and in the life of God's Son, Jesus.

Two of today's readings remind us that we are the spiritual descendants of a
    people for whom the Scriptures were *the* authoritative voice in life,
    providing ongoing guidance, solace, and challenge.
Consider today's reading from the book of Nehemiah, written to record
    what happened to some of the Jewish community who returned from
    the Babylonian exile around 458 BC.

People who had been forcibly removed from their homeland over fifty years
   earlier have been allowed to return to Jerusalem and to rebuild.
One of the first things that happened was their priest gathering them
   together and reading the Word of God to them, so they could renew
   the covenant with the Lord.
Ezra, the priest, gathered the men, women, and those children who could
   understand, and he read to them from the Torah, the book of the Law
   of the Lord.

We are told that Ezra read to them from daybreak until noon, about six
   hours, and the people stood, listening, with tears streaming
   down their faces, tears of sorrow because they had not been
   faithful to the Word of God.
But Ezra says to them, "Do not be sad, and do not weep."
Ezra recognizes this as a day of great joy.
He tells the people to eat rich food and drink sweet drinks.
Why? Because "Today is holy to our Lord."
God's children gathered around the Word, listening to the Word.
It is a Word in which they found their identity and purpose.

And we continue to do this when we come together to worship God.
   We listen to God's Word, written down long ago but still a living
   Word for us now.
And just as Ezra the priest interpreted the Word of God for his people,
   someone stands here and interprets it—or tries to interpret it—for us
   and our lives.
The Word of God remains a light in the darkness and a lamp to guide
   our feet.

In the Gospel we see Jesus turning to the Word.
He has come back home after being baptized in the Jordan.
At that event the Spirit came upon him.
And this Spirit blew him out into the wilderness, where he was tempted for
   forty days.

Then the same Spirit blew him into his home territory.

Luke tells us, "Jesus returned to Galilee in the power of the Spirit."

The native son has finally come to his hometown, Nazareth.

The stories of him teaching wisely and working wonders have preceded him.

And what does he do first?

He goes to the Sabbath service at the synagogue.

This is an important moment.

Here Jesus proclaims who he is, both to the home folk and to all who hear
his voice.

He takes up the scroll of the prophet Isaiah and turns to chapter 61.

He opens it and reads the passage where the prophet speaks of one whom
God will anoint in the power of the Spirit.

This anointed one will do three things:

First, he will preach: he will bring Good News to the poor, proclaim liberty
to captives,
and announce a year of favor from the Lord.

Second, he will liberate: he will let the oppressed go free.

And, third, he will give sight to the blind.

This text articulates the threefold ministry of Jesus:

the ministry of preaching Good News of the coming of God's kingdom;

the ministry of social justice, bringing freedom to those held captive by
forces of evil;

and the ministry of bringing sight to the blind, that is, a ministry of
compassion.

In speaking of bringing sight to the blind, Jesus takes a phrase from an
earlier passage of the prophet.

In chapter 42, the prophet speaks of a servant who will come for all peoples,
one who will not break a bruised reed or crush a smoldering wick.

This ministry is marked by gentleness, forgiveness, nonviolence.

This ministry of compassion keeps the preaching ministry from becoming
pie in the sky, and the social-justice ministry from slipping into anger
and violence.

This threefold mission of Jesus remains the mission of those who follow Jesus.
As the church, we continue to bring the Good News of God's love to others,
    to work for justice and reconciliation in our world,
        and to reach out with compassion to all, even those who reject us.

We are the Body of Christ, as Paul reminds us,
    a Body with different members with different gifts.
But all gifts are given for the common good: of the church, of our society, of
our world.

The Word of God calls us to know who we are,
    to be attentive about who God is, who Jesus is, so we can know who
    we are.
Then God calls us to act and let this Word bear fruit in our lives,
    to be a force for peace in our world.

The philosopher Albert Camus once spoke to a group of Dominicans about
    what non-Christians expected of Christians.
He offered this as a job description of Christians:

> "What the world expects of Christians is that Christians should speak
> out, loud and clear, and that they should voice their condemnation in
> such a way that never a doubt, never the slightest doubt, could arise in
> the heart of the simplest man or woman. That they should get away
> from abstraction and confront the blood-stained face history has taken
> on today. The grouping we need is a grouping of men and women
> resolved to speak out clearly and pay up personally."

What does it mean to be a people of the Book?
What does it mean to be formed by the Word of God?
Look to Jesus, formed by the words of the prophet Isaiah.
He came to hear God's calling through the words of the prophet,
    and to engage in a ministry of preaching, liberating,
        and embodying God's compassion.

So what do you listen to?

Whom do you listen to?

Does God's Word have your ear?

JAW

Questions for Reflection

1. What are some of the texts of the Bible that help you to know who you are?

2. How can you make the Word of God a more important part of your life?

3. How do you see the church continuing to live out the threefold ministry of Jesus: preaching the Word, social justice, compassion?

Other Directions for Preaching

1. The law of the Lord is not simply a burden to be borne; hearing the Word of God and taking it to heart can provide us with a sense of who we are. The Psalm Response tells us that the words of the Lord are Spirit and life.

2. Paul reminds the Corinthians that they are Christ's Body and that their diversity should not lead to division. We are all given to drink of one Spirit, and we each have a part to play for the common good of the Body.

3. Luke gives emphasis to Jesus as prophet and invites preachers to consider the prophetic ministry of the church and how that relates to and challenges one's own community.

Not Following Sensitivity Guidelines
FOURTH SUNDAY IN ORDINARY TIME

READINGS:
*Jeremiah 1:4–5, 17–19; 1 Corinthians 12:31—13:13;
Luke 4:21–30*

The New York State Regents test for high school students was changed "to
meet sensitivity guidelines."
They purged or changed language they considered potentially offensive,
including references to Jews and Gentiles, from a passage by Isaac
Bashevis Singer.
When some protested this purging as a distortion of art, computer-savvy
students just could not understand what the fuss was all about.

After all, with the click of a mouse we can now reshape photos, music,
literature, history, and biography.
Students know that with simple software, you can edit your own version of
Homer's *Odyssey* or Eminem's *White America.*
The delete button on our laptops is so handy!
Even higher powers are not immune.
When Joy Behar, a host of ABC's "The View," thanked Jesus for helping her
lose weight, the network bleeped the reference on its taped West Coast
broadcast.

Even though our computer age has made easy the purging of material that
would offend sensitive ears, this is not a new phenomenon.
The compilers of the Lectionary, for example, frequently purged passages
from Scripture they didn't like or that didn't fit their themes.
We find an example of this today in the First Reading, about Jeremiah.
The compilers leave verse 6 out of our reading today.
That verse reads:

"'Ah, Lord GOD!' I said, 'I know not how to speak;

I am too young.'

But the LORD answered me,

Say not, 'I am too young.'

To whomever I send you, you shall go;

whatever I command you, you shall speak."

By purging this verse from the reading we tend to forget that Jeremiah, like
all great prophets, was reluctant to follow his calling.
Even the great Moses protested to the Lord that he couldn't be a prophet
because he had a speech impediment.
And so we are robbed here of Jeremiah's own inner struggles;
we might even forget his depression and how he once cursed the day
he was born.

Although the compilers of the Lectionary do not purge any of the verses of
our Gospel today, it would have been easier for us if they had.
For isn't this a strange story?
First, the people praise the homily Jesus preaches to them.
Then they switch gears and turn into an unruly mob and seek to throw him
not just out of town but over the hill.
And what about the ending of the story?
The solitary Jesus walks away from the mob and goes on his way untouched.

There is a wide body of material from biblical scholars on how to unravel
Luke's story.
Some claim Jesus preached two homilies.

The first homily was preached during Jesus' "honeymoon period,"
while the second was preached once they understood just what he was
telling them.

The first was accepted by his neighbors, but the second was not
because he told them that they did not have priority with God;
indeed, it is in another rival town, Capernaum, where many pagans
lived, that Jesus performed his wonders.

Some might think the people in the crowd turned on Jesus because they just
couldn't get it in their heads that such wisdom could come from a
hometown boy: "Isn't this the son of Joseph?"

But others claim this is not why the crowd turned on Jesus.

They claim that the people of Nazareth were not cynical about the
preacher's origins.

The people were simply surprised and amazed at their hometown boy.

Actually the people in the story are a lot like us today who believe that an
expert is somebody from out of town carrying a briefcase.

And of course the story ends with the remarkable line:
he "passed through the midst of them and went away."

Some used to think that it was a miracle that Jesus was able to escape being
hurled over the hill.

Joseph Fitzmyer's translation makes Jesus seem more like a magician.

He writes that Jesus "slipped through the crowd."

Others claim that Luke wants to offer a theological point:
Just as Jesus walked through their midst and continued his mission,
later on his crucifixion would also fail to stop his mission, which was
to bring salvation to all people.

We cannot sanitize this story from Luke.

We cannot purge from it the harsh realities of being a prophet.

We cannot escape the fact that Jesus' own neighbors rejected him because
he disturbed them.

The people spoke highly of Jesus and were amazed by him when he spoke
  of liberation.
It is when they realized that this liberation to which they were called
  also included people outside their little circle that anger and
  violence erupted.

In our own time we have witnessed the martyrdom of someone who once
  was a reluctant prophet:
  Archbishop Oscar Romero of San Salvador.
He once preached:
  "It is very easy to be servants of the word without disturbing the
  world; a very spiritualistic word, a word without any commitment to
  history, a word that can sound in any part of the world because it
  belongs to no part of the world. A word that creates no problems,
  starts no conflicts."
Jesus did not offer us a spiritualist word, a word without any commitment
  to history.
He got into trouble once he became specific: "a widow in Zarephath in the
  land of Sidon" and the leper Naaman the Syrian.
After all, how could the God of Israel's plan of salvation embrace the
  pagans, the Gentiles?

I suppose there are times when all of us would like to purge from the
  Gospels stories like today's because they anger us, frighten us, disturb
  us because they are specific.
They challenge our comfort, self-assurance, and smugness.
We come to Eucharist to be comforted, to be amazed at God's gracious words.
But today we are reminded that Jesus and those who continue his mission
  have another important charge:
    to disturb us when we are locked in our own little circle
    and not to offer sensitivity guidelines but a prophetic call.

RPW

Questions for Reflection

1. Who are the prophets of our day and how do we receive them?

2. Why is it that prophets rarely gain acceptance in their native place?

3. This reading from Paul's First Letter to the Corinthians is one of the most familiar and beloved passages in the New Testament, often read at weddings. It sounds so clear and so obvious—"Love is patient, love is kind"—yet it is so hard to live. Why?

Other Directions for Preaching

1. While some scholars suggest that today's readings are about vocation, these readings are also about rejection. Jeremiah is called from the womb to be a prophet, but God makes it clear to him that he will suffer and be rejected by the very people to whom he is sent. Jesus returns to his home place to preach and slips away before he can be hurled from a hilltop.

2. The psalm and the passage from Paul's first letter to the Corinthians offer the consolations that God gives to those who risk rejection for God's sake. The psalm is filled with images of God as refuge, stronghold, deliverance, and hope. Paul speaks of love as the foundation on which prophecy must rest. These consolations enable the prophet to endure the pain of rejection.

When the "B Team" Is the Better Team
FIFTH SUNDAY IN ORDINARY TIME

Readings:
Isaiah 6: 1–2a, 3–8; 1 Corinthians 15:1–11; Luke 5:1–11

Sometimes I think about what I might have done as a Redemptorist priest, if
    I had not gone into teaching.
And although I always start off thinking about the kinds of ministry we do—
    working in a retreat house, preaching parish missions, working in a
    parish—I eventually end up thinking not only what I would do but
    with *whom* I would like to do it.
I think about working either with X who has such a good mind,
    or with Y who is so great with people,
    or with Z who is so creative, and the list begins to form.
In short, I begin to compile my very own "A team."*

But I was reminded recently that the "A team" doesn't always work out.
There was a new musical coming to Broadway that was generating real
    excitement.
It was a musical version of the 1950s movie *Sweet Smell of Success.*
I bought a ticket to it months ahead of time.

---

    *I am indebted to my former student Greg Jakubowicz, OFM, for the idea of the
"A team."

It had a top-notch director, music by a successful composer, set design by
   one of the great talents, the terrific John Lithgow, and a new talent,
   Brian D'Arcy-James.
And guess what happened?
It was a flop.
It just didn't come off.
You could see all the talent and energy and money that went into it
   up on stage.
But it didn't click. No magic! And a very short run.

God does not seem too concerned with putting together an "A team,"
   at least that is the conclusion I come to when I read the Scriptures.
Consider the three featured in today's Readings.
They describe themselves as "doomed," "unfit," and "sinful," respectively.
Hardly the qualities for a starting line-up drafted by the Divinity.

Consider Peter in today's Gospel.
Jesus, who has been preaching and teaching the crowd, apparently feels
   hemmed in.
So when he spots two boats, he gets in the one belonging to Simon and asks
   him to pull out from shore so he can have some breathing room.
When he is finished, out of the blue, he tells Simon to go out further and to
   lower the nets for a catch.
Imagine Simon's reaction to a carpenter's son turned itinerant preacher,
   telling him where to fish.
Not surprisingly, Simon resists, politely saying,
   "Master, we have worked hard all night and have caught nothing,"
   but then—we don't know why—he changes course, "but at your
   command...."
And Simon signals for the nets to be thrown out.

The result? So many fish the nets were tearing.
So many fish that, even with the help of their partners, "the boats were in
   danger of sinking."

But the boats weren't the only things weighed down.
Peter sank to his knees before Jesus and said,
    "Depart from me, Lord, for I am a sinful man."
Note the change in title here.
First Peter refers to Jesus as Master, but now he calls him Lord,
    a title reserved to God.
Peter's awe was contagious—astonishment seized them all.
And then, we get the climax of this story.
As surprising as it was for a carpenter's son to join in the job of fishermen,
    now Jesus invites them to join him in the job of catching people.

We may be so used to these stories that they no longer surprise us.
But you must admit that Jesus made some strange choices.
Why would he go with fishermen as his first disciples—
    four of them!—two of whom were hotheaded and a third rather
    bull-headed?
Was he that much into metaphor?
And we might further ask, why would he go on to choose a political zealot
    who wanted to overthrow Rome, along with a tax collector who
    collaborated with Rome?
These were some strange choices for a group dedicated to fishing for people.

In the short run, it did not seem to pay off very well.
One would betray him, another deny him, and a third doubt him.
When the chips were down, they all ran away.
Peter could have been speaking for them all when he said to Jesus at their
    first meeting,
    "Depart from me, Lord, I am a sinful man."

Then there was the next wave, spearheaded by Paul, formerly Saul, who
    writes to the community at Corinth,
    "I am the least of the apostles, not fit to be called an apostle,
    because I persecuted the church of God."
Paul sat there while they stoned Stephen,

and then took up a career rounding up and imprisoning the followers
of Jesus.
At the outset, another questionable choice.

Perhaps it was in Jesus' genes.
His Father consistently made odd choices, as the Old Testament records:
> Abraham sent out both the mother of his first child and the child
> himself into the wilderness; Jacob was a scoundrel to his own brother
> and parented fratricidal sons; Moses was a murderer on the run before
> going down at eighty to liberate a people.
Then, consider most of the judges and even some of the prophets.
You have a very odd assortment.
Not exactly "A list" people.

While Isaiah seems a fairly good choice—he was a member of the royal
> court, well educated, and obviously pious—even he knew himself to be
> a sinful man.
When he went into the Temple to pray that day and had this vision of God
> and the angels, his immediate response was,
>> "Woe is me, I am doomed! For I am a man of unclean lips."

But "not as man sees does God see," as God reminds the prophet Samuel
> just as he is about to anoint Eliab, an "A list" choice, as successor to
> Saul (1 Sam 16:7).
God had chosen instead the youngest son, the one out tending the sheep,
> who wasn't even brought in to parade before the prophet.
God chose the one who as king would murder a loyal soldier after taking
> his wife to bed.

When you look closely at God's choices, at the three we heard today, a
> certain pattern emerges.
Each of the three chosen has basically the same response:
> I am unclean, sinful, not fit.
Perhaps that is the criterion God is looking for.

People who recognize that, whatever happens, it is certainly not going
　　to be on their own steam and through their efforts alone that it
　　comes about.
They knew they needed all the help God could give them.
Peter's response is touching in its openness and honesty.
He knew this person standing before him was someone unique, and he had
　　no hesitation in doing what needed to be done in the presence of the
　　Divine; he fell at Jesus' knees.
And we hear this same attitude coming through in both Isaiah and Paul.
Paul's words—Where sin abounds, grace abounds all the more—could serve
　　as mantra for all today's chosen.

Jesus, like his Father, wasn't looking for sinless workers, not even
　　skilled ones.
Simon's sin obviously didn't disqualify him.
When he fell at Jesus' feet, Jesus lifted him up into discipleship,
　　or at least put him on the road, a long road for Simon, with its ups
　　and downs,
　　and one that ended at his own cross.
Paul's response led to an experience of God's power in his life that he could
　　write: "By the grace of God I am what I am,
　　and his grace to me has not been ineffective.
　　Indeed, I have toiled harder than all of them;
　　not I, however, but the grace of God that is with me."

The point seems to be that Jesus needed help then and still does.
The call continues to come, to work with God for the salvation of all.
The question this morning is: have we heard it?
For Isaiah, it came when he was praying in the Temple.
For Peter, it came in the midst of his daily work.
For Saul, it came when he was literally heading in the wrong direction
　　and needed to be knocked off his horse.

Maybe, too, another question precedes asking whether we have heard
   God's call.
The first question to ask ourselves might be: are we listening?
Are we giving our attention to God?
The word *attention* comes from the Latin word meaning "to lean toward."
Do we lean toward God, who sometimes speaks in the barest of whispers,
   although one must recognize that God is not above banging us on the
   head, when the situation gets really desperate?

It seems, if the past functions as precedent, that God does not give up.
Just as Jesus did not give up on the Twelve, who eventually came through
   for him—except for the one, reminding us we remain free to say no—
   so too, he keeps calling to us.
Every Eucharist we hear his words, "This is my Body, this is my Blood."
They are given to us so that we become more fully his Body in the world.
Every Mass we are sent forth "to love God and serve one another."
An agenda remains to be fleshed out with, in, and through our own bodies.

So, take a few moments in the course of the coming week,
And whether it is when you are at prayer, or rushing around, or simply
   going about life as usual, keep one eye attentive, one ear perked up.
You never know when God might be trying to get your attention.
God often picks the strangest people for his team, the "B team"—as in
   blessed.

JAW

Questions for Further Reflection

1. When have you heard God calling to you? What has your reaction been?

2. Have you ever had an experience of the holiness of God?

3. What are some of the ways God's grace has been effective in your community?

Other Directions for Preaching

1. Simon is obedient to Jesus, even though not fully understanding. We find a similar reaction in Mary as Luke presents her to us. The followers of Jesus are called to obedience even when understanding is not complete.

2. Through the Gospel that has been preached to us, we are being saved if we "hold fast to the Word." How do we as a community help each other to "hold fast"?

3. Response to the call in these accounts is total. Isaiah became God's spokesperson; Paul converted to become an apostle, born out of time; and Simon and the others left all and followed Jesus.

Blessed Are You Whose Hearts Are Loving
Sixth Sunday in Ordinary Time

Readings:
*Jeremiah 17:5–8; 1 Corinthians 15:12, 16–20;
Luke 6:17, 20–26*

I have always loved Saint Valentine's Day.
I like sending cards—and receiving them, along with making phone calls to
   loved ones.
True that we know very little about the saint, but the day has taken on a
   life of its own, probably due as much to Hallmark as to anything else.
Still, the day appeals to our hearts, which too often can be put on "hold,"
   calling us to put our affection for family and friends into words, and
   even deeds.

In light of this, imagine my first reaction when I read the Readings for today.
Jeremiah the prophet is quoting God, saying:
   Cursed is the one who trusts in human beings....
   He is like a barren bush in the desert that enjoys no change of season,
   but stands in a lava waste, a salt and empty earth.
And a Happy Valentine's Day to you too, Jeremiah.

This homily was preached on the Sunday before Valentine's Day—which was also
the World Day of Prayer for the Sick—accompanied by a celebration within Mass of
the anointing of the sick.

Even Jesus' words today are "woe-full," at least half of them:

> "Woe to you who are rich..., woe to you who are filled now...,
> Woe to you who laugh now..., woe to you when all speak well of
> you...."

Don't look for these readings to be quoted in next year's valentine cards.

But, as strange as it may seem, when you scratch a little below the surface,
they are pretty good readings for Valentine's Day.

First of all, we must remember that the Bible is a love story.

It is about God's love for everything God made, all creatures of the sky and
sea and earth.

And it is especially the story of God's love for those creatures made in the
divine image.

But from early on, there have been relationship problems, with accusations
of hardened
hearts, possessiveness, jealousy, and infidelity.

God chose the prophets as go-betweens, serving as spokespersons of
God's heart;

Again and again they are sent to speak God's heart to the chosen
people Israel.

Even so, God's people tended to put their trust in political alliances with
foreign powers, or even in the gods of other nations, with names like
Baal or Moloch.

God's people were fickle, disloyal, and unfaithful, leading Jeremiah to say:

> "More tortuous than all else is the human heart, beyond remedy;
> who can understand it?" (17: 9).

But God keeps trying again and again to woo Israel.

And the prophet similarly cries out:

> "Cursed is the one who trusts in human beings, who seeks his strength
> in flesh, whose heart turns away from the Lord."

But there is an alternative:

> "Blessed is the one who trusts in the LORD, whose hope is the LORD.

He is like a tree planted beside the waters that stretches out its roots
to the stream: it fears not the heat when it comes; its leaves stay green;
in the year of drought it shows no distress, but still bears fruit."

God is speaking to us with the urgency of a passionate lover:
    Don't put your trust in others.
    Trust me first, last, and always.
    Root yourself in me.
    Give me your heart.

Which gets us back to Valentine's Day, that celebration of the heart.
As a kid, I remember it as a day of suspense and even peril.
Sitting at my desk in school before the valentine cards were given out, I was
    in a state of dread, true existential angst, that I might not get one from
    whoever at the moment had captured my heart.
There was also the fear that I would get one from someone I hadn't sent
    one to.

When I look back, I think Valentine's Day was a training ground for the rest
    of life.
It provided the opportunity to think about whom I wanted to
    give my heart to.
As the years have gone on, I now think of it as a day to thank God that I
    have a heart, one that can give and receive love and bring love into
    the world.
It is also a day to think about the last time I said "I love you" to God.
The founder of the Redemptorists, Saint Alphonsus de Liguori, was a
    passionate Italian who came to recognize that God was a passionate
    God, crazy in love with us.
And God wants us to know this, so he sent Jesus.
And God wants a return of our love, yesterday, today, and always.

But God also wants *our* hearts to go out to all of creation, especially
    those in need.

Jesus is speaking for God's heart when he says:
>   Blessed are you who are poor, you who are now hungry, now weeping,
>   Blessed are you who are rejected because you have accepted me.
>   Rejoice! I will take care of you.
>   You will inherit the kingdom and be filled with joy and laugh and
>   have a great reward.
But if you are rich now, and full now, and live in laughter and approval
>   now, watch out; you already have your reward.
Your hearts must go out to others as mine does, as the heart of your
>   heavenly Father does, to those who need a loving heart.

It is not that God does not want us to be happy or satisfied.
But God wants *all* of us to be in that state.
And until *all* are full and satisfied, then our hearts are to be restless.
The human heart is to mirror the heart of God with a love that goes out
>   to others.

Today at this Mass we do a loving thing when we turn to anoint the sick.
We invite anyone who has a serious illness, or who suffers from the
>   weakness of aging, or who is about to have a serious operation, to
>   come forward.
In the name of our parish family gathered here, I will do two things.
I will stretch out my hands over each of you and place them on your head
>   and ask God to send the Holy Spirit upon you to strengthen you.
And I invite all here to extend your hands over our brothers and sisters as I
>   do this, and join me in praying for those about to be anointed.

Then I will put oil on your foreheads and on the palms of your hands and I
>   ask all present to join your prayer to the prayers I will say.
This sacrament is a way of putting our arms around those who are sick and
>   letting them know our love joins with God's love to embrace them at
>   this time.
Our faith joins with their faith to give them support, to hold them up
>   in faith.

Sometimes, when you are sick, you might find it hard to pray, so we pray
for you.
Sometimes you might wonder if God is around, and you can lose heart.
We want to support you with our faith and assure you God is near.
In this way we act as God's children, as faithful followers of Jesus.
We become walking valentines, and we join our hearts to the heart of God.

Valentine's Day is a day that calls for a song.
I often wonder what song God might sing on Valentine's Day.
There are so many beautiful ones God could choose,
but I think God would chose a simple song.
Do you know what was named the most popular song for Valentine's Day
just a few years ago?
An old song by Irving Berlin called "Always."
We can hear it for what it was, the song a man wrote in memory of his wife
who died at a young age.
It contains the ongoing pledge of his love for her—always.
But I think in the final words we can also hear God's love given timeless
expression.
Like Berlin's love for his wife, God's love for each of us is "not for just an
hour, not for just a day, not for just a year, but always."*

JAW

---

*Irving Berlin, "Always," in *Reading Lyrics,* ed. Robert Gottlieb and Robert
Kimball (New York: Pantheon, 2000), 73.

Questions for Further Reflection

1. Where does the love in my life come from? What does it go toward?

2. Who are the poor, the hungry, the weeping, the hated, and the excluded in our world today? Who are the rich, the filled, the laughing, and the praised? Where am I in relation to these two groups?

3. Who is the God I worship? Is it a God I recognize as passionately in love with me? with us? with all of us?

Other Directions for Preaching

1. Barren bush or fruitful tree? Jeremiah says it depends on whether we put our trust in the Lord or elsewhere.

2. Paul reminds us that the resurrection of Christ is at the heart of our faith and that the firstfruit of his resurrection is the hope we have of our own resurrection.

3. Each list of beatitudes and woes in Luke's Sermon on the Plain can be seen as a community profile, depending on whether we have joined in the prophetic ministry of Jesus or not.

The Logic of Redemption
SEVENTH SUNDAY IN ORDINARY TIME

READINGS:
1 Samuel 26:2, 7–9, 12–13, 22–23;
1 Corinthians 15:45–49; Luke 6:27–38

There is an extraordinary moment in today's first reading.
But first a little background.
King Saul has been stalking David, his rival, who has been hiding out in
the desert.
Saul had already tried to kill David several times,
even at the dinner table by throwing a spear at David while he was
playing the lute—so much for music having "charms to soothe the
savage breast"!
This time the king has gone out to the desert with a party of three thousand
men to search for him.

The king realizes that not only has David won the hearts of his people,
who sang, "Saul has killed his thousands but David his ten thousands"
(1 Sam 18:7), but, most devastating of all, Saul knows the hand of
the Lord now rests on David.
This is the final encounter between these two heroes who have become
deadly enemies.

David has crept into the camp of Saul and his three thousand men.
And this is where the extraordinary moment occurs.

David stands over the sleeping king, looking down on him.
His loyal and ruthless kinsman Abishai whispers to him:

> "God has delivered your enemy into your grasp this day.
> Let me nail him to the ground with one thrust of the spear."

But David will not allow it:

> "Do not harm him, for who can lay hands on the LORD's anointed and
> remain unpunished?"

David has a chance to kill his enemy, but he doesn't.
He is even given a rationale for doing so:

> "God has delivered your enemy into your grasp,"
> but he doesn't do it.

What he does do is significant.

David takes Saul's spear, the symbol of the king's authority and power, used
    in battle, and he carries off his water jar, so necessary for survival out
    in the desert.
He goes a distance and calls across to the camp.
First he berates Abner, Saul's general and a noble man,
    for not guarding the king.
Then he speaks to Saul himself, who has awakened, evoking Saul's touching
    confession, all of which, unfortunately, is left out of today's reading.
We do hear, however, the bottom line, when David says to Saul:

> "The LORD will reward each man for his justice and faithfulness.
> Today, though the LORD delivered you into my grasp,
> I would not harm the LORD's anointed."

This incident provides an example for us of what Jesus is calling for in
    today's Gospel.
We are called to enter into what may be called the logic of redemption.
Today we are at the heart of what is called the Sermon on the Plain.
Luke's sermon is only one-quarter as long as Matthew's Sermon on the
    Mount, twenty-seven verses compared to one hundred and
    twenty-nine.

But we find in the few verses of Luke's sermon an agenda for transforming
　　the world.

In Luke, this sermon is given to the disciples of Jesus, his followers.
Our Lectionary divides it into three parts.
Last week we heard of God's love for the least:
　　the poor, those who weep, who hunger, who suffer for Jesus' sake.
Christ's heart—and the hearts of his disciples—must go out to the least, the
　　little ones.

Today's and next week's Gospels focus on the rest of the world.
Next week the emphasis is on loving other disciples—those
　　"inside our camp."
But this week's reading directs our attention to those "outside our camp."
If we have any enemies, either as individuals or as a community, we are to
　　love them.
In this light, David is offered to us as an example of such love in action.

Jesus' words need little comment, if you recognize that you have
　　enemies in life.
Not that it makes his words any less demanding—seemingly impossible
　　at times.
But it can be helpful to realize something quite specific about this
　　command.
It doesn't speak about transforming an enemy into a friend.
It says to love your *enemy* precisely as *enemy;* you are to love the
　　one who hates you.
And how does that play out?

It means that one must do good, pray for, even bless that person.
Of course, there are ways one can slip under that bar.
　　"Love my enemy? Well, I don't really have any enemies. Perhaps there
　　are people I don't care for, would prefer not to be in the same room

with, have stopped talking to, a few of those, maybe. But enemy? No,
   siree, my life is enemy-free."

But, then, when I think about it, I do know that inner voice that whispers:
   "Strike out." "Nail them." "Don't let them get away with that."
I must confess I do know the satisfaction of keeping score and getting even.
   Not going to war.
   Not even to battle.
   More like occasional skirmishes.
But such skirmishes can sting, cause harm, provoke vengeance in return.
Equally bad is what such moments do to us, on the inside, how they
   transform us.

A certain kind of dislike can harden or fester within,
   resulting in an ongoing habit of striking out as a modus operandi
   for coping.
It releases a poison into our system, settling into our heart and changing it.
A heart can become cold or hard over the years, shriveled in its capacity
   to love.
Such cannot be the heart of a disciple of Jesus Christ.

What we are talking about here is adopting a logic of redemption that
   reveals itself ultimately as a logic of nonviolence.
Consider how violence works:
   I push, you shove;
   I hit, you strike back;
   I smash, you crush.
The movie *Thirteen Days* about the Cuban missile crisis brought this out:
At one point President Kennedy says to an aide:
   "If we go in, they will shoot, then we shoot back, then they fire their
   missiles, then we retaliate, then Russia comes in here and into other
   places in the world, and all of us are on the way to a nuclear
   holocaust."
This is the logic of violence.

Jesus offers a logic of redemption.
Violence and destruction are only brought to an end by those who refuse
    to participate,
        by those who will not return evil for evil.
Violence will cease only with those who are willing to absorb the impact of
    the blow
        so that it stops here and now, not going any further.

This week's *Post* had two wonderful stories about human achievement.
One was about biologists who are making incredible strides in
    understanding the types of
    human genes that make us who we are.
They discovered that there are about 30,000 genes in the human person.
They were expecting much more, like 100,000—after all, the fruit fly has
    13,000 and a laboratory roundworm has 19,500.
The wonder lies in being able to discover these 30,000 genes, but it is
    also interesting how little separates us from a fruit fly, much less a
    lab worm!
Then, on the other side of the scale, another article reported how NASA has
    landed a spacecraft on an asteroid approximately 200 million miles
    from earth.
This event was compared to passing through the blades of a spinning
    propeller.

Both of these are incredible feats in terms of the exploratory spirit of
    humanity.
Even so, I found myself thinking of an old quotation of the great
    philosopher, paleontologist, and mystic, Father Pierre Teilhard de
    Chardin, a Jesuit.
He once wrote:
    "Someday after mastering the winds, the waves, the tides, and gravity,
    we shall harness the energies of love.
    And then, for the second time in the history of the world,
    we will have discovered fire."

To harness the energy of love that can transform both lover and beloved,
    even when the one beloved is an enemy—
That will come about
        when the Gospel of Jesus Christ takes root in the human heart,
        when we recognize that, in addition to the many thousands of
        genes we carry,
        in addition to our ability to travel far beyond this lovely planet,
        we also have the capacity to be the dwelling place of God's Spirit,
        and an instrument of that Spirit at work in the world and beyond.

Does this mean that there is no room for hatred in life?
No, there are things to hate:
        a system that allows a young child to die in an abusive home;
        a cultural attitude that fosters hatred for any group—whether on the
        basis of nationality, ethnicity, religious faith, gender, or sexual
        preference; a policy that allows for preemptive strikes and the use of
        instruments of death that kill so many innocent people, especially the
        elderly, the defenseless, and the young.
We buy into these systems. We tolerate them, even actively support them.
Systems can be worthy of hatred. So can policies. And cultural attitudes
        and values.
And the things people *do* can also be worthy of our hatred.
"I hate what you did to me." "I hate what you said about them; it was
        cruel, callous."
But as for the people: Love your enemies, do good to them, bless them, pray
        for them.

Sometimes transformation does come.
At the end of the story, after David speaks to Saul, Saul's final words to
        David are:
        "Blessed be you, my son David.
        You will do many things and will succeed in them" (1 Sam 26:25).
We witness transformation whenever we come here:
        bread and wine changed into the Body and Blood of Christ.

May it be said of us as disciples of Jesus,
>   as a people who eat at the table and drink from the cup:
>   Blessed may we be.
>   May we do many things and succeed in them for the kingdom of God.
>   May we grow in love, for each other and for all others, especially
>   our enemies.

JAW

Questions for Reflection

1. Do you see yourself as having enemies? Who are they? Why are they?

2. Where is God calling us to expand our boundaries, to reach out beyond those whom we love and who love us?

3. Have you ever found yourself, like David, in a position to do harm but discovered you had the strength to hold back?

Other Directions for Preaching

1. To put our trust in God completely, as David did, rather than following the natural inclination to strike first, can seem naive in today's world. Can a case be made for walking this path?

2. Consider how we are bearers of both the image of the old Adam, the earthly creature, and of Christ, the new Adam, the heavenly creature, and how we can grow as a community into the fullness of Christ.

3. We are called to give when there is no hope of any return, to manifest the mercy of God in a world whose generosity is often offset by the tendency to "call in a debt."

Heart Storage
EIGHTH SUNDAY IN ORDINARY TIME

READINGS:
Sirach 27:4–7; 1 Corinthians 15:54–58; Luke 6:39–45

When my uncle died recently, my aunt said to me on the phone,
    "You know, he never said a nasty word about anyone his whole life."
They were married for over fifty years, so I figured she ought to know.
It was really a wonderful tribute from her.
It also reminded me that what we say has its roots in who we are.

Today's readings connect speech and character.
Sirach, a teacher of wisdom, wrote about two centuries before Jesus.
Today we hear him reflecting on the way speech reveals character.
He compares shaking a sieve, which retains the worthless husks while the
    grain passes through, to the act of speaking, which shows our faults as
    it offers our thoughts.
One can hear it as an invitation to talk less.
I can remember a wise priest once saying that we have few secrets
    from each other.
Perhaps he had been reading Sirach, or just listening to
    what others were saying.

Sirach also says we can think of our speech as the fruit of our mind.
And what we speak is organically related to what we think,
    speech as the harvest of our thoughts.

By our words we manifest our minds—and hearts.

Thus, he cautions his students to refrain from judgment until they hear
people speak: "Praise no one before he speaks, for it is then that
people are tested."

Jesus is developing a similar theme of connection between what goes on in
our minds and how it bears fruit, not always sweet, in what we say.

"Why do you *notice* the splinter in your brother's eye," he first asks,
"but do not perceive the wooden beam in your own?"

Why do you fasten on the microscopic flaw when you look at your brother
or sister, yet miss the magnitude of your own mess?

But then he goes further and asks, "How can you *say* to your brother,
'Let me remove that splinter in your eye,'
when you do not even notice the beam in your own eye?"

Our minds bear fruit in what we say, and what we say leads to what we do,
for good or ill.

In other words, we are willing to do splinter surgery while being half blind.

From noticing to saying to acting—that is the flow.

This also takes us into the ancient understanding of the heart and the
importance of God giving the people a new heart, a heart of flesh
rather than a heart of stone, impenetrable and hardened.

The Jewish understanding was that thoughts were located in the heart.

The heart was the seat of intelligence and decision, and *heart* was used in
the Bible where in English we would use mind and will.

The heart, then, is the source of thought, desires, and deeds.*

And the movement is from what our heart notices to what we speak to how
we act in the world.

So the bottom line seems to be to check out what we store in our heart.

What we hold onto in the space we live in is revealing of what we value.

---

* See John L. McKenzie, *Dictionary of the Bible*, "Heart" (Milwaukee: Bruce Publ.
Co., 1965), 343–44.

Many of us tend to hang onto certain things because of their emotional
value, storing them away in whatever available space our living
conditions allow, whether in a drawer, a bureau, a closet, a room, or
some rented storage space located some distance away
from where we live.

I remember my grandmother used to save string and ribbon.

My mother would say to her, "Mom, what on earth do you plan to tie up
with all this string?"

My grandmother would just smile.

But my mother had her own things stored away.

At the time of her death I discovered cards and letters she had saved over
the years.

I save play programs, every one since 1961 when I saw Mary Martin in *The
Sound of Music* at the Lunt-Fontanne Theater in New York City.

Far more important are the things we store in our hearts—memories of
events, of words spoken, of hurts sustained, dreams of achieving
success, winning approval, overcoming obstacles, judgments rendered,
attitudes absorbed, values accepted, loves and hatreds.

Jesus' final words in today's Gospel emphasize the crucial importance of our
heart storage: "A good person out of the store of goodness in his heart
produces good, but an evil person out of a store of evil produces evil;
for from the fullness of the heart the mouth speaks."

What we store within does not stay still there but bears fruit in
word and deed.

The church's tradition of *lectio divina* (sacred reading) helps to store the
words of the Scriptures in our hearts.

This is a practice of reading Scripture aloud, slowly, savoring the words,
chewing on them, digesting them, letting them enter our hearts and
minds for further meditation and prayer during the day.

One takes a text and repeats it over and over, until one is able to carry
away a phrase from it for further nourishment during the day, calling
it up in the hours ahead.

Consider the words of Jesus in the Sermon on the Plain that we have been
hearing the last few weeks (Luke 6:20–49), which includes the words
of today's Gospel.
They call us to care for those least in the eyes of the world—
the poor, the hungry, the weeping, the persecuted—
and to let our love embrace even our enemies, those who hate us and
whom we hate.
Jesus' words today speak to us about those within the community—
those we think we know all too well, gifted as we are with this
sensitivity for splinters.
If we absorb the twenty-nine verses of this sermon and store them in our
hearts, we shall have a heart shaped by the Gospel, one that thinks
and acts in the spirit of Christ.

The heart of Christ was dedicated to doing the will of the Father.
And this remains the mission of the church as the Body of Christ
in the world.
The great preacher William Sloane Coffin reflects on what this means in a
recent book:

"The more we do the will of the Father in this life, the less unfinished
business we will leave behind when we die. If our lives exemplify
pastoral charity and the pursuit of social justice, then death will come
not as an enemy but as a friendly angel who will take us to the One
whose greatest hope is to say to each and every one of us, 'Well done,
good and faithful servant, welcome into the joy of your Master.'"*

Each and every Sunday we gather here to celebrate the power of God
revealed in Christ.
Here we see the power of God at work in transforming bread and wine for
the purpose of transforming us, that we might grow to fullness as the
Body of Christ.

---

*William Sloane Coffin, *Credo* (Louisville, KY: Westminster John Knox, 2004),
169.

This power enables us to live out the call of the Gospel, to be a force for life
in the world.

This power allows us to sing out with Paul:

"Where, O death, is your victory?

Where, O death, is your sting?"

For indeed, through our Lord Jesus Christ, God has given us victory over
sin and death.

So, let us therefore resolve to "be firm, steadfast, always fully devoted to the
work of the Lord, knowing that in the Lord our labor is not in vain."

Amen. Alleluia.

JAW

Questions for Reflection

1. What is occupying space in your heart these days?

2. What does your speech reveal about you? What role does making
judgments have in your life?

3. What words of Jesus found in Luke's Gospel are important for
your life?

Other Directions for Preaching

1. Paul's words to the Corinthians invite preachers to consider the
transformation that is our destiny because of the Resurrection, "when this
which is corruptible clothes itself with incorruptibility and this which is
mortal clothes itself with immortality."

2. Community life calls for a balance between tolerance and what used
to be called fraternal correction. What does that mean for a community's self-
understanding and behavior today?

3. Productivity is a key value in capitalist societies. What defines
Christian productivity?

Faith Seeking Healing
NINTH SUNDAY IN ORDINARY TIME

READINGS:
1 Kings 8:41–43; Galatians 1:1–2, 6–10; Luke 7:1–10

Listen again to the final words of Solomon's prayer that we heard today.
Solomon is praying for the foreigners who will come to the Temple to honor
the God of Israel.
He asks God:
"Listen from your heavenly dwelling.
Do all that the foreigner asks of you,
that all the peoples of the earth may know your name,
may fear you as do your people Israel,
and may acknowledge that this Temple which I have built is dedicated
to your honor."

So prayed Solomon the wise in the Temple he built for the God of Israel.
The king is thinking of the day when people would come from all around to
see this holy place.
Early on, there was some recognition by Israel that God was a God for all
peoples.
We see this same awareness in the Gospel today in the figure of the
centurion.

We don't know this Roman soldier's name.
But we know he was a man of importance.

He served under Herod or Pilate and, in turn, had one hundred
    men under him.
He also had slaves who answered to his needs.
And he was a man with connections among the Jewish elders.
Given that the Romans were an occupying force in the land of Palestine,
    it may come as a surprise to hear not only that he loved the Jewish
    people, but that they had such high regard for him.
It appears that he had won them over, even built them a synagogue,
    so when his servant fell ill, he asked them to intercede for him with
    the healer, Jesus.

The elders say to Jesus: "He deserves to have you do this for him, for he
    loves our nation and built the synagogue for us."
But after the Jewish elders had asked Jesus to come with them and he was
    on his way, the centurion sent friends to Jesus telling him it was not
    necessary to come to his home.
Some commentators suggest he did this because he was sensitive to Jewish
    law, which considered a person defiled who entered the house of a
    Gentile.
But the story itself hints of other reasons.

As a soldier, he knew the power of the voice of authority.
He acknowledges this in his message:
    "I say 'go,' and they go, 'come,' and they come."
But he was confirming more than his recognition of a
    kindred spirit in Jesus.
His words reveal him to be a man of faith:
    "I am not worthy to have you enter under my roof...
    but say the word and let my servant be healed."
Jesus heard the voice of a believer, and he was amazed by this foreigner.
And Jesus honored him:
    "Not even in Israel have I found such faith."

I like to think Jesus would give that same response this morning, when he
    hears us say those same words:
    "Lord, I am not worthy to receive you,
    only say the word, and I shall be healed."
I hope he might say this day: "Such faith I find in this parish, among these
    people!"
I hope that he sees our trust in the power of his Word repeated during the
    Eucharistic Prayer:
    "This is my body which will be given up for you.
    This is the cup of my blood. It will be shed for you and for all."
I hope that he witnesses our faith in how his Word can work in our lives
    and in our world, to bring healing, peace, and reconciliation.

And may Solomon see in us the fulfillment of his prayer:
    that all the peoples of the earth know God's name,
    and fear the mighty God of Israel who worked such wonders for
    God's chosen people and continues to work such wonders in our
    midst, if we call out in faith.

Do we see these things in ourselves?
Do we recognize ourselves in this centurion's need for help, healing,
    wholeness?
Or, more important at this time, do we recognize God's desire to bring in all
    the peoples of the world, to draw them closer?
This is a real challenge when we often hold the rest of the world in
    suspicion, especially those who threaten us.

Paul reminds us of something important today in his outburst at
    the Galatians.
This is a letter that has no word of thanksgiving at the beginning.
Usually after his greeting, Paul expresses his gratitude to God for how God
    has worked among a particular community.
Not here!

Paul launches immediately into his disappointment at how this community
    is forsaking the Gospel.
This was a community that Paul had founded.
But others had come into it and told the Galatians that they needed to be
    circumcised, and to follow more exactly the demands of the Law
    of Moses.

In response, Paul insists that God was doing something new for all
    peoples—in Christ.
Christ was now the new Temple in whom all could gather and pray to
    the Father.
They did not first have to become Jews by being circumcised.
Paul reminds us that the Holy Spirit is to be found at work in all who have
    been baptized in Christ.
And, while we are called to spread the Good News of Jesus Christ, we also
    acknowledge that the Spirit of the Lord is at work in other places.
And it is possible that we can all gather together and pray together as
    peoples of faith to the God who made us all.

The centurion stands before us today as one who depended on the kindness
    of a stranger.
Jesus the stranger is a way we can continue to think about him.
He does not conform to our cultural codes and modern perspectives.
We often try to domesticate Jesus into Jesus the Nice,
        a Jesus stripped of his otherness and of the mystery that lay at his core
        as the Son of God and God's Anointed One.
But it is Jesus the stranger who came—and continues to come—calling on
    us to change our lives and to accept the kingdom of God, which is near.

He belongs to all because he came for all,
        but he will not be manipulated by any.
He came to bring the presence of God to whoever calls on him,
        inviting that person, that community, to draw near.
He comes this day to all those who put their trust in the power of his Word.

So it is with fear and trembling that we continue to cry out to him,
   "Lord, I am not worthy to receive you,
     but only say the word, and I shall be healed."
You never know where it may lead once his healing power touches
   our spirit.

The number of those in need of his healing power continues to grow,
   not only in the sickness of the body but in the sickness of our spirits,
   in intolerance, hatred, racism, prejudice,
    in all attempts to transform the world by terror and abusive violence.
His healing power is needed in many of the lives of those that return from
   fighting in the present war.

There must be another way of living in our world.
Solomon recognized it in the vision of all peoples gathering on holy ground,
   and acknowledging God's name.
Jesus recognized it in his day, reaching out to heal all who came to him
   in faith,
   Jew or Gentile, soldier or slave, elder or sinner.
Pope John Paul recognized another way by calling on believers to be heralds
   of hope and agents of peace.
And so, today, we are sent out into the world once again,
   to work to make it God's holy place,
    where all can live together in justice, reconciliation, and peace.

JAW

Questions for Further Reflection

1. How has Solomon's prayer already come to fulfillment in our world?

2. Have you experienced faith in any surprising places?

3. Do you find the attitude of faith expressed by the centurion in your relationship with God?

Other Directions for Preaching

1. Paul reminds us that being a slave of Christ can put us in opposition to pleasing others.

2. Consider how we witness the work of the Holy Spirit in other faith traditions.

3. Reflect on the authority of the Word of God in the life of the church.

I'll Meet You at the Gate
TENTH SUNDAY IN ORDINARY TIME

READINGS:
1 Kings 17:17–24; Galatians 1:11–19; Luke 7:11–17

Over thirty years ago the massive apartment-commercial complex known as
the Watergate became a prominent name around the world.

Ever since that time, whenever a scandal breaks out in America, the suffix
gate is used: Travelgate, Monicagate, etc.

In 1974, when Watergate became the code word for the Nixon White
House scandal, I was visiting Poland.

One day, in a remote farming village, an eleven-year-old boy, a distant
relative of mine, asked me very earnestly,

"Father, tell me exactly what is Watergate?"

Wojtek had heard the word but couldn't decipher the code.

With many biblical texts we need to decipher the code to appreciate their
full meaning.

Biblical scholars who use a literary methodology to decipher a text's code
often use today's reading from Luke to demonstrate their method.

The story of the widow of Nain is a perfect example of how words need to
be deciphered for a richer meaning of the text.

Almost every word is a code of deeper meaning.

We might miss the fact that this miracle occurred at the gate of the city.

Gate is not just an accidental setting; it is a code for a deeper meaning.

The city represents the place of life, where meaning is found in people's lives through the day-to-day struggle of relationships and community.

The cemetery represents the place of death, of the ultimate termination of relationships and community.

There were two large crowds, Luke tells us.

The one large crowd that accompanied Jesus had the city, the place of life, as its destination.

The other large crowd that accompanied the widow and her dead son had the cemetery, the place of death, as its destination.

And then it happened (does anything ever really just happen?) that the two crowds met at the gate of the city.

The gate is the place that is not quite inside or outside the city.

It is the place in the biblical stories where beggars and sick people are.

They are not accepted in the city because they are not whole.

Nor is it suitable that they live in the cemetery, because they are not yet dead.

They stand there begging, appealing, longing to be made whole, to enter the city where we live out our lives in the give-and-take of community.

The gate, therefore, is a biblical code for those in-between places in our lives where decisions are made, where we are tested, where we long for a change that will make us whole again.

In Luke's masterful story, Jesus stops at the gate and looks not so much on the dead son but on his mother, who is a widow, which is a biblical code word for someone who is truly at the mercy of others because now, without a husband or a son, she has no means of support.

Jesus sees *her*, is moved with pity for *her*, speaks to *her*, and, after commanding the son to life, gives him to *her*.

The very fact that Luke uses the code word *her* so many times demonstrates that this is a story about *her*.

It is unfortunate that in our time, we have taken the suffix *gate* and
associated it only with the perverse crises in our age.

Luke's story today shows how the place of the gate in our lives, the in-
between place, certainly is a place of crisis.

But this miracle story beautifully illustrates the possibilities of what can
happen when, at the gate, we make the decision to choose life, to go
the way of mercy and of healing, to notice the widow in our midst.

Often in my ministry I have heard people tell me that they are standing at
the gate, the place where they have to make a major decision about
where they are going in life.

They don't use the code word *gate,* but that is what they mean.

Over the years I have tried to ask them one major question when they stand
at the gate: "Where do you think God wants you to go?"

In other words, what is the destination that will bring you to peace of
heart?

Then, I try to pay very close attention to the first words that flow from
their mouth.

I am convinced that the first words are the most significant because they
represent what is foremost in the person's heart and also the gift that
God is giving that person.

Luke's story ends today with the two large crowds becoming one crowd as
they exclaim, "A great prophet has arisen in our midst,"
and "God has visited his people."

We come to Eucharist this morning, a blend of many crowds, standing at
many gates.

By the time we say amen, may we recognize the power of God to make us
one large crowd who can call Jesus, our visitor, the one we have met
at the gate.

RPW

Questions for Reflection

1. How often, when we are seriously afflicted in some way, do we ask, "Why me?" "What have I done to deserve this?" or "Is this a punishment for my sins?"

2. Are we sometimes suspicious of the conversion stories of others, for example, jailhouse conversions and stories of born-again Christians? Do I have a conversion story?

3. When we witness the tragedies in the lives of others, do we feel overwhelmed and powerless? Or do we do what we can, however little it may seem?

Other Directions for Preaching

1. *Widow* is a code word in ancient Israel for one who lives a precarious existence and is dependent on the generosity of others, without rights, and subject to harsh treatment and exploitation. The Hebrew Scriptures tell us over and over that the wrath of God is reserved for those who neglect or oppress widows, orphans, foreigners, and strangers. Who are the widows among us? How do we fulfill this gospel mandate?

2. We are reminded by these readings to cherish and renew our belief in a God who is always life giving and re-creating. This belief is essential to keeping us from hopelessness and despair in the face of both personal tragedy and national or international disasters, such as the tsunami of December 2004 and the destruction of New Orleans by hurricane in 2005. It is the same God who continues to rescue us now, as in the time of Elijah, and through Jesus.

Tears in the House of Love
ELEVENTH SUNDAY IN ORDINARY TIME

READINGS:
*2 Samuel 12:7–10, 13; Galatians 2:16, 19–21;
Luke 7:36–50*

The repentant woman depicted in Luke 7:36–50 has become an icon of the
    repentant, even ecstatic, soul in the presence of grace.
In her tears we can find a range of those who have had a change of heart,
    from King David's conversion up to our own.
Our Lord's poignant encounter with the woman whom the poet Richard
    Crashaw once called a "weeping fire" carries sufficient fragrance to fill
    any Gothic cathedral without much gloss or heavy exegesis.
The text calls and, I dare say, even shouts to all of us,
    to recognize who we are in the presence of the Holy
    and to respond with heartfelt thanksgiving and service.

Perhaps the most obvious thing to say about this little drama in Simon the
    Pharisee's house is that at its core we find a woman's tears and the
    two men who make sense of them.
Simon and Jesus are interpreters of her tears.
We seem to have caught her in the midst of something, motivated by what,
    precisely—a provocation, an insight, a revelation?

The reason for her weeping reveals the tension between Jesus and his host
    and offers the Lord an opportunity to say something about
    forgiveness.

For the Pharisee, she is a prostitute—*that* kind of woman, he says,
    as if to reduce her human status to a subgenre,
    a genus used to identify insects.
For Simon, her tears could only be manipulative, devoted to the seduction
    of his newly arrived guest.
According to Simon's reading, our Lord loses his prophetic and social status
    because he has willingly become associated with a known sinner.
We soon learn, however, that Jesus is not a bit naive about the woman's
    identity or her past and tells a parable to demonstrate his point.
Jesus implies that the woman's enormous debt was canceled;
    he indicates that her weeping and subsequent actions are in direct
    response to that forgiveness.

Although unnamed (and frequently misidentified as Mary Magdalene, who
    brought her own tears to the tomb at the garden where the Lord had
    risen), this woman is the most compelling of gospel characters.
Like King David, we catch her in the *midst* of conversion,
    or, more mysteriously, at its bright fringes.
Wonderfully, she enables us to watch the fruits of a graced encounter unfold.
What makes this woman different from many conversions in the Gospel is
    that we see the good works that result from sorrow for sin.

David's house paid a heavy price for his sin.
Bad, treacherous kings followed David.
But not Simon's house.
Jesus has sanctified the home of the Pharisee with his loving presence, which
    the woman recognizes.
We can see that the woman's passionate attention to Jesus is the offspring
    of tears.
She is unique even among the famous who have converted in the Gospel.

What happens to the prodigal son after the big fiesta is over, when the
   bones of the fatted calf are long dried up, and that great ring begins to
   tarnish?
Who knows?
And again, that formally paralyzed, now forgiven, man with his mat and his
   restored body.
Where does he go? How does he spend his years?
On the other hand, the woman in Simon's house places us in a unique
   position.
We gently inhale the baroque results of forgiveness,
      feeling the dizzying effects of God's mercy in all its socially rough,
      embarrassing details.
The fruits of repentance are before us like a well set albeit extravagant table.
In the end, the effects of her conversion are so powerful that this woman
   has become the new host at the dinner, as Jesus himself suggests.
She has constructed a house of love built of faith and cemented with tears.

This response to forgiveness is not only the result of repentance, but a
   reaction to endless mercy.
Jesus not only accepted the woman as she was but allowed himself to be
   shamefully associated with her.
That is sacrificial giving that extends, fabulously, beyond just a moment of
   forgiveness for a checkered past.
She obviously sensed that mercy without measure, and so the tears begot
   more tears—this time in response to unconditional love.
As for Simon, he is not only a bankrupt host but vanquished to the dark
   pantheon of cynics and gossips and all those who fail to love.
We know the type.
They are professional "dis-creditors," living only to dismantle other people's
   reputations.
Bad zeal blinds them from imagining goodness in anyone but themselves.

We respond, astonishingly, as if to a canceled debt.
And all at once we are in union with the Psalmist.

"'I confess my faults to the Lord,' and you took away the guilt of my sin."
That we weep as fallen creatures for the world and ourselves,
      and then respond in grateful praise to the Creator who acts only in
      love, may alone justify our call to live out our baptism.
God is always recreating, reinventing, and reimagining us in Christ.
Isn't it incredible that what starts out as sorrow becomes transformed into
      creative service for the sake of the beloved?
Christian life is a kind of dialogue: knowing we are sinners and then
      responding to God's mercy and love in absolute freedom and in the
      fruitful, abundant creativity of good zeal.
Like the woman in Simon's house, our adoration comes in silence and with
      a freely given gift of the self at ground zero, in complete authenticity.
As Jesus suggests, the degree of our response indicates the intensity of our
      awareness of the love that has been given us.
For when the true self encounters Christ—
      known only to ourselves and God alone—
      we will find ourselves new hosts in the house of love,
      anointing him with a more perfect prayer.

GD

Questions for Reflection

1. Have I ever been moved to tears by something I felt sorry for? What was that experience like?

2. Have I judged people before I really knew them?

3. Where is true hospitality lacking in my household?

Other Directions in Preaching

1. Just because I invite the Lord into my house does not mean I have made him welcome. That gift must come from the heart—a contrite heart.

2. The gift of grace is unimaginable, unearned, and Americans have a hard time with getting something for nothing.

3. Imagine yourself as the servant in the room at Simon's house. You are witnessing all these events. What would you say?

Nomination Brings Obligation
TWELFTH SUNDAY IN ORDINARY TIME

READINGS:
Zechariah 12:10–11; 13:1; Galatians 3:26–29;
Luke 9:18–24

"What's in a name?" Juliet asks Romeo, after discovering he is a Montague,
a sworn enemy of her family, the Capulets.
"A rose by any other name would smell as sweet.
So Romeo would, were he not Romeo called, retain that dear
perfection which he owes without that title.
Romeo doff thy name, and for thy name which is no part of thee, take
all myself" (Act 2, scene 2).
Of course she is both right and wrong.
Romeo might still retain that "dear perfection" were he called Fred, or
maybe not!
But one cannot conclude that names do not matter, or that a name is "no
part of thee."

We come by our names in different ways.
There are the names given us at birth, over which we have no control.
There are nicknames, sometimes serendipitous, sometimes earned,
sometimes regretted.
There are the names given because of our relationship with another:
husband, wife, mother, father, son, daughter, best friend, mentor.

Then there are those names that come with a particular office or position, often sought after, then given either by appointment or election.

In these instances we speak of being nominated (that is, named) for a
    particular office, such as mayor, governor, senator, and, of course,
    president, in the political realm, or cardinal, bishop, pastor, provincial,
    in the ecclesiastical world.

These latter names can become one's primary identity in the world—
    "Mr. President, come this way."
    "The bishop will now say a few words."

Even in a culture where almost all signs of formality have disappeared into
    the mush of chummy camaraderie, some names still have holding
    power.

Being nominated still retains a certain honor and dignity,
    and being named for these positions brings both glory and celebration.

Nomination brings privilege but also expectation and obligation.

Today's readings concern how Jesus is being named and what that means
    for him.

He initiates the questioning, asking first how the people name him.

How others name him reflects what they think of him.

So, he asks the question, "Who do the crowds say that I am?"

Notice that all the responses point to figures from Israel's past:
    John the Baptist who was beheaded by Herod,
    Elijah who was the first of the great prophets,
    and, finally, one or another of the prophets of old.

Then he asks a more loaded question: "But who do you say that I am?"

Only Peter answers: "The Christ of God."

And we are immediately told:
    "He rebuked them and directed them not to tell this to anyone."

Why the rebuke?

Jesus asks a question; then, when he gets an honest answer, he gets huffy,
    rebuking them and telling them not to talk about this.

His reaction goes back to the name.

"The Christ of God" is Luke's translation for what the Jewish people called
     the Messiah.

Both *christ* and *messiah* mean "anointed one."

Since Luke was writing for a non-Jewish audience, he used the term *Christ*.

This Messiah was the long-awaited Savior the Jewish people had been
     yearning for ever since the time of David, through the years of the two
     kingdoms, through the exile, through the oppressive occupations of
     such powerful kingdoms as the Assyrians and Babylonians to the
     Persians, Greeks, and now the Romans.

The Jews were hoping for a Messiah who would come and throw out their
     oppressors, usher in the kingdom of God, and restore all that had been
     lost since their glory days under King David.

All this rode in on the title *Messiah*.

But Messiah was a name Jesus did not accept.

Jesus then substitutes another name: the Son of Man, whom he describes as
     one who must suffer, be killed, and then raised on the third day.

The Son of Man, from the book of Daniel, would in itself be a welcome
     one, for this was the name of one who was to come at the end of the
     world in glory and majesty.

But the Son of Man to whom Jesus refers is one who will suffer and die
     before he comes into his glory.

Names are important because nomination brings obligation.

Nomination brings responsibility.

Jesus did not accept the responsibility of being a political savior, so he
     rejected Peter's nomination as Messiah.

God was going to do something new through him, and central to this plan
     was the suffering he would endure.

Jesus, then, gave himself a new name: the suffering Son of Man.

And he takes it even further.

If we are to be named as his followers,
     then it means a willingness to deny ourselves and take up our
     cross *daily*.

Whatever form the cross takes, dying of some kind is involved,
a giving up, a surrendering.
Within our most important relationships we often find the cross waiting.
In all our efforts to love in a way that gives life, freedom, mercy to others,
a dying to self is needed, and out of that dying new life comes.
Theologian John Shea writes that the cross is "what happens to those who
persist in righteousness in an unrighteous world." *

Jesus taught his disciples about the cross in words on the way to Jerusalem,
and in deed from a cross on a hilltop outside the city.
In him we find the Messiah who redefined his role: not slaying those who
opposed him but loving them into new life, if only they would accept
him with the eyes of faith.

Paul expands further on what it means to belong to Christ, to be Christian.
Through faith we are all children of God in Jesus Christ.
By being baptized into Christ, we have clothed ourselves with Christ.
And for all of us who are named Christian, there is to be no division
according to race, gender, or social class.
No division by way of labels like liberal or conservative,
progressives or traditionalists,
fanatics or pagans.
Christian names us as belonging to God the Father through the Son in the
power of the Spirit.

What's in a name?
A great deal if you allow it to shape you in accord with its
paradoxical power.

JAW

---

* John Shea, *The Spiritual Wisdom of the Gospels for Christian Preachers and
Teachers: On Earth As It Is in Heaven* (Collegeville, MN: Liturgical Press, 2004), 265.

Questions for Reflection

1. What are some of your names? Do you notice the difference in how they fit you? Do you wear some better than others? Do you reject any of the names you had growing up?

2. How does the name Christian define you? How do you define the name?

3. What does it mean to be part of a Christian community? Does it call for more of a response than simply seeing yourself as an individual Christian?

Other Directions for Preaching

1. God promises through his prophet Zechariah to pour out a spirit of grace and petition. This text can be seen to apply to the celebration of the Eucharist, where we look on the crucified and risen Lord under the forms of bread broken and wine poured out for us.

2. Consider what baptism brings with it: a deep sense of unity, a connection with a past rooted in the patriarch Abraham, our father in faith, and the promise of a future looking to the return of the Lord in the power of the Spirit.

3. What does it mean today to take up the cross? Is God calling us to be victims, people committed to lives of pain and suffering?

What Freedom Do We Celebrate This Fourth of July?
THIRTEENTH SUNDAY IN ORDINARY TIME

READINGS:
*1 Kings 19:16b, 19–21; Galatians 5:1, 13–18;
Luke 9:51–62*

The General Congress that met in Philadelphia in 1776 declared to the world that we were free and independent states.

We celebrate this weekend that bedrock principle of our American way, our freedom.

But we know that Americans don't have a neat and single definition of freedom.

All we have to do is look at the many 5–4 decisions coming from our Supreme Court to realize our differences when it comes to defining what freedom really is.

Last week, our highest court by a 5–4 vote said that the University of Virginia violated the free-speech rights of a student group by refusing to provide funds for it.

They also ruled in a 5–4 vote that the state of Georgia's creation of three majority-black congressional districts violated the equal protection rights of white voters.

If the "mighty nine" have different and distinct views about freedom, we shouldn't be shocked that the rest of us ordinary citizens do, also.

But freedom has its price, especially the cost of hard decisions.

In totalitarian states people don't have to make hard decisions;

    Big Brother makes decisions for them, and thus, life seems a lot less

    complicated.

Supreme Court Justice Anthony Kennedy once said,

    "The hard fact is that sometimes we must make decisions we do not

    like. We make them because they are right, right in the sense that the

    law and the Constitution compel their results."

Because the church is in the world, it too agonizes over what Saint Paul

    once called

    "the glorious freedom of the children of God" (Rom 8:21).

He proclaimed to the Galatians:

    "For freedom Christ set us free; so stand firm

    and do not submit again to the yoke of slavery" (Gal 5:1).

The Christians in Galatia were biting and tearing one another to pieces,

    and so Paul reminded them that, when they became Christians,

    they were freed from the yoke of slavery;

    but now, because of their divisiveness,

    they were putting on a second yoke of slavery.

For Saint Paul, the freedom of Christians was not to bite and tear one

    another to pieces, but to serve one another.

Saint Paul raises some age-old questions that still haunt us today:

    What is freedom for?

    Is freedom an inalienable right?

    Does freedom have restraints?

    And, if so, who decides what those restraints are?

Perhaps the people who wrestle most with the meaning of freedom are

    the artists.

It is the tough but glorious vocation of the artist to raise questions that we

    would rather not think about.

There is a story in a novel by the science fiction writer Isaac Asimov that
reveals the problem of freedom in a technological society.

The Naked Sun is about a planet where robots protect humans.

They are programmed with the Laws of Robotics.

The first two laws are:

> 1. A robot may not injure a human or allow a human to come
> to harm.
>
> 2. A robot must obey the orders given by a human, except where such
> orders conflict with the first law.

In one episode, a robot serves a glass of water to a human.

The human is poisoned.

Even thought it did not know the water was poisoned, the robot short
circuits because he has brought harm to the human.

In this episode Asimov demonstrates the dangerous side of freedom in a
society where we think we can do and make anything we want.

To solve the problem so that no more people are poisoned by robots, what
does he do?

Program the robot to make decisions?

But if he does that, don't we forfeit our human capacity for freedom?

And so, even the marvels of modern science that are supposed to free us up
bring about a new yoke of slavery.

All those work-saving kitchen gadgets have to be washed and stored.

Medical advances allow us to live longer, but now we have the new
yoke of slavery that comes with all the technological developments of
recent years.

We have the treasures of the Internet, all that information in an instant, but
some are getting so addicted to cyberspace that they have little other
space to play, pray, listen, or be at peace.

We must not look for off-the-rack, ready-to-wear solutions to these
problems of freedom in our time.

We must listen carefully, however, to the rich traditions of freedom in the
   Gospel as we make our hard decisions in life.

Saint Paul meant it when he told us that we "were called for freedom"
   (Gal 5:13).
Jesus freed us so that we can be like him,
   free to live by the Spirit the life within, which nobody can take
   from us.
Jesus demonstrates this freedom today when the "sons of thunder," James
   and John, want to destroy the Samaritans for not welcoming their
   Master.
Whenever freedom is threatened, we often turn to simplistic solutions,
   especially violent ones, as we plot to destroy the freedom of others.
Jesus rebukes them and shows them what it means to live in freedom, to
   live the life within.
He says no to simple answers, especially those that have the effect of
   destroying others.

Of course, Saint Paul knew the dangers of freedom.
He wasn't speaking about self-indulgent freedom,
   but a freedom that is built on the love and service of others.
"For the whole law," he said,
   "is fulfilled in one statement,
   namely, *you shall love your neighbor as yourself*" (Gal 5:14).
A good note to end on,
   as we celebrate this weekend our freedom as Americans,
   and as we celebrate always our freedom as daughters and sons of God.

RPW

Questions for Reflection

1. What do I need to walk away from in order to walk toward Christ with total commitment?

2. Even though I have been freed by Christ, what are the other forms of enslavement that I choose to grasp?

3. Am I prepared to pay the costs of discipleship? And to do so wholeheartedly?

Other Directions for Preaching

1. Both Elijah and Jesus immediately make clear that in order to become disciples, we must be willing to commit ourselves completely to the demands of discipleship. At times there can be conflicts between our responsibilities to God (Christ) and the other responsibilities in our lives. Living in and through these conflicts is very difficult.

2. The human desire to punish and wreak revenge upon those with whom we profoundly disagree is very powerful. Both Jesus and Paul reprimand their followers for acting on such desires. We are free from causing pain and suffering to one another; we are free for loving one another as we love ourselves. Easy to say, but very hard to live.

On Not Glossing Over the Healing
FOURTEENTH SUNDAY IN ORDINARY TIME

READINGS:
Isaiah 66:10–14c; Galatians 6:14–18;
Luke 10:1–12, 17–20

An old man in India sat down in the shade of an ancient tree whose roots
    disappeared far away in a swamp.
Suddenly he sensed a commotion where the roots entered the water.
He noticed how a scorpion had become helplessly entangled in the roots.
The old man made his way carefully along the tops of the roots to the place
    where the scorpion was trapped.
He reached down to free it.
But each time he touched the scorpion it lashed his hand with its tail,
    stinging him painfully.
Finally, his hand was so swollen he could no longer close his fingers,
    so he withdrew to the shade of the tree to wait for the swelling to
    go down.
As he arrived at the trunk, he saw a young man standing above him on the
    road, laughing at him.
"You're a fool," said the young man, "wasting your time trying to help a
    scorpion that can only do you harm."
The old man replied, "Just because it is in the nature of the scorpion to
    sting, should I change my nature, which is to cure?"

In Luke's Gospel, Jesus makes it clear that the primary mission of his
   disciples is to cure the way he cured—despite the scorpion's sting,
   despite the howling of the wolves.
The disciples were to follow their nature;
   they were to bring peace to all who would accept peace,
   and they were to preach that the kingdom of God was at hand.

What is unique about today's Gospel from Luke is the number seventy-two.
The other evangelists speak of Jesus sending out his twelve apostles to
   preach.
It's only Luke who has this story of Jesus sending out seventy-two disciples.
The number is significant.
In the book of Genesis, Noah's descendants numbered seventy-two, and the
   Bible says that after the flood seventy-two people started to spread all
   over the earth.
So, for Luke, the number symbolizes the fact that Jesus was sending his
   disciples not to only the twelve tribes of Israel, but to the entire world.
He was sending them out to follow their nature, which was to cure.

What amazed me as I studied the best biblical commentaries on this
   particular Gospel today is how the commentators all seemed to gloss
   over verse 9, which says that the disciples were to "cure the sick."
The commentators are so anxious to remember that Jesus told them to
   announce that "the kingdom of God is at hand for you" that they
   gloss over the fact that we are first called to cure the sick among us.

Why do they gloss over this verse?
Is it because we live in a time when only professional medical people are
   called to cure the sick—those who make artificial hearts, those who
   research the potential healing from stem cells, those doctors and
   nurses and techs and hospital chaplains who have a professional
   calling to cure the sick?

But doesn't that let the rest of us off the hook?

After all, by using the number seventy-two, Luke is making sure that we
    understand Christ's call that all of us, whether we are professionals or
    not, are called to cure the sick.

We are always surrounded by sick people, in our families, our parish, our
    communities.

How do we respond to the gospel call to follow our nature, which is to cure?

Here, may I offer just two insights I have learned, not from a book, but
    from my own three-year battle with leukemia, chemotherapy, and the
    people who have surrounded me during this time of trial.

Here, may I offer just two practical ways in which we can all take part in
    the healing of the sick.

First, allow sick persons the freedom to be and to feel and to say
    what they want.

Don't impose your own fears, your own clichés, your own needs upon them.

There is a natural awkwardness when we are confronted with illness,
    especially a life-threatening one.

And so we say awkward and sometimes confusing things.

When I first told a family member about my diagnosis, she said,
    "Well, as I always said, when your time's up, your time's up."

When my friend Nancy told her aunt she had breast cancer, her aunt said,
    "Well, you must have bumped your breast."

Those are awkward and stinging examples of what the scorpion might say,
    not the disciple of Christ.

Instead, simply say to the sick person, "Tell me about it."

Very simple, very open-ended.

But what is *it*? you might ask.

Believe me, the sick person will tell you what *it* is on that particular day
    and *it* will not be the same for every person.

This invitation to a sick person is a simple act that helps us to follow our
    nature, which is to cure.

The second insight I share with you is the power of prayer in curing the sick.
Simply tell the sick person in front of you that you will pray for him or her.
Cardinal Bernardin wrote from his hospital bed as he was battling with
    cancer: "Pray now while you're healthy; it is not always easy to pray
    when you are sick."

How true that is.
There have been times in the past three years when I simply could not pray;
    I was too sick.
But I can also share with you that very often in those moments I
    remembered so many people who had promised me their prayers.

There were times when I actually felt those prayers: a power coming not
    from my weak body but from the Body of Christ,
    the church, the Communion of Saints,
    the prayers to Saint Anne from my sister-in-law,
    the prayers to Blessed Titus Brandsma from the Carmelites,
    the Rosary prayed each day for me by an eighty-seven-year-old
    Sulpician priest,
    the prayers of the monks of Conception Abbey, the nuns at Carmel,
    the prayers of the Dutch Reformed in the Netherlands and the
    Presbyterians in Japan,
    and most especially the Prayers of the Faithful—your prayers each
    Sunday Eucharist at Holy Trinity Parish.

So, two simple insights on how we can all cure the sick:
    give them freedom to speak and give them prayers.
This is how we might follow our nature: not to sting like a scorpion but to
    save, to cure, to heal, like Jesus.

RPW

Questions for Reflection

1. Have I experienced the healing presence of others at times of sickness?

2. Have I found within my nature the capacity to cure?

3. Do we always recognize the workers who are sent by God to the harvest in this church?

Other Directions for Preaching

1. Times of natural disaster seem to bind us together with people who live in places that we would have previously been hard pressed even to locate on a map. The cross of suffering enables us to learn much more about our sisters and brothers at home and around the world. Once this bond has been established, it can become easier to invest ourselves in caring and acting on behalf of all those who suffer.

2. Fortunately for all, the people to whom the seventy-two followers of Jesus were sent recognized and welcomed them. Sometimes, we believe that we know what a minister sent by Christ should look like. We can fail to recognize the gifts that Christ has already poured into the vineyard.

Graced Hospitality
FIFTEENTH SUNDAY IN ORDINARY TIME

READINGS:
*Deuteronomy 30:10–14; Colossians 1:15–20;
Luke 10:25–37*

In the early part of the sixth century a document appeared that would
    change the course of human history.

It would guide Western Europe through a tumultuous period of unusual
    savagery and war.

It would offer a blueprint for common Christian life and be noted for its
    genius in moderation and practicality.

It would leave a lasting impact on spirituality for centuries to come.

Even with all the many accolades that have been lavished on the *Rule of
    Saint Benedict* over the years, one feature in particular stands out:
    a unique and stunning vision of hospitality.

The treatment of the guest is so important that anyone, no matter who that
    person may be, is to be treated as Christ himself.

It would be hard to exaggerate the importance of hospitality in antiquity.

There are swatches illuminating the importance of the guest in the Hebrew
    Scriptures, beginning with Abraham.

Even the wicked, like King Herod, observed hospitality when he swore an
    oath before his guests to give away up to half his kingdom.

His loyalty to hospitality ultimately forced him to behead John the Baptist
    as a gift to a teenage girl and her mother.
The Gospel takes a very ironic twist because of the crucial importance of
    hospitality.

Jesus himself appears to have a radical sense of hospitality and
    demonstrates its importance in the parable of the good Samaritan.
Placed in the context of Luke's Gospel, the parable is followed by a famous
    domestic dispute between Martha and Mary, which Jesus resolves.
Mary has chosen the better part because she is most attentive to the guest.

The question "Who is my neighbor?" raised by a scholar of the Law invites
    us to ponder just how far the limits of hospitality really extend.
Relatives? Even the ones we have quarreled with?
Friends? Even those who have hurt us?
Neighbors? Even those who disagree with us?
The men that passed the beaten Samaritan on the road have already made
    their decision about the limits of love.
They have chosen to live in a tiny world.
Perhaps it was because they were too "religious" to get their hands dirty.

We all have our reasons for not welcoming others, and the best ones often
    come wrapped with righteousness.
That is the way we have justified war as well, isn't it?
Patriotism can be an excuse for whatever aggression we please.
A popular saying in the 1960s during the Vietnam War was "My country
    right or wrong."
And it always helps, of course, if we think God is on our side of the road,
    doesn't it?
As a corporate body—a nation, a state, a community—we have walked past
    millions of Africans who have starved or been massacred within the
    last few decades.
It is not because we are malicious, but because we just did not seem to want
    to cross over to the other side of the street.

Only radical hospitality interprets the limits of love.

You cannot measure out hospitality in a law book, and that is why Jesus
tells this parable in the first place.

The story of a man, a sworn enemy of the Jews, who picks up one who is
not his own and cares for him like a brother—where is the legislation
that tells us about that?

The fact is that God's Son had to become one of us in order for us to see
the endlessness of love.

Interestingly enough, the patristic tradition read the good Samaritan
parable through an allegorical lens, symbolizing God's hospitality
to humanity.

For Saint Augustine and Saint Ambrose, the good Samaritan was a figure of
Jesus himself, who healed our mortal wounds from sin with the wine
of his own blood.

God makes us welcome by restoring us to health and bringing us into the
shelter of the church, the home that keeps us safe in divine love
through the mysteries hidden in Word and sacrament.

Divine hospitality transcends the Law, which either passes the downtrodden
unrecognized or willfully ignores the plight of the poor.

God has set the blueprint for compassion as deep as the ocean.

We will never understand the depths of love, but we can respond to its
mystery by receiving others more capaciously, more generously,
even those who have been beaten up by sin on life's road,
one perhaps more dangerous than Jericho,
and with difficulties more hidden and dark.

Our own hospitality might even prove heroic.

We may not be called, like Blessed Damian of Molokai, who lived and
ministered to lepers and eventually caught the disease himself.

He crossed over to serve them as a priest.

It did not matter who they were.

They were his brothers and sisters.

We can welcome the stranger in our lives as well,
     even one we don't particularly care for.
And, beyond a personal commitment, we also have a corporate responsibility
     as a Christian people to invite the immigrant into our midst as our
     brother and sister.
Christ passes no one on the roadside.
Surely, care for the foreigner is a reminder to all people of good will that we
     are our brothers' and sisters' keeper.
We have all come to this inn of welcome, this shelter we call church, and
     now we gather around this altar.
God has come to heal our wounds, even as he has given his Son to feed us
     for the journey.
We are strangers no longer but guests at God's table.

GD

Questions for Reflection

1. Have I knowingly avoided certain people on social occasions because they were different from me or because I did not want to be seen with them? Why?

2. What can I do to help heal the wounds of division in our society?

3. If I were asked to forgive the person who has hurt me most deeply, would I be able to do it?

Other Directions in Preaching

1. Christ is made manifest in a thousand different faces, and it is our responsibility to see these neighbors as graced occasions and invitations.

2. All of us have been beaten up on the road of life one way or another. At those moments we ought to allow God and our neighbor to care for us and bring us into shelter for healing.

3. What would the three characters—the priest, the Levite, the Samaritan—each say as they notice the beaten man on the road to Jericho?

Setting the Record Straight
SIXTEENTH SUNDAY IN ORDINARY TIME

READINGS:
Genesis 18:1–10a; Colossians 1:24–28;
Luke 10:38–42

Each summer, I invite a person from the Gospel of the day to preach
the homily.
It fits the tradition, especially in Protestant congregations, of having a guest
preacher preach while the pastor is on vacation.
A friend of mine pointed out to me, however, that over the last few years, I
have invited only men characters in the Gospel to preach.
Since I am a sensitive person, I thought I would take my friend's advice and
invite a woman to preach today's homily.
And so, let me introduce to you tonight's guest homilist, a woman named
Martha.

Thank you, Fr. Bob.
Well, where on earth, do I possibly begin?
This Gospel from Luke you just heard is preached every three years all over
Christendom and, let me tell you, I am not always pleased with what I
hear from preachers on this day.
So many of them make me into some kind of neurotic, obsessive, household
dominatrix.

But, believe me, I was not the kind of person who ran around the house
with a glue gun and a copper soufflé pan.

I am not Martha Stewart; I am Saint Martha.

Saint Martha! Remember that, you card-carrying contemplatives.

I don't know why, but Luke really never cared for me that much.

But, remember, his was only one of the four Gospels.

In John, I get a better role.

In John's Gospel, I make the first formal confession of Jesus as "the
Messiah, the Son of God,
the one coming into the world."

For you fundamentalists in the congregation, that's John 11:27.

So, remember, I am not just a woman named Martha from a certain village;
I am invoked in all the litanies of the church down through the ages as
Saint Martha.

A week from today the church will celebrate my feast day, the feast of Saint
Martha!

I was named Saint Martha because I did what all my ancestors had done:
welcomed the stranger, welcomed the prophet, welcomed the itinerant
preacher, who just happened to be Jesus, the Son of God.

I did what my ancestors Abraham and Sarah had done: welcomed the weary
traveler with food, water, and hospitality.

The ancient world of Palestine was a dangerous place, filled with robbers,
arid land, and sun-blazing trails.

It was built right into our religion to welcome those on a journey and to
attend to their needs.

It was the only way in which we could survive as a people.

And I was good at what I did: recognizing the neighbor's needs, attending to
them as honored guests.

But it wasn't easy.

I had no help, no servants, like Abraham and Sarah.

Oh, yes, I did have a brother, Lazarus, who eventually became Saint Lazarus.

But that day, when I welcomed Jesus into the house, Lazarus was nowhere
    to be seen.
There's a part of me that would love to tell you the juicy gossip about
    where Lazarus was that day and why he didn't help me.
But I can't because, alas, saints are not supposed to gossip!

And then there was Mary.
By the way, she was not Saint Mary Magdalene, as some preachers still
    claim, like the one today on Mother Angelica.
Oh, yes, once in a while I do tune in to the Eternal Word Network just to
    see how they get it so wrong.

One other assumption that a lot of preachers make is that there was this
    fierce sibling rivalry between Mary and me.
But that is simply not true.
Mary usually assisted me in the preparation of the stew, the setting of the
    table, the washing of the dishes.
We had a wonderful relationship; she was not only my sister but my
    best friend.

But on that day, something came over Mary.
She simply refused to help me with my chores.
She sat, not like the traditional woman of the day, but like a male disciple,
    sitting by the Lord's feet, listening to him.
It simply wasn't like Mary.
I couldn't take it.
I was overcome by my burdens, and blurted out to Jesus,
    "Don't you care that my sister has left me by myself to do the serving?
    Tell her to help me."

As soon as I said that, I knew I had made a mistake.
I'm sure all of you have had that experience.
Just as the words roll out of your mouth, you say to yourself, "Oh, no, why
    did I say such a dumb thing?"

Instead of going to my sister, I made the faux pas of asking a stranger to intercede in a family dispute.

I know Jesus' words seem harsh to you, but I didn't take them that way.
He wasn't putting me down, nor my hospitality, my hard work, my frustration.
He was simply reminding me that in my work for the Lord I forgot to pay attention to the Lord of my work.

When I went to heaven, I got interested in poetry.
I read it all the time.
It helps me to focus.
One of my favorite poets is T. S. Eliot, who once wrote:
"Teach us to care, teach us not to care, teach us to sit still."*
I cannot imagine a more important piece of gospel advice to you people here at Holy Trinity who are so engaged in your faith, your religion, your hospitality to others.
Of course, we must care; that is why I am Saint Martha.
But there are so many times in our busy life,
even our busy religious life,
when we have to not care,
when we have to sit still,
when in silence, in awe, in wonder, we have to tear off our given cultural and ecclesial roles and simply listen to the Lord in our midst.
If we don't do that, we won't have anything to give to the neighbor in our midst.

So, here I am, a kind and generous woman who made one faux pas in my life and preachers have put me down ever since.
But Jesus never put me down. He simply reminded me to care, and not to care, and to sit still.

---

*T. S. Eliot, "Ash Wednesday" [1930], I:40 and VI:29; pp. 86, 94 in *Collected Poems 1909–1962: The Centenary Edition 1888–1988* (San Diego, CA: Harcourt Brace Jovanovich, ©1968 by Esme Valerie Eliot).

That is why I am so honored to have this opportunity tonight to tell my
story, to set the record straight.

And you know, one of the nicest things about being in heaven is that I don't
have to change.
I don't need a psychiatrist, a spiritual director, a quiet weekend, a twelve-
step program.
I can still be the same Martha.
Just because you're in heaven doesn't mean you've changed.
I'm still anxious and worried about many things, especially about you.
And I mean *you!*
But I've also learned my lesson and I am at peace.
I am sitting at the feet of my Lord and waiting for you to join me.

RPW

Questions for Reflection

1. How have I encountered the Lord while offering hospitality to those who come my way?

2. What are the matters about which I am anxious and upset?

3. How do we balance time for prayer and meditation with the requirements of ministry and hospitality to others?

Other Directions for Preaching

1. This Gospel challenges the gender expectations of that time. Martha welcomes Jesus into her home. In the patriarchal society of that time, it would be customary for the man of the house to greet visitors. While not impossible, it would have been unusual for a woman to own a home. And Mary sits at the feet of Jesus, the customary place of a disciple.

2. Anyone who invites others to their home for a meal knows that there is a lot of work involved. It is easy to become so caught up in cleaning and food preparation and service that, at the end of the evening, the host sometimes thinks, "I didn't even really have a chance to converse with my guest!" Today's Gospel reminds us that hospitality should always be focused on the person to whom the hospitality is being offered, in this case, Jesus.

It All Depends on Friendship
SEVENTEENTH SUNDAY IN ORDINARY TIME

READINGS:
Genesis 18:20–32; Colossians 2:12–14; Luke 11:1–13

Last week Irma Goff sat through a two-hour memorial service and heard four
friends give eulogies for her husband and three daughters who were
bludgeoned and stabbed to death in their Potomac, Maryland, home.
One wonders what went through her mind and heart when she heard one
preacher say of her fifteen-year-old daughter, Alyse, that she was Mrs.
Goff's best friend.

To be called somebody's best friend is perhaps the most touching tribute
that can ever be made.
Just think of all the marvelous names two lovers share:
spouse, husband, wife, beloved, sweetheart.
But all of these names, lovely as they are, dim when someone says to his or
her spouse: "You are my best friend."

But there are friends and there are friends.
It was Aristotle who first told us that.
He said that were three kinds of friendship:
friendships based on the pleasure another gives us;
friendships based on another's usefulness to us;
and friendships based on a shared love of the good, the true,
and the beautiful.

Aristotle defended the last type of friendship as the one required for the moral life.

It's the same kind of friendship that's necessary for a spiritual friendship with God.

Although our Scripture readings today focus on how we relate to God in prayer,
    if we look and listen deeper to these readings
    we find that friendship with God is the framework of our prayer life.

First, we have the story of Abraham bargaining with God to save the cities of Sodom and Gomorrah.

This story might strike us as strange because at first it doesn't seem right that we should bargain with God over anything.

After all, even the great patriarch Abraham wasn't equal to God; he was only a creature in the presence of his Creator.

But the story can only be understood in the framework of friendship.

In the book of Isaiah, it is God himself who says to the patriarch,
    "Abraham, my friend" (Isa 41:8).

When you are in the presence of someone you consider a friend, distinctions don't matter.

Older-younger, richer-poorer, smarter-dumber, male-female, parent-child, creature-Creator, the distinctions vanish like a magician's rabbit.

You are yourself in the presence of your friend.

Elisabeth Kübler-Ross says that one of the first things people do when they are faced with a terminal illness is to bargain with God.

It's a natural thing to do, to be yourself in the presence of God who is your friend.

Our Gospel today about prayer can also be focused more clearly through the lens of friendship.

After Jesus teaches his disciples to pray,
    he tells them a parable in which "friend" is mentioned four times.

The story begins in the middle of the night.

Travelers often journeyed late in the evening to avoid the sweltering sun.
In Jesus' parable the traveler arrived at his friend's home late and was in
    need of a meal.
In the Middle East, hospitality is a sacred duty.

This put the householder between a rock and a hard place.
He had to supply a lavish meal for his friend, but he had no bread on hand.
The householder goes to his friend's house, and even though the doors are
    shut because it is the middle of the night, he knocks and knocks until
    his friend opens the door.
The story says he doesn't open up his door because of friendship but
    because of the man's persistence.
Actually, a better translation of the Greek would say that he opened up his
    door because of the man's shamelessness at knocking at this late hour.
The man within, in turn, was ashamed that his neighbors would hear this
    ruckus and accuse him of not being a good friend to the householder
    who stands begging for what ought to be freely given.

We must not make the mistake of thinking that Jesus was comparing this
    sleepy friend to God.
What Jesus was saying was:
    even if an ashamed friend eventually will listen and open up the door,
    how much more will your heavenly Father listen to you? So, be
    shameless in begging God for what you need.

There have been times in my life when people have said to me that they
    don't pray because they never have heard God answer them.
I have often been tempted to say that if they treated their friends the way
    they treat God, their friends would not say anything to them either.
In the world of friendships, we don't develop much of a relationship if we
    do all the talking.
Prayer is talking to God our friend, but mostly it is listening to God
    our friend.

And remember, when we are in the presence of a true friend,
>   we can be completely ourselves.

Friendships require that we share emotions freely,
>   yet many people attempt to hide their emotions from God.

Abraham is not afraid to bargain with God, because God is his friend.

Just as I worry about those couples who say they never argue or express
>   anger with each other,
>   I worry about those who cannot even imagine swearing at God.

Do we really love God enough to be angry with God?

We come to Eucharist as a community of friends because that's what Jesus
>   called his followers.

We come to pray for the necessary bread we need, as they say in A.A.,
>   "one day at a time."

RPW

Questions for Reflection

1. What does the First Reading tell us about God's justice? Is it like our own?

2. Do I cling to hope, even in the midst of unrest and fear?

3. When we hear "Ask and you shall receive," do we think of the Holy Spirit as the gift that will be given to us?

Other Directions for Preaching

1. The play *The Exonerated* tells the stories of six innocent women and men who were wrongly sentenced to death row. The sixth man's story is told by his wife because he has already been executed. If God spared the lives of all in Sodom and Gomorrah in order to avoid killing ten innocent people, how does God view the death penalty?

2. We must be convinced of the effectiveness of prayer. Jesus makes clear the necessity of prayer: worshiping, asking, seeking, knocking. Do we simply pay lip service to prayer or do we believe, at the core of our being, that God hears and responds to our prayers?

The Clock's Ticking
EIGHTEENTH SUNDAY IN ORDINARY TIME

READINGS:
*Ecclesiastes 1:2; 2:21–23; Colossians 3:1–5, 9–11;
Luke 12:13–21*

I have been watching the new HBO series *Six Feet Under*.
Let me caution you that it is a show that has strong language and what is
circumspectly called adult situations.
But it is the only TV series I know that portrays the impact of death.

Each week the plot deals with a death—a father, the wife of an elderly black
man, a young Hispanic gang member—and the effect that death has
on the living,
on those who loved and/or lived with that person.
The setting is the Fischer Funeral Home, run by the very dysfunctional
Fischer family:
Ruth, the newly widowed mother;
her two sons, Nate and David;
her daughter Clare;
and a periodic appearance by the deceased father, Nathaniel.

This past week a six year old found a gun under his mother's bed and
accidentally shot himself.

226

The boy's father, who had not been on the scene for two years, goes after
      his oldest son in the funeral home, blaming him for not watching
      his brother.
The older Fischer son, Nate, grabs the man and takes him into the office
      and, after letting the father voice his grief, rage, and impotence, says
      to him: "Some of us live to be a hundred; some never make it through
      the first day; but everybody dies—that is a fact of life.
      Your boy's dead; your chance to be part of his life is over.
      Did you use that time well or did you just throw it away?
      Your life is a ticking clock—everyone's is."

I think if Qoheleth, author of the First Reading, were alive today, he would
      be watching *Six Feet Under* and nodding.
Qoheleth had a sense of the ticking clock.
His name, Qoheleth (Ecclesiastes in Greek), means preacher.
And his experience of life led him to preach,
      "Vanity of vanities! All things are vanity!"
Scholars say vanity here can be translated as empty, absurd, meaningless.
The oldest meaning links the word with all that is passing, fleeting,
      transitory.
Vanity is used five times in the first sentence of eight words.
Fleeting, fleeting, fleeting—all is fleeting, is the cry of this preacher.
In other words, the clock is ticking.
Which prompts the question: How are you using your time?

In the Gospel, Jesus has been speaking to his disciples about some
      weighty matters.
He has been telling them that they are not to be afraid of those who
      kill the body,
      that they are to have courage in times of persecution.
In the midst of this a man shouts out,
      "Tell my brother to share the inheritance with me."
Jesus curtly responds: I am not here to arbitrate family quarrels.
Then he takes off from this and warns the crowd:

Don't be greedy. Life is more than possessions—even when you
have a lot!

The word for greed in Greek is *pleonexia,* the vice that always seeks
more possessions.

Plutarch wrote that *pleonexia* never rests from getting more.

"More, more, more," a voice whispers, "you can never have enough."

The story Jesus tells is about a man whose land suddenly gives him more:
"a bountiful harvest."

And what does he do with it?

We hear him talking to himself:

Look at all I have. But my barns are too small. What shall I do? I've
got it! I shall build more barns, bigger barns. I shall take all my grain
and all my good things and put them in the barns. Then I shall eat,
and I shall drink, and I shall be merry! And I shall party, party, party.

Listen to him:

I...I...I...I...I....

This man only looks to himself—to stockpiling all he has.

No word of thanks to God, who gave the bountiful harvest.

No invitation to his friends to come celebrate his good fortune.

No sharing with his workers, no inviting them to join him, no giving
them a bonus.

Nothing but *me, me, me!*

And so we hear the blazing voice of God cut in:

"You fool, this night your life will be demanded of you;
And the things you have prepared, to whom will they belong?"

Now, this might sound like the "Gotcha God," who is just waiting for
things to be great and then comes and snatches you away.

But it is more about what we allow to matter most, what we give our
hearts to.

As Jesus concludes:

"Thus will it be for all who store up treasure for themselves
but are not rich in what matters to God."

It is a shame that the reading does not continue here.

Jesus goes on to say what it means to be rich in what matters to God.

Listen to his words:

> "Therefore I tell you, do not worry about your life and what you will
> eat, or about your body and what you will wear. For life is more than
> food and the body more than clothing. Notice the ravens: they do not
> sow or reap; they have neither storehouse nor barn, yet God feeds
> them. How much more important are you than birds!...Notice how
> the flowers grow. They do not toil or spin. But I tell you, not even
> Solomon in all his splendor was dressed like one of them. If God so
> clothes the grass in the field that grows today and is thrown into the
> oven tomorrow, will he not much more provide for you, O you of
> little faith? As for you, do not seek what you are to eat and what you
> are to drink, and do not worry anymore. All the nations of the world
> seek for these things, and your Father knows that you need them.
> Instead, seek his kingdom, and these other things will be given you
> besides. Do not be afraid any longer, little flock, for your Father is
> pleased to give you the kingdom" (Luke 12:22–24, 27–32).

To be rich in what matters to God is to trust in God's providence.

The clock is ticking, so live trusting in God.

> Seek the kingdom and what you need will be given.

How are we using our time?

Are we growing rich in what matters to God?

The question is posed to us as individuals, but also as a nation.

What do we do with the harvests that come our way?

Do we store up more and more and more?

How do we use the miracles of modern technology,

> the breakthroughs in medical research?

The parable has been called "The Man who Mismanaged a Miracle."

So much was given, but he only talked and listened to himself.

He only looked to his own good.

I remember an August cover from the *New Yorker* a few summers ago.

It was a beach scene: four adult figures towering over a little child standing
on the sand.

All the adults have cell phones in their hands; all look intense, anxious,
even angry.

Three of the adults are in motion, pacing; the fourth is seated at a laptop.

The child, however, has a smile on her face;

she has a conch shell to her ear, listening to the sound of the ocean.

The artist, Carter Goodrich, named the drawing "Higher Calling."

The Letter to the Colossians calls us to think of what is above:

"If you were raised with Christ, seek what is above,

where Christ is seated at the right hand of God.

Think of what is above, not of what is on earth.

For you have died, and your life is hidden with Christ in God.

When Christ your life appears, then you too will appear with
him in glory."

With these words we hear the invitation to focus on Christ, who is
with God.

Baptism plunges us into the saving paschal mystery, into his dying
and rising.

In the meantime, the mean time, the time in between, there is an agenda.

Use your time to "put to death...immorality, impurity, passion, evil desire,
and that greed that is idolatry."

Use your time to "put on the new self, which is being renewed...in the
image of its creator."

In the meantime, use your time to live in a way that treats all equally—
not discriminating, not causing division, but living in a way that
proclaims Christ is truly all and in all.

The author Qoheleth was not just one note of gloom.

In other places of his book he calls on people to eat, drink, and be merry.

And that is what we do here.

We eat, we drink, and we are merry, rejoicing in all God has given.
For we can find security not in what we own but in the God who loves us
    and calls us to share our riches with others.
In doing that, we will truly have our fill and be God's merry people.

JAW

Questions for Reflection

1. Are you sensitive to the clock ticking? How are you using your time?

2. What do you count as your treasures?

3. What does it mean to seek what is above? How does this relate to how we are living now?

Other Directions for Preaching

1. Ecclesiastes also invites us to consider our theology of work and what work means in our lives. Why do we work? Does our desire to be productive control our lives?

2. Living in the paschal mystery takes on a practical face in the reading from Colossians, which speaks of putting on the new self "which is being renewed, for knowledge, in the image of its creator." At the heart of this process is living in Christ, who "is all and in all."

3. The image of the man storing his grain confronts us with how we respond to the needs of the hungry and needy in our world. The basic needs that so many in the world are lacking demand a stronger response from us as a nation in danger of being "not rich in what matters to God."

Watchwords
NINETEENTH SUNDAY IN ORDINARY TIME

READINGS:
Wisdom 18:6–9; Hebrews 11:1–2, 8–19; Luke 12:32–48

Luke's Jesus intends for us to go about our daily business of loving and
    working, even as we keep an eagle-eyed watch for his coming.
It is easy to forget that each of the Gospels was written at a particular time
    and place.
Luke's Gospel was composed well after the days of the historical Jesus, after
    a generation of eyewitnesses had died.
So these early Gentile Christian disciples faced the inevitable: the crisis of
    waiting and longing for the coming of the Lord.
And so the Lukan community keeps vigil, lighting the candle of faith with
    the burning fire of charity and a practical Gospel as its guide, loaded
    with domestic images of prudent servants and wise stewards:
    "Do not be afraid any longer, little flock," Jesus tells his hearers, "for
    your Father is pleased to give you the kingdom. Sell your belongings
    and give alms. Provide money bags for yourselves that do not wear
    out, an inexhaustible treasure in heaven that no thief can reach nor
    moth destroy" (Luke 12:32–33).

Jesus' advice could have been written for us today.
We surely share with the Lukan community a certain despair of heartfelt
    waiting for the Lord to return, where we imagine, in our despair, that

the course of centuries has worn away the edges of the Gospel,
 the way the pounding of waves erodes the shoreline.
The nineteenth-century poet Algernon Charles Swinburne spoke for an age
 of hopelessness when he wrote his popular poem "Hymn to
 Proserpine": "Thou hast conquered, O pale Galilean; the world has
 grown grey from thy breath; We have drunken of things Lethean, and
 fed on the fullness of death."*
And Swinburne's inheritors in the twenty-first century have themselves grown
 quite white and ashen: dead to faith; dead to hope; dead to charity.
A veritable culture of death, a well-known phrase often used by Pope John
 Paul II.

Yet to every last one of us—from those in darkness,
 seeking an answer to those who still keep their candles burning—
 the Lord provides a saving word.
That saving word comes from the Word himself: sacred memory.
The key to keeping faith and waiting for the coming of the Lord is
 remembering the wonders God has done until he comes again in
 Christ Jesus.
Remembering the Lord has been part of the Judeo-Christian tradition from
 the beginning.
It is witnessed by the Wisdom tradition in Israel.
The First Reading, taken from the book of Wisdom, is a meditation on
 God's wondrous actions of deliverance from Egypt:
 "Your people awaited the salvation of the just and the destruction of
 their foes" (Wis 18:7).
It is the faith community that makes sense of the Exodus event, the
 movement of deliverance from darkness into light.
Waiting for the salvation of the just becomes clearer under the moon glow
 of the light of faith.

---

*Algernon Charles Swinburne, "Hymn to Proserpine," in *The Norton Anthology of English Literature*, 5th ed., ed. M. H. Abrams et al. (New York: W. W. Norton, 1986), 2:1546.

Faith needs time to ponder the workings of God.

Faith must have space to breathe in the mystery of the Holy.

Faith has to recollect itself long after the goodness of the Lord has unfolded
in our midst.

And so the Letter to the Hebrews gravitates toward a kind of reinvigorated
wisdom tradition when it says:

"Faith is the realization of what is hoped for and evidence of things
not seen"(11:1).

Only in the passing of years and the day-to-day remembrance of the
goodness of God did it become apparent that the entire nation of
Israel was built on God's promise.

Abraham, Isaac, and Jacob—all of them heir to one enormous,
divine promise,
the first stewards of the work God has given to all humankind.

As a church we are in a long line of stewards, caretakers of God's house,
waiting for the Master to return.

The degree to which our stewardship will be successful is based on our faith
in a promise,
the covenant made by Jesus to come again.

Clearly, Jesus imagines a variety of responses to God's promise.

There is the prudent servant who keeps vigil, trusting,
the way Abraham kept faith,
surrendering to the unknown power of God.

There is the defiant servant who, as it were, rewrites God's will.

He has decided that the Master has been delayed.

This servant believes in no promise except his own, and Jesus reckons him
as one of the unfaithful.

Then, there is the ignorant servant who never really takes the time to
remember God's promise.

The faithful, the unfaithful, the ignorant—there you have a pretty broad
range of human personalities.

More to the point, it may be that we glide in and out of these behaviors
    several times in the course of a lifetime.
Perhaps the reason we sit in so much darkness in our century, that people
    face so much anxiety and depression, is that we are really not much
    good at trusting the promises of others.
We tend to think of the root of infidelity in marriage, for example, as an
    inability to keep our vows, but maybe some of that infidelity emerges
    from not trusting our spouse in the first place.
Maybe the difficulty with faith is finding the courage to believe that God
    will keep God's covenant to the very end.
We need to trust the One who made the promise as well as the
    promise itself.

As a faith community, as a contemporary wisdom community, we assemble
    here to confirm the wonderful works God has done in Christ.
The Eucharist was sealed with the Blood of the Lamb.
Here is the manna given to us by the hands of the Savior himself,
    divine food for the journey.
That is our promise until he comes again.
We have come here to acknowledge that God continues to do wonderful
    works, to bring us out of our Egypt.
It is a sojourn we do not make alone.
We walk with the community of love,
    with a pillar of faith to guide us.
Until he comes again.
We wait.
We watch.

GD

Questions for Reflection

1. Do I think of myself as a trusting person when it comes to my relationship with God? with others? If not, why?

2. How do I live out a covenant of fidelity from day to day? Does this promise inform the rest of my life and my behavior?

3. Do I encourage a lifestyle of simplicity? Could I do better? In what way?

Other Directions for Preaching

1. Faith is a journey that Abraham took because of God's initiative, and so all of us make that same passage supported by grace.

2. The day will come when our faith will be put to the test. There are a cloud of witnesses in Scripture and tradition to show us how to stand firm until the Day of the Lord.

3. Our culture and our human nature encourage us to collect many things, but these will only weigh us down on our route to meet the Master.

A Faith on Fire
TWENTIETH SUNDAY IN
ORDINARY TIME

READINGS:
Jeremiah 38:4–6, 8–10; Hebrews 12:1–4;
Luke 12:49–53

When I prayed over today's Scripture readings, I remembered a young
  Paulist seminarian I had in my preaching class a few years ago.
He was so earnest and determined to follow in the footsteps of Paulist
  founder Fr. Isaac Hecker, who brought the old Gospel alive to a new
  American church.
The young seminarian came to me with both fire and anxiety in his eyes
  and pleaded: "I need your help. How can I preach this Gospel? It is so
  hard for me to hear."
In my best pastoral voice I replied: "Get used to it; they're all hard to
  preach."

I wonder where this young man is this morning and what he is preaching.
For, as we just heard, nothing harder is ever proclaimed from the pulpit
  than today's Gospel.
One commentator put it this way:
  "If one were to list ten of the hardest sayings in the Gospels, the first
  portion of today's selection would undoubtedly be on the list. The
  statements that Jesus came to bring fire, a distressful baptism, and
  division, even among families, are hardly welcome words for any

congregation. We are happier with Jesus as a peacemaker than as a
home breaker."*

Usually a Sunday Gospel ends with a felicitous or hopeful flourish.

But today it just ends abruptly with a word that makes many folks squirm:
the word is *mother-in-law.*

One of the major points a preacher strives to make is that a Gospel on any
particular Sunday relates to us today.

But how in the world can we possibly relate what Jesus is saying to our
own times?

The situation described here is so different from our own.

Like his ancestor Jeremiah, Jesus was ripping apart the very fabric of
religious, social, and family life.

When you accepted Jesus, you had to accept the cost of alienation,
persecution, death itself.

There are still places in our world where this Gospel rings true and could
easily be applied by any preacher.

This very morning Christians in the Sudan, Indonesia, China, Saudi Arabia,
and Myanmar are literally dying for their faith in Jesus as the Lord of
their lives.

We must not only remember these tortured disciples in our Prayer of the
Faithful today but cry out to our governing officials to come to their
assistance.

But for most of us assembled today, following Jesus does not alienate us
from anyone.

As Americans, we've learned to become polite and tolerant and inclusive in
matters of religion.

This summer I attended a wedding ceremony where the presider told the
congregation prior to communion,

---

*Charles B. Cousar, Beverly R. Gaventa, J. Clinton McCann, and James D.
Newsome, *Texts for Preaching: A Lectionary Commentary Based on the NRSV—Year
C* (Louisville, KY: Westminster/John Knox Press, 1994), 476.

"You are all welcome to receive because here in this church
   it does not matter what you believe."
Can you imagine?
It *does* matter what we believe, and that is why we recite the Creed together
   at the Eucharist.
In the same congregation, a minister of the cup,
      not wanting to offend anyone,
      could not bring himself to say,
   "The Blood of Christ," and so he said, "The blood of life."

There is a sense in which our American political correctness is forcing us to
   water down Jesus Christ in our lives.
A few months ago, when I was in chemotherapy at Georgetown University
   Hospital, a eucharistic minister came to my room, gave me the
   consecrated host, and said,
   "Well, good luck!"
I called that minister back to my bed to remind him that it was the doctors'
   job to bring me luck but it was *his* job to bring me Christ!

In our sincere desire to be inclusive, not to offend or embarrass anyone, to
   say, "Everything you believe is OK with me,"
   have we not lost what it means to be followers of Jesus? Certainly
   Jesus brought to this world a profound sense of inclusiveness:
He taught us to accept the Samaritan, the divorced woman at the well, the
   leper, the so-called other, into our lives and our hearts.
But today's Gospel is a reminder that inclusiveness does not mean
   abandonment of our fundamental beliefs or of our loyalty as disciples
   of Jesus.
In the same solid tradition of Jeremiah slushing in the mud in the bottom of
   the cistern Jesus reminds us that following him will cost us something.

The word *religion* literally refers to that which binds us together.
There is a sense that exclusiveness is a hallmark of every religion:
      Orthodox Jews don't want to be forced to give up their dietary laws;

Quakers don't want to be forced to serve in the military; Fundamentalist Christians don't want evolution to be taught to their children.

Adhering to a belief system is what religion is all about.

And what about us Catholic Christians?

Why are so many of us afraid to bless ourselves and pray grace in public, whether at Wendy's or Morton's? Why were some Catholics working at CNN intimidated last Ash Wednesday when mogul Ted Turner laughed at the sign of ashes on their forehead and called them religious fanatics?

When the person at the checkout counter greets us with "happy holidays," why are we afraid to respond, "Merry Christmas to you"?

And why do we think that Jesus came to bring us a false peace where nobody is offended, no one is called to task, no one is told: "That is not what Christians believe or how Christians ought to act"?

And, for heaven's sake, why do we think we have come to hear an easy Gospel, be lulled into a false security, belong to a religion that costs us nothing?

The Gospel today calls all of us to a faith that is not cheap, not wimpy, not politically correct.

Which is why only fire can describe it so well!

RPW

Questions for Reflection

1. Am I willing to take the risk of being prophetic in my preaching, or would I rather be popular?

2. In times of struggle what spiritual practices might we use to avoid despondency?

3. When is division essential to the Christian life?

Other Directions for Preaching

1. Jesus clearly knew that there are times when the Gospel of challenge and discord needs to be preached. There are sinful practices that have become so common in our society (adultery, cheating on school exams, acceptance of pornography) that they are rarely addressed. Today's Gospel invites the preacher to consider thoughtfully how to speak the word of challenge in some of these areas.

2. Paul uses the image of sin as an encumbrance in the race toward Jesus. We can develop this image by picturing Lance Armstrong competing in the Tour de France with a flat tire on his bicycle. Or a wide receiver racing toward the end zone with all kinds of weights hanging on him.

On Saying Goodbye
Twenty-First Sunday in Ordinary Time

Readings:
Isaiah 66:18–21; Hebrews 12:5–7, 11–13;
Luke 13:22–30

Of all the words we have to utter in our lives,

　　perhaps the most difficult one to say is *goodbye.*

We avoid it whenever we can because there's something about us that

　　doesn't like finality, that wants to go on forever.

In a few weeks some of you mothers will walk your child to the school bus

　　for the first time and bravely wave and say goodbye.

Somewhere at this very moment a father is on the phone with a son who

　　has disappointed him.

Harsh words are exchanged.

Then there is silence.

Then the father will say, "Well, goodbye."

And all over the world at this moment in airports, bus stations, train

　　stations, lovers kiss and say the words that break their hearts,

　　"Well, this is it. Goodbye."

The Jesus we meet in our Gospel today is a man who is about to say

　　goodbye to his friends and followers.

He is still at work teaching, but Luke tells us that he is making his way
toward Jerusalem, the place of his destiny, the place of his crucifixion
and death.

Everything he says and does as he makes his way through the cities and
towns can only be understood if we realize that he is a man about to
say goodbye.

And so when some smug person taps him on the shoulder and says,
"Excuse me, but can you tell me if only a few will be saved?"

Jesus gives a jarring answer because he is a man about to say goodbye.

Jesus knows that soon he will enter his destiny through the
narrow door of death.

It is from his own perspective of dying that Jesus tells the person:
Listen, you are asking the wrong question.
You are trying to convince yourself that just because you say your
prayers, pay your taxes, and belong to the "right" religion, you'll be
saved, but the rest of the world will be damned.
You see that gate over there leading into this village?
It's a narrow gate, not *wide* open, but open.
You and anybody else, even those not in your religion, not of your
color, not of your country, not of your morality,
can enter through it.
You'll be surprised who is going to enter the kingdom through the
narrow door.
And you'll be surprised who is not going to enter the kingdom
through the narrow door, because they carry too much smug baggage
with them.
I can tell you all this because I'm on my way to Jerusalem.
There's no time for small talk because I'm getting ready to say
goodbye.

I have been so blessed these past years
    serving at this parish on weekends.
Your faith, your vibrant sense of community,
    your challenges and supports have strengthened my own faith
    and commitment to God's church and God's world.
It's not easy to say goodbye to you.
I do so in the spirit of the Gospel today,
    in the spirit of Jesus, who had no time for small talk.

It seems to me that we are living in a time when many are so convinced that
    theirs is the only door to go through.
Listen to any radio or TV talk show.
Most of them are "one door" talk shows.
Some pro-choice and some pro-life people speak as if they alone have God's
    ear; they speak in war-like mantras.
New brands of racism and sexism are also emerging in our time.
They, too, seek to divide the church and the world between two camps,
    the saved and the damned.

But Jesus tells us as he heads toward Jerusalem that life is not that simple,
    that black and white.
I recall once reading about a physicist who said,
    "The opposite of a truth is a lie;
    the opposite of a profound truth is another profound truth."
We must not divide our church and our world so glibly and so smugly.

All three Scripture readings today remind us that God's ways transcend our
    feeble imaginations.
God is greater than the little images we have of the Divine.
The door is narrow.
A lot of life is struggle and part of life is learning how to say goodbye.
But the door is open to everyone.

"It was a long while ago that the words *God be with you* disappeared into the word *goodbye*, but every now and again some trace of them still glimmers through."*

RPW

Questions for Reflection

1. In her short story *The Displaced Person*, Flannery O'Connor seems to suggest that we are all displaced people. What are the gifts that the fugitives or displaced people can bring to one another and to the community?

2. Does a rigid set of rubrics and teachings offer a false sense of security, seeming to guarantee to those who adhere to them a place in the reign of God?

3. Do some of the world religions preach exclusive access to the reign of God out of fear that the narrow gate is not large enough to accommodate both them and "others"?

Other Directions for Preaching

1. When put together, the images offered by the First Reading and the Gospel seem a recipe for disaster. Isaiah tells us that people from every direction will be pouring into Jerusalem to worship the Lord. Jesus then tells of the narrow gate through which everyone will be trying to pass in order to find safety in the kingdom of God. Clearly, God's way of sorting this out is very different from our own. Those who find safety in the reign of God may not be "the usual suspects." God's view is much more inclusive than our own.

2. The gift of salvation is just that—a gift from God. It is not earned. Therefore, when we think about who is saved, today's Gospel becomes more understandable. We sometimes forget that God is far beyond our conceptions and interpretations. God can offer this gift to anyone of any faith tradition— or of no faith tradition.

---

* Frederick Buechner, *Whistling in the Dark: An ABC Theologized* (San Francisco: Harper & Row, 1988), 55–56.

What God Means by Humility
TWENTY-SECOND SUNDAY IN ORDINARY TIME

READINGS:
Sirach 3:17–18, 20, 28–29; Hebrews 12:18–19, 22–24a;
Luke 14:1, 7–14

There was a good reason why they observed Jesus closely
    when he went to dinner.
He already had gained a reputation for ignoring the dinner rules of
    "Miss Manners."
There had been those two previous meals where he had shocked the guests.
There was that meal where he allowed a sinner to perfume his feet.
There was also the meal where he began eating without the ritual washing
    of his hands.

And now there was this meal at a leading Pharisee's house,
    which was not just an ordinary meal but a Sabbath dinner.
They wondered what new act of bad manners the rabbi from Nazareth
    would commit at this sacred meal.
That's why "they observed him closely."

But the irony of today's Gospel is that Jesus was observing *them* closely.
He noticed how these sophisticated religious people were acting like
    children, trying to grab the best seats at dinner so they could feel high
    and mighty.

As usual, Jesus tips the tables.

He always reverses the order we think should be in place.

He tells them to sit at the lowest places so that they will be invited by the
host to come up higher.

We must not make the mistake of thinking that Jesus is offering some sort
of Dale Carnegie course on how to win friends and influence people
by putting on a mask of humility.

Throughout the history of Christianity there have been many people who
have put on that mask.

There's a great story about a pastor who, in a fit of passion, rushed in
before the altar and started beating his breast, saying,
"Lord, I'm nobody. I'm nobody!"

When his assistant saw this, he was so impressed by the pastor's example of
spiritual humility that he too joined the pastor on his knees, crying
out, "Lord, I'm nobody. I'm nobody!"

The church janitor was watching this scene of submissiveness, and so he too
joined the other two on his knees, crying out,
"Lord, I'm nobody. I'm nobody!"

Just at that point, the pastor nudged his assistant with his elbow, pointed to
the janitor, and said,
"Just look at who thinks he's nobody!"

In other words, for the pastor it was just an act, a mask of humility.

In today's Gospel, Jesus is not offering a course in dinner etiquette or telling
us just to act humble.

What he is really telling the Pharisees and us is,
"Remember where you stand and in whose presence."

Even though the Pharisees observed him closely, they failed to recognize that
they were standing in the presence of not just the host of a dinner
party but the host of the heavenly party, Jesus himself.

One summer in the early 1970s, I lived in Princeton, New Jersey, where I
was writing my doctoral dissertation.

I celebrated daily Mass for the Religious of the Sacred Heart at Stuart
    Country Day School.
That particular order was always known for its sophistication.
Some even called the sisters the Jesuits of women religious.
Because of its prestigious location, the rich and famous would join us at
    Sunday Mass.

I remember one day when such people as Svetlana Alliluyeva (the daughter
    of Joseph Stalin) and Mrs. Johnson (of Johnson and Johnson), one of
    the richest women in the United States, celebrated liturgy with us.
During the Prayer of the Faithful, Mrs. Johnson prayed for her dear and
    close friend who was then grieving the death of her husband.
And so Mrs. Johnson prayed,
    "For my dear friend, the Duchess of Windsor, let us pray to the Lord."
She didn't do it to impress anyone; it was a humble prayer of her heart.
But I couldn't help thinking as I stood there,
    "What am I doing here among these elite?"
After all, I am the son of a poor coal miner from Pennsylvania.
The closest my parents ever got to Mrs. Johnson was a box of Band-Aids.

But then during the Communion Rite,
    it dawned on me that at this meal of the Lord, we are all the same.
Poor, middle class, the rich and famous, the religious and not religious:
    no one is greater than the others.
That is why it's so foolish to beat our breasts and say, "I'm nobody."
That is why it's so silly to push everybody aside because we think we are
    better than the rest.
In the presence of the Host of this eucharistic meal, the Lord tells each one
    of us, "Remember where you stand and in whose presence."

And because the Eucharist is supposed to spill out into the rest of our lives,
    during all the meals we will share this week,
    at home, at work, at the school cafeteria,
    at McDonald's, or if you're lucky, at a fancy restaurant,

"Remember where you stand and in whose presence."
Then we can take off our masks
    and know what God means by humility.

RPW

Questions for Reflection

1. A contemporary economist has said that, in this country, we are afraid of the very poor. Do you think that this is true? How does today's psalm respond to this?

2. A well-known writer on spirituality has suggested that our addictions provide a space inside us where God can work. Is acknowledging our addictions an act of humility?

3. Recognizing God as the complete and ultimate model of generosity, what do today's readings teach us?

Other Directions for Preaching

1. Jesus calls us to go beyond reciprocity in our giving. What about our debt to the poor? Is it more comfortable to send checks (though this is important) than to have actual contact with people who are without a home, in need of a meal, or unable to do something for us in return? If so, why?

2. Humility is honesty about ourselves. It enables us to have a clear-eyed view of ourselves and others. It is especially essential that we have this honest perspective about ourselves in God's order of things. By recognizing our neediness, we can be open to God's overwhelming generosity.

True Discipleship
TWENTY-THIRD SUNDAY IN ORDINARY TIME

READINGS:
*Wisdom 9:13–18b; Philemon 9–10, 12–17;
Luke 14:25–33*

Some time ago, *US News and World Report* carried a special issue
    on heroes.
These men and women appear as bright suns in the human constellation.
There is Marion Pritchard, a timid Dutch woman who concealed a Jewish
    family in her home for three years.
There is Allan Tibbels, a disabled co-director of Habitat for Humanity,
    who works tirelessly to rebuild the inner city.
And there is Dana Christmas, who almost died four years ago while trying
    to revive the sleeping students in her college dormitory at midnight
    from a blazing fire that someone intentionally set.
Along with these, we might add the numerous self-sacrificing people we
    have known over the years who have followed their conscience even in
    the face of life's terrifying consequences.

After we get over the details about how these folks managed to face such
    obstacles, we face a more baffling question: *Why* did they do it?
Preferring altruism instead of a Darwinian version of the survival of the
    fittest, the highest good instead of knowable, scientific consequences,
    these folks become for some a perplexing scramble of motivations.

Giving away ourselves seems so unnatural.

And it is.

But unnatural, supernatural self-sacrifice is at the core of Jesus' challenge to
   discipleship in today's Gospel.

Christ himself is obviously the blueprint here, the one who was obedient
   unto death,
      surrendering everything to the will of God.

Jesus becomes the unique, single-minded, faithful witness—a divine Son—to
   a loving, faithful God.

Heroism has tunnel vision.

No wonder that our Lord's exhortation on discipleship sounds so severe:
      "If anyone comes to me without hating his father and mother,
      wife and children, brothers and sisters, and even his own life,
      he cannot be my disciple."

Let's admit it, my friends, this is unnatural, rough language from the Savior
   who commanded us to love our enemies.

Yet that is what it takes to serve completely and utterly this Christ our
   Lord.

In the context of Luke's Gospel, Jesus is setting forth the conditions of
   honest-to-God, real discipleship without games.

It is what we risk if we take the kingdom of God seriously.

We might indeed be ostracized by family and friends because the choice that
   the disciple has to make may be between natural, good, perfectly
   normal inclinations, and singular attention to the person of Jesus.

Christian discipleship sometimes involves chipping away at what is most
   dear to us in order to unearth our true allegiance.

Tough language, yet there is no getting around it, lest we settle for what
   Dietrich Bonhoeffer would call "cheap grace."

As Saint Benedict has reminded us in his usual sober manner:
   the way to God is often harsh and bitter.

Obedience is the yoke that any mature person must put on.

Sometimes that obedience calls us to do something dramatically heroic,
and at other times we are just called to live inside a difficult moment.
It is easy for us to romanticize sublime altruism into an act of heroism
alone, especially in this country where the myth of individualism is
so powerful.
Yet we know that our Lord did not become obedient unto death for himself
but to free us from our sins and so that the church might be born.
Jesus delivered us into a world of sanctification as we died with
him in baptism.
And the church continues to teach, to preach, and to sanctify in
Christ's name.

Contemporary culture has forced the Catholic Christian community to think
more globally and collectively about discipleship.
We owe a lot of this universal Christian witness to Pope John Paul II,
who managed to bring the church into dialogue
with other religions and nations worldwide.
As disciples of peace we must proclaim gospel peace tirelessly,
despite national interests.
I wonder how many of us would falter if we had to choose between God
and country.
Are we capable of leaving our mother country behind and following the
poor Christ?
The days in which society nurtured religious and ethical behavior are
finished.
We might as well face that reality squarely and realize that our call is to
reevangelize with the Gospel of Christ.
Christians today find themselves gathering around justice issues that will
help to define them collectively as radical believers.
I am thinking here of our national apathy toward Africa and ethnic
cleansing.
I am thinking about American aggression in the fragile Middle East.
I am thinking about not blinking twice about using human embryo stem
cells for the purpose of research.

I am thinking about electrocuting people for revenge.

And I am thinking about terminating a pregnancy that is just too inconvenient.

Rational, pragmatic America has been our mother, our brother, and our sister for years; it has nurtured us so we are like well-fed children.

But the time has come to leave the sweet home of nation and rationalism to its own devices, if we would be disciples of Christ Jesus.

During the Vietnam war there was a popular bumper sticker that proudly proclaimed: "My country right or wrong."

Patriotism, like talk, comes cheap on the back of a sedan in the suburbs.

And if politics would solve our problems, then Jesus would have become governor of Judea instead of being crucified by the state.

Like sacrificial love, our discipleship costs our very lives.

Our lives and nobody else's.

Christian witness calls us to ratify the presence of God, the Giver of life, in all things, and Jesus, who redeemed all creation by the power of divine life that is still lurking, working within us.

That acknowledgment will occasionally fly in the face of all reason, even our natural proclivities and loyalties to our mother country.

As the book of Wisdom says,

"What is within our grasp we find with difficulty" (9:16).

We need to adopt the kind of compassionate unity that is shaped by unique disciples willing to surrender what they hold most precious for the highest good: Christ above all.

And, if we asked Marion Pritchard, Allan Tibbels, and Dana Christmas, they would tell us that it was single-mindedness that got them where they are today.

Perhaps a community of Christian disciples can discover such collective zeal as well, even as we put on the mind of Christ and seek God in mystery and in truth.

GD

Questions for Reflection

1. What is the most difficult thing Jesus would ask me to do? Could I do it? If not, why?

2. How do I make ethical decisions? Do I count my discipleship as part of the process of making up my mind regarding moral issues?

3. Suppose a family member would not speak to me because of my beliefs. What would I do?

Other Directions for Preaching

1. It is said that blood is thicker than water. Jesus has bound the church together with his own life-giving sacrifice on the cross. We are all related.

2. Paul proposes reconciliation based on class differences. Shattering social stereotypes is part of living the Gospel and telling the Good News.

3. The book of Wisdom keeps us honest. We will never know God's will or the magnitude or mystery of divine Love; we can only pray and discern in the context of our relationship with the Trinity.

No "Idol-ing," Please
TWENTY-FOURTH SUNDAY IN ORDINARY TIME

READINGS:
Exodus 32:7–11, 13–14; 1 Timothy 1:12–17;
Luke 15:1–32

We get two contrasting images of God today.
The God presented in the reading from Exodus is in a state of fury,
     ready to destroy the people Moses just led out of Egypt.
The people are barely out of Egypt and they are already breaking the first
     two commandments,
     having other gods and making images of them.
     God knows they have made a molten calf and are worshiping it and
     sacrificing to it,
     identifying it as the God who brought them out of Egypt.
"Let me alone, then, that my wrath may blaze up against them to consume
     them," the Lord says to Moses.
Moses has to bring up God's promises before God relents and turns away
     from anger.

Then we have the God behind the three parables Jesus tells.
I say "behind the three parables" because Jesus tells the three parables as an
     answer to the complaint that he welcomes and eats with sinners,
     something no law-abiding Jew would do because it would render
     him unclean.

Jesus tells these stories as a way of explaining his understanding of
  his mission.
But, in understanding his mission, we also understand the God whose Spirit
  has anointed Jesus to carry out this mission.
The images of the shepherd, the woman, and the father speak to us not only
  of Jesus but of the Father who sent Jesus.

But doesn't that leave us with two contrasting images of God?
I found myself wondering why these readings were put together.
Usually the First Reading is chosen because it mirrors the Gospel in
  some way.
That's when Kathleen Norris helped me.
In her book *Amazing Grace* she has a short chapter on idolatry.
She writes succinctly, "Idolatry makes love impossible."*

When the Israelites made that golden calf, they tried to freeze God into
  an image.
And God rejected that—violently.
God was not about to be set into a mold, hardened into the form of a calf.
The first commandment was first for a reason:

> "I, the LORD, am your God, who brought you out of the land of Egypt,
> that place of slavery. You shall not have other gods besides me. You
> shall not carve idols for yourselves in the shape of anything in the sky
> above or on the earth below or in the waters beneath the earth; you
> shall not bow down before them or worship them. For I, the LORD, your
> God, am a jealous God, inflicting punishment for their fathers'
> wickedness on the children of those who hate me" (Exod 20:2–5).

In one respect it might seem safer to worship an idol,
  safer than to love a real person who is not predictable, who can
  surprise you,

---

*Kathleen Norris, *Amazing Grace, A Vocabulary of Faith* (New York: Riverhead,
1998), 88.

who often acts in unexpected ways,
who not only loves you and demands love in return,
but who can change, or, at least, change from our expectations.
But God won't stand for it.
Idolatry makes love impossible because it reduces the other to something
lifeless.
And God is a living God.

Jesus tells three stories today in an effort to crack the idolatry of the scribes
and Pharisees.
"Why are you eating with tax collectors and sinners?" they asked.
For them, this was against the Law and thus against the will of God.
God was a God of strict rules:
rules about what you did on the Sabbath,
rules and regulations to keep you pure for performing the
required rituals,
and these included with whom you sat down to eat.

Eating with tax collectors and sinners was not part of the profile of a
religious person.
Now, these were not ignorant people—the scribes were the theologians of
the community, and the Pharisees were laity who took their faith
very seriously,
going beyond the written words of the Law to honoring the cherished
traditions.
Still, a certain self-righteousness had crept in.
"Why is he eating with *these* people?" you can hear behind the words.

And so Jesus answered them by telling three stories about loss,
tales of three losers who were not content with loss:
a shepherd, a woman, a father.
Jesus offered them as images of himself and of his ministry;
he was also offering them as images of the One who had sent him.
These are images of the Father.

The shepherd who had lost a sheep was a questionable figure in one respect, since shepherds were considered unclean by the Law.

But since the prophet Ezekiel spoke of God as a good shepherd, this would have a certain legitimacy, although it raised the issue of whether Jesus was equating himself with God.

This shepherd, however, would be seen as foolish for going out in search of only one sheep and leaving the ninety-nine to be preyed upon.

But this points to a God passionately in love with the people, each and every one of us.

The woman is also an interesting choice as a God image.

A coin was worth a day's wages, so she lit a lamp to search for it.

The windows were high up, making it difficult to find something that had probably rolled into a crevice or some dark spot.

She finds it.

So happy is she at finding what was lost that she throws a party.

Again, somewhat foolish, since it would probably go beyond the worth of the coin.

These first two stories are quite similar.

Something is lost, and someone goes in search.

When what's lost is found, there is a party, with friends invited in to rejoice.

Rejoicing is the only appropriate response to recovery of what is lost.

The third presents a father who has lost two sons.

The younger has demanded his share of the inheritance— a great insult to his father, the equivalent of wishing his father were dead—and has gone off to squander it.

The other has stayed at home with the father but is equally far off, as we discover.

The father's response to both sons is similar, though also different.

He waits for the younger one to "come to his senses," leaving him free to live with his choice.

Once he sees this son coming down the road, however, he runs to meet him.

What is significant here is that in the Middle East culture for an old man to run was seen as a loss of dignity.

He would have to lift up his garment and his underwear would show; he would become a figure of foolishness, like the shepherd and the woman.

But such is this father's love, such is God's love revealed in Jesus.

And, again, a party follows.

And this is where we see how far away his older son has grown.

He refuses to go into the house but stays outside sulking because he feels slighted.

He should be standing by his father's side welcoming those coming to celebrate.

This is a great insult to his father, deserving of a father's anger.

But here the father makes the first move, going out to his older son.

He answers his son's grievance with a generous "Everything I have is yours," and asks him to enter into his father's joy.

Jesus tells these three stories to explain why he eats with sinners.

We can see the three parables as a catalog of how people get lost from God.

We wander off like sheep and can't find the way back, or find ourselves at some point "in the dark" and wait for rescue, for someone to come along and lead us into the light.

Or there are those times when we deliberately get lost.

We go out in search of adventure and end up in a foreign place, or our hearts leave home, even when we stay in place.

But we are not made to stay lost.

There is One who seeks us, who sent his own Son to search us out.

This seeker has been called the "Hound of Heaven" by the poet Francis Thompson, relentlessly tracking us down.

But the final note of our being found is the same: rejoicing, a party, a house filled with song and laughter.

So, while we may be endlessly inventive in our idol making,
> dedicated to setting things, people, friends, spouses, celebrities, sports heroes, presidents—and even God—up on pedestals,
> casting them into a mold, hardened by our expectations,
> God will not stand for this.

God slips away from us.

But once we realize our loss, God will be there, the first to respond to our move, ready to party, reminding us that calves are for eating, not adoration.

JAW

Questions for Reflection

1. What or who are some of your idols?
2. Is God living, or have you cast God into an idol of some kind?
3. Have you experienced God seeking you out?

Other Directions for Preaching

1. Moses is presented as a mediator who reminds God of God's promises. In the Eucharist we gather to call on God to remember the promises made in Christ.

2. Paul witnesses to the mercy of God given through Christ, which is evident in the vocation God has given him. Consider how our various vocations signal the mercy of God.

3. Repentance leads to rejoicing. The elder's son inability to enter into joy is rooted in his failure to experience his own need for repentance.

WWJS?
TWENTY-FIFTH SUNDAY IN ORDINARY TIME

READINGS:
Amos 8:4–7; 1 Timothy 2:1–8; Luke 16:1–13

This is one difficult parable to preach on.
Why would Jesus hold up a crook for admiration?
More ink has been spilled over this parable than
      any other one Jesus told.
You've seen those buttons, WWJD (What Would Jesus Do?);
      well, this parable deserves its own button, only it would be WWJS
      (What Was Jesus Saying?).

To get Jesus off the hook, some say the steward/manager really isn't a
      crook, that, according to the business practice of the time, people
      would borrow money and return the payment in goods.
And it was common to add on to the debt to be repaid not only a
      commission for the manager but an additional tax for the master.
So when the manager told the debtors to take out their pens and
      change the amount owed, he was either letting them take off his
      commission, or he was knocking off the tax of the master, a
      tax that was itself against the Torah, specifically the book of Leviticus,
      which forbids a Jew to make money
      off a fellow Jew.
Are you following all this?

261

Whatever...it is hard to get around the fact that at the very end the text says very specifically: "The Master commended that *dishonest* steward for acting prudently."

The work of the steward was to increase the holdings of the master, but this steward reduced them for his *own* benefit.

So what does it all mean?

Well, even Luke was not sure.

He takes four runs at it, with all those sayings at the end.

And most scholars say that none of them really fits the parable, although they do have something to say in a general way about being a trustworthy servant and attaining *true* wealth.

But let's go back to the parable.

At the end the master commends the dishonest servant, but he does not commend him for his dishonesty.

He commends him for being shrewd, astute, prudent.

The word used comes from a word that means the steward has "practical wisdom."

And Jesus (or Luke) is clearly saying that the children of this world have more practical wisdom than the children of the light.

How so?

We can focus either on the steward or the master.

First, consider the manager's shrewd estimation of the master.

He realized that what he was doing would win the master honor from the debtors.

They would assume the manager was doing what the master had told him to do.

By changing the amount they owed, the debtors would have started to party the minute they left the manager's house.

And word would go forth what a generous and noble master this was.

So, if the master were to come out and say, "No, big mistake! You still owe
    me the money," the grumbling would be great.
But if he lets it slide, he will find himself greatly esteemed.
He will be held in high honor.
And honor was its own currency in this society.
Thus, the steward was shrewd, astute, had practical wisdom in estimating
    the master as a man who wished to have honor.
Jesus urges the children of light to have as much incentive as this man
    of the world.

But there is another way to think about this master, not as one hungry for
    honor but as a different kind of master.
And this would be a more fitting explanation of why Jesus told the story.
When the master found out the steward was squandering his money, he
    could have had the manager thrown in jail or sold into slavery.
He doesn't—why?
Because he is merciful and kind.
In this way the master is similar to the father in the story of the prodigal son.
There, too, someone squandered money and the father had every right to
    reject him when he came crawling home, but the father didn't—he was
    merciful.
And the son counted on this.
Today we see the same thing.
The steward counts on the master's mercy as he takes care for himself.
He has practical wisdom—knows who it is he works for and acts on it.
The servant knows his master.

How does he act on it?
By doing something that helps others.
He's not a saint, but neither is he totally selfish.
He cuts their debt and makes friends with them.
Yes, he is taking care of himself, to be sure, but he does this by doing
    something for the others.

So what we have here is a parable that praises practical wisdom:
    to be wise with the long term in mind.
To use wealth "to be welcomed into eternal dwelling places."

We live at a time when you wonder if it can get much worse for
    many people.
Take Florida and Alabama with the flooding and tornadoes, or Hurricane
    Katrina in New Orleans;
        then there is Iraq, Afghanistan, Sudan, Israel, West Bank, Baslan on
        the world scene.
It is bad enough that nature is doing such terrible things to us,
    but what terrible things we continue to do to each other.
The home political scene is as mean-spirited as I can ever remember.
Perhaps it is a time when the appeal to self-interest is the best we can do.
Do good to others so that others will do good to us.

We have this parable that calls on us, not just to use wealth with the master
    in mind, thereby serving God and not mammon or self in whatever
    form; rather, it calls us to use our wealth with an eye out for others.
It is not just for the sake of honoring God but so we might imitate divine
    mercy and generosity, knowing that God's generosity will not
    be outdone.

This parable is paired with a reading from the prophet Amos, who spoke
    the word of the Lord to the people of Israel in the eighth century.
We only hear from him a few Sundays in the three-year cycle of readings,
    but this week and next he comes on strong enough that his voice
    might echo for a while.
Amos is really heated up over the merchants of his day, blasting them for
    living as if only money matters.
They rush from worship to gouge the poor, fixing scales, fooling with
    weights, all at the expense of others.
God's wrath will settle on those who do not care for but rather
    cheat others.

God's wrath will come down on the people when they don't take care
   of the poor.

Today we are asked to sign some letters as part of a letter-writing campaign.
People from Bread for the World are here asking for our signatures.
BFW is a Christian advocacy organization that speaks out in favor of the
   hungry and poor throughout our country and the world.
Holy Trinity Parish not only has a membership in the organization but,
   once a year, participates in this letter-writing campaign to our senators.

After the liturgy you are invited to sign a letter to our senators, urging them
   to support full funding for programs designed to combat world hunger.
One of these programs is President Bush's Millennium Challenge Account.
A motion was sent to Congress to provide funding for countries that meet
   the conditions assuring that the money given would be used properly.
While it was announced in 2002 that we hope to give $5 billion a year by
   2006, and $3.3 billion this year, all we put into the budget was $2.5
   billion—and the Senate pared this down to $1.12 billion.
Because of this, of the sixteen countries selected for aid, only a little more
   than half can be helped.

The United States only gives 1 percent of its national budget for foreign aid,
   and half of that goes to Israel and Egypt.
Unfortunately, people don't get elected by having a strong stand on foreign
   aid, and consequently there is not a lot of interest in doing more, nor
   much political capital to be gained.
But today we hear a Gospel calling us to use our money to make friends
   who will greet us in the eternal dwelling place.
Here we have a choice: allow this Gospel to have an immediate impact on
   our lives or not.

This Friday is the feast of Saint Robert Bellarmine, a bishop and theologian.
He took down the tapestries in the bishop's residence, giving them to the
   poor to wrap themselves in.

"Why should the walls be warm and the poor cold?" he asked.

He added, "Better to be fooled a thousand times by someone who may be
taking advantage of us, than to miss the chance just once to help a
genuinely poor person."

In our own time the prophetic voice of William Sloane Coffin rings out:
"The way we are cutting taxes for the wealthy and social programs
for the poor,
you'd think the greedy were needy and the needy were greedy."*

So, as we go into the week, consider the call to be a person of practical
wisdom.

Keep your eyes on the Master of creation and the one he sent, Jesus the Lord.

If we put people ahead of profits, we could become prophets in our own day.

May God be praised in all we do.

JAW

---

* William Sloane Coffin, *Credo* (Louisville, KY: Westminster/John Knox, 2004), 61.

Questions for Reflection

1. What is your reaction to the dishonest steward? To the master?

2. How do you make use of what has been entrusted to you?

3. Some translations of the Our Father contain the words "Forgive us our debts as we forgive our debtors." How do these words challenge you?

Other Directions for Preaching

1. The words of Amos still challenge communities, cities, states, and nations—any person, persons, or political entities whose god is wealth, especially any who amass their riches on the backs of the poor.

2. Paul's words remind us of our obligation to pray for all those in positions of authority, both in civil government and in the church. Partisan divisions must not stop the flow of prayer for the well-being and the gift of wisdom needed by those called to serve the common good.

3. "You cannot serve both God and mammon" is one of the most frequently quoted lines in Scripture, but what does it really mean in our time? How does a follower of Jesus hear and heed this statement?

Mind the Gap
TWENTY-SIXTH SUNDAY IN ORDINARY TIME

READINGS:
Amos 6:1a, 4–7; 1 Timothy 6:11–16; Luke 16:19–31

I was in London this past summer, getting around by subway or "tube."
Whenever one comes to a stop, from within the car you hear a soothing
    voice saying, "Mind the gap, mind the gap."
Its aim is to guide you safely across the divide between the tube and the
    platform.

That message is at the heart of today's readings: mind the gap.
The story of the rich man and Lazarus is about a man who did not mind
    the gap.
Jesus told this parable to the Pharisees, described in Luke's Gospel as
    "lovers of money."
It's a tale of reversals.

The rich man, his body dressed in purple (a sign of wealth) and linens
    (another sign), eats a banquet meal every day in a house on the hill,
    his property secured by a gate.
Outside this gate lies Lazarus, his body covered with ulcerated sores, which
    wild dogs, considered unclean, come to lick.
Lazarus longs to eat what falls from the rich man's table.

Between them, however, stands a gate.
An important image—that gate!
It marks the gap between the one who is rich and the one who is poor.

Both men eventually die.
Lazarus is carried away by angels to Abraham's bosom.
The rich man is buried and wakes up in hell.

Some things have changed and some haven't.
For the first time, the rich man speaks Lazarus's name, so he must have
     known him.
But he treats him as a servant: Father Abraham, tell old Lazarus to come on
     down here with a little water.
Abraham yells back:
     Can't be done.
The gate has become a very large gap—indeed, a chasm, an abyss.
Nothing to be done, no movement possible.

Jesus' story is an old one, scholars say, found in other cultures:
     Egyptian, Greco-Roman, to name a few.
What is Jesus doing with it?
Luke's Jesus doesn't say here that money is evil.
And the rich man isn't portrayed as mean or abusive.
But he is blind.
He doesn't see Lazarus.
Nor does he show any sign of caring about what is beyond his property.

This was a story meant to challenge the listeners, to get them off
     their couches.
Today it is matched up with Amos's harsh words to the rich of the northern
     kingdom.
The wealthy of Amos's day are complacent, too, very pleased with
     themselves—a pampered, perfumed people also lolling on their

couches, drinking wine from bowls, not goblets, plucking at their guitars, while the poor perish.

So, how do *we* hear these texts? How do they speak to *us*?
Isn't it hard not to feel a twinge of discomfort, even guilt, whether we are rich or not?
Still, for the most part, our lives are comfortable.
And our world up until recently has felt secure.
But whether *we* see ourselves as wealthy is beside the point.
So much of the world, which *is* poor and desperate, tends to see us as rich, comfortable, complacent, and insulated.
How we are perceived may not be who we are "when you really get to know us," yet it is who we are for those who see us from across the poverty line.

And there are those across the world who want to create a new version of this story.
In this new version Lazarus will no longer be content to lie at the gate.
He will be marching through it, entering the house, bringing death and destruction.
The poor will no longer wait on something to trickle down to them.
The most chilling image televised in the days after 9/11 was of children dancing for joy in unknown streets in the Middle East.
Last week Arab world expert Jon B. Altermann, an analyst at the US Institute for Peace, was quoted in the *Washington Post,* saying: "They don't hate us because we are a democracy and have a congress. They hate us because we seem so indifferent to their problems and their suffering."

But let us return to that gate which marks the gap.
The gap doesn't have to remain an abyss.
In the parable this uncrossable divide occurs only after death.
Here and now, it still depends on what happens at the gate—during life.

In Latin the word for gate was *porta;* we get our word
    "opportunity" from it.
An opportunity is a gate, an opening to a new possibility.
In his life the rich man never went to the gate, never went through it to the
    other side, never responded to the opportunity of helping Lazarus.
Do we? Can we?

Certainly efforts have to go beyond making our own country more fortified.
Some are saying a new Marshall Plan is needed. Or a new Peace
    Corps venture.
The building of coalitions to root out the evil of terrorism is certainly
    important.
But even more is needed.
It's not just *mind* the gap. We need to *mend* the gap.

At the end of the parable the rich man asks Abraham to send
    Lazarus to his brothers.
Abraham responds, "They have Moses and the prophets.
    Let them listen to them."
We are called to listen to the voices we have been given.
God's voice continues to call out:
    "This is my Son—listen to him."

Today we heard Paul's voice.
Immediately before these words, Paul writes:
    "The love of money is the root of all evils."
Then he tells Timothy:
    "Avoid all this. Instead, pursue righteousness, devotion, faith, love,
    patience, and gentleness....Lay hold of eternal life."
The letter concludes with these words:
    "Tell the rich in the present age not to be proud and not to rely on so
    uncertain a thing as wealth but rather on God, who richly provides us
    with all things for our enjoyment. Tell them to do good, to be rich in
    good works, to be generous, ready to share, thus accumulating as

treasure a good foundation for the future, so as to win the life that is
true life."

Not just mind the gap but mend the gap.
This is our work as the people of God, disciples of Jesus, children of the
kingdom.
These readings challenge us and give us hope.
In this life, there's always a gate, an opportunity.
Even during those days immediately after the tragedy of 9/11 the sound of
hope could be heard.
Fifth-grader Sapier Jamie Behr, a student from one of the public schools
within blocks of the World Trade Center, wrote this in class:

> My heart is racing,
> Tears in my eyes,
> Sirens yelling in my ear,
> I felt it.
>
> Fear in me,
> Friends in my arms,
> More tears from each of us coming,
> I knew it.
>
> I'm shaking,
> I hear nothing,
> My world got shut down,
> I saw it.
>
> Sadness came a hold of us.
> Terrified was I,
> *But good things will blossom out of this,*
> *I know it.*

God continues to visit us at every Eucharist.

Then we are sent forth to love God and serve one another.

In short: Mind the gap....Mend the gap.

JAW

Questions for Reflection

1. Today's readings call our attention to an aspect of life we acknowledge when we ask pardon for "what we have failed to do." We can live lives of benign neglect of those who lie "outside the gates" of our lives. How can we mend the gap?

2. What are the actions of my country in relation to the poor of the world? Do I make my opinion known to legislators who are working for or against aid to the poorer nations?

3. Paul calls us to "compete well for the faith," using an athletic metaphor. In an age often criticized for lack of physical fitness, we might reflect on our spiritual fitness.

Other Directions for Preaching

1. Amos draws attention to the self-indulgence of the rich of his time. In pronouncing "woe," Amos is using the language of a funeral dirge. Wealth's danger is that it produces inner death in those still living.

2. Paul's words to Timothy offer an agenda for the Christian life: living a virtuous life, defending the faith, seeking after eternal life, and honoring the commandments. These are the four directions of a disciple's moral compass.

3. Luke's Gospel also draws our attention to what it means to be a people faithful to the covenant: caring for the poor, the widow, and the orphan, God's little ones.

Rethinking Faith
Twenty-Seventh Sunday in Ordinary Time

Readings:
Habakkuk 1:2–3; 2:2–4; 2 Timothy 1:6–8, 13–14;
Luke 17:5–10

Our culture is known for its practicality, a disposition that may be at odds
    with Jesus' very unpragmatic Gospel.
That way of thinking goes back a long way.
In his *Journals* of 1828, Ralph Waldo Emerson—that architect of the
    American imagination—said that he preferred "a man who likes to see
    a fine barn as well as a good tragedy."
We like our prose fiction simple and direct, the way Hemingway wrote
    about the snows of Kilimanjaro or bullfights in northern Spain,
    eliminating all the words he "could not stand to hear."

Even our traffic laws are clearly defined models of predictable road
    etiquette.
Red means *stop*, green says *go*, behavioral signals that stand in stark
    contrast, for instance, to the—shall we say, impressionistic—traffic
    patterns of Rome at high noon.
Quid pro quo could well stand as our national motto.
We want to know precisely how much we are getting for our dollar.
Change?
Forget it.

Anyway, who wants to argue over a price as they do on the dry, sandy
    market tables in Morocco?

So, when the apostles ask Jesus to increase their faith, the practical among
    us might be inclined to see this request as something close to the
    politics of holiness.
Read one way, "increase our faith" may appear as a security against doubt,
    a kind of installment plan for persons who experience an ebb tide
    in the seemingly vast ocean of faith.
To ask for an increase insists on a quantitative edge.
But surprisingly, "increase our faith" comes in Luke's Gospel as the result
    of a challenge to the apostles surrounding one of the most difficult
    of issues.
Recall that just before the apostles ask him to increase their faith, our Lord
    says that they must forgive everyone, unconditionally,
        "and if he wrongs you seven times in one day
        and returns to you seven times saying, 'I am sorry,' you should
    forgive."

Now, consider the contrast in Matthew and Mark, where the same request
    for faith comes after the disciples are unable to exorcise a demon.
The difference here is obvious: the terribly difficult mandate to *forgive* in
    Luke's Gospel provokes a plea for an increase of faith.
They just don't have enough compassion for the journey.
The Twelve know that they have failed to love.
And surely, the apostles' situation is all too familiar in our own ears in the
    face of life's impossibly sad moments.
Give me more faith so that I can cope with the death of my loved one,
    O Lord.
Increase my faith so that I can be reconciled and at peace, my God.
Grant me more faith so that I can comfort the city that now sits like a
    widow overlooking a once proud skyline, Christ Jesus.
We need an increase of faith to get us through the night of haunted
    memories.

This all-too-human litany is an impassioned cry to send our withering
   roots rain.

All of which Jesus answers, not with a cool spring shower,
      but, stunningly, with a mustard seed.
Jesus is transplanting both our thinking and the order of power.
"If you had faith the size of a mustard seed...."
I do not think that the Lord is being petulant here, shaming us into belief.
Jesus wants to show us just how easy it is:
      we can move from faith as a position of strength,
      from considering how much we *think* we need,
      to something much more mysterious, merciful, and relational.
If you have faith that is literally next to nothing, a mustard seed,
      you can do astonishing and wonderful things.
Even forgive your enemy.
It is that easy.

Faith does not come by the spoonful.
Jesus' notion of faith is much closer to a Jewish religious experience than
      our own pragmatic ways of making ourselves better,
      like an interest on a loan.
It is better to see the complexity of faith as Jesus would have meant it to be
      seen, through the eyes of a pious Jew.
Habakkuk says that the Lord wants the people to "live by faith."
And the meaning of the word translated as "faith" in Hebrew here is
      emunah, which means steadfast loyalty, holding on obediently to the
      Lord's Law, even when it apparently pays no dividends.
At the end of the book of the prophet Habakkuk, the prophet says,
      "For though the fig tree blossom not nor fruit be on the vines, though
      the yield of the olive fail and the terraces produce no nourishment,
      though the flocks disappear from the fold and there be no herd in the
      stalls, yet will I rejoice in the Lord and exult in my saving
      God"(3:17–19).

Mustard seed faith is reckoned here closer to the language of love and
    fidelity than it is to faith measured in quantities.
We cannot ask for grace as if it were an allowance for a rainy day.
We live by faith; we don't measure by faith.
That is love.

Faith seeking understanding suggests precisely what is at stake:
    charity, pure and simple.
A longing for a kind of faith that seeks power to control or conquer even
    difficult, razor-edge emotions fails to be faith at all because it
    fails to love.
No wonder Paul himself discounts the amount of faith we may judge so
    important when he says in 1 Corinthians: "If I have all faith so as to
    move mountains, but do not have love, I am nothing" (13:2).

Faith grows from love, and like the earth and its abundant fruits, they are
    wedded forever.
Faith comes from love like a tiny shoot bursting from a seed.
We serve the table precisely because we are loved at the altar.
The storm of divine lightning is what gives us all the power for our dark
    nights and cold winters.
Bernard Lonergan has reminded us that religious experience is falling in
    love without restriction.
That dynamic is what allows faith to emerge.
Even mustard-seed faith is born of love.
Jesus' farewell gift to us is the Spirit of his love, from which has sprung the
    church, the believing heart, the community of faith.
We carry that on here at the altar of God, the God who renews the joy of
    our youth.
At this Eucharist, together we profess our faith as an acknowledgment of
    the One who is the perfect offering on the altar, endlessly thanking the
    One who has loved us so that we might believe all the more.

GD

Questions for Reflection

1. If I asked Jesus to increase my faith, what would I be expecting, exactly?

2. Do I see God working through me and others even in the small details of my life? How has that encounter happened today?

3. What does it mean for me to fall in love without restriction?

Other Directions for Preaching

1. Paul reminds Timothy of the power of the Gospel that speaks out, even when we feel inclined toward passivity when it comes to proclamation.

2. The Holy Spirit guides our everyday actions if we live by mustard-seed faith, a gift that cannot be measured by human standards. Living by the Spirit increases our awareness that faith is a gift.

3. Faith is severely tested in times of violence or when we think God is silent.

After 9/11:
Are the Clouds Really White?
Twenty-Eighth Sunday in Ordinary Time

READINGS:
2 Kings 5:14–17; 2 Timothy 2:8–13; Luke 17:11–15

This past summer my dear friend and colleague Fr. Jim Wallace and I went
    to the Netherlands for an international conference for professors of
    preachers.
I am always energized by this group, whose name is Societas Homiletica,
    because I am always amazed at how our love for our profession,
    our passion for preaching, our vision of church,
    is so beautifully tapestried by so many colors, languages, accents,
    and customs.
Even sampling what we consider "foreign" food makes us so much richer.
There is an African saying: "He who has not traveled thinks his mother is
    the best cook."

Local art is another treasure.
And in the Netherlands, of course, the local paintings of such giants as Van
    Gogh and Vermeer have become exquisite samples of our universal
    longing for beauty, truth, and light.
On the way to the Netherlands I read Tracy Chevalier's *Girl with a Pearl
    Earring,* the current best-selling novel about Griet, a simple peasant
    girl who starts out being Vermeer's cleaning girl, then helps him to

mix his paints, and finally becomes the subject for the famous painting
Girl with a Pearl Earring, which is considered the Dutch *Mona Lisa*.

It might seem odd at this point that I am babbling about a Dutch
    masterpiece and a current novel.
What about the terror that our nation and our world is braving through
    right now?
And what about not only the "other nine,"
    but the "one" Samaritan who came back to give thanks?
But, strangely, it was a scene from *Girl with a Pearl Earring* that I
    remembered as I prayed over the story of the ten lepers in light of our
    international terrors.

One morning Griet is mixing the paints for her master's palette.
She assumes what colors he will use.
It is then that Vermeer takes Griet over to his studio window to watch
    clouds disappearing behind the new church tower.
"What color are those clouds?"
"Why, white, sir."
But the artist raises his eyebrows slightly and asks,
    "Are they?
    "Come Griet, you can do better than that."
Slowly, Griet realizes that there is blue in the clouds, and yellow, and even
    some green.
And then she says:
    "I had been looking at clouds all my life, but I felt as if I saw them for
    the first time at that moment." *

One of the reasons we come to worship as a community gathered around
    the Word and table is to ask ourselves:
    "Are the clouds really white?"

---

* Tracy Chevalier, *Girl with a Pearl Earring* (New York: Penguin Putnam, 2001)
p 101.

We think they are because we were told they are and because we hardly
   ever gaze on them.
I'm not just talking about the clouds in the sky but things on our earth that
   are most real in our lives: people, events, terrors, miracles.
We speak abstractly sometimes of revelation but the word *revelation* simply
   means taking away the veil to reveal what is really before us in light of
   the Gospel.

Naaman was a five-star general in the Syrian army, but he was also a leper.
He couldn't believe it when a messenger of the prophet Elisha came to tell
   him to bathe in the Jordan River seven times in order to be healed.
Now Naaman absolutely knew that there were rivers in Syria that made the
   Jordan look like a cow stream.
But with his miracle of healing there came a revelation,
      the veil of suspicion was taken away;
      the clouds were no longer white,
      and Naaman now knew that his god had been too small.

Some think that the story of the ten lepers is all about being well bred:
      writing thank-you notes to those who have helped us;
      practicing gratitude, especially as we approach Thanksgiving.
But the truth is that the leper who came back after recognizing his healing
      was not well bred;
      he was considered by the people around Jesus to be "half-bred" since
      he was a Samaritan.
He belonged to a group who were marginalized because they weren't pure-
   bred believers.
They had mixed blood; today they would be considered heretics,
   schismatics, sinners.
They didn't worship God in Jerusalem but on Mount Gerizim.

The real miracle of this story is that Naaman was cleansed not just of
      his leprosy
      but from his ignorance of who God is and how God can be worshiped,

whenever and wherever we see that the clouds are not always white,
that God is waiting to show goodness and mercy in the strangest
and most terrifying places in our lives.

The terrors of 9/11 have challenged our old stereotypes
and even our vision of the clouds.
A TV reporter recently asked a young girl what we should do to end the
terrorist attacks:
Her answer: "Send in Bruce Willis."
Just a few months ago President Bush announced on his ranch in Texas:
"This is the real America. Washington, DC, is not the real America.
All those folks on the East Coast soaking up their sun rays are not the
real America."
Now, thank God, our president is beginning to see that the clouds are not
always white.
He is no longer dividing us into Americans of the so-called heartland and
"other" Americans;
he is calling us to be a unified, compassionate, and just nation.

Jerry Falwell has blamed 9/11 on gays, lesbians, abortionists, feminists, and
a lot of other people whom he doesn't like.
But now it is reported that the Franciscan priest, Fr. Mychal Judge,
who gave his life as a chaplain to firemen, was a gay activist,
struggling to live authentically himself and to live for others.
It is also noted that Mark Bingham, one of the passengers who overtook the
hijackers in the skies of Pennsylvania, was a member of the Gay
Rugby team in San Francisco.

And then there is Mayor Giuliani, a man some considered to be a right-
wing thug, a man more stubborn at times than Naaman or any
Samaritan.
But after 9/11, Giuliani has been called "Churchill in a baseball hat."
We are told that his favorite hymn is *Ave Maria*.

He has been invited to speak before the United Nations and is now one of
    the most widely admired men in our country.

Our lives have changed since 9/11.
Simplistic answers will no longer do.
We are not yet ready to stop our grieving or drop our anger.
Our pain and our frustration are real, and so is our fear.

We don't come to church for any simple human solution to this new threat
    of violence and hatred in our midst.
We come for a divine response.
We bow down with the Naamans of our world before Jesus and simply ask
    his mercy on our beloved country, on our shattered world.
The clouds are no longer simply white, but that can make us strong and
    help us to grow up and find a bigger God, one with far greater variety
    and mystery.

RPW

Questions for Reflection

1. How has God's saving power been revealed to the nations in our time?

2. How is it that Paul suffers the humiliation of imprisonment but, at the same time, seems to rejoice in his suffering?

3. Much of our prayer is made up of petitions. How often do we throw ourselves at the feet of Jesus and give thanks? Is that what we are doing in the Eucharist?

Other Directions for Preaching

1. Amid the stories of loss and survival on 9/11 and following other natural disasters, some came to believe in God, like Naaman, while others lost faith. Does disaster, and its aftermath, have a lasting effect on our faith? (You might want to watch the documentary *Faith and Doubt at Ground Zero.*)

2. I wonder what became of the other nine who were cured in the Gospel. Did they go on their way thinking, "Wow! Wasn't I lucky?" What is lost from our lives if we do not experience and express gratitude?

Our Lady of Consistency
Twenty-Ninth Sunday in Ordinary Time

READINGS:
Exodus 17:8–13; 2 Timothy 3:14—4:2; Luke 18:1–8

Back in the late sixties and early seventies it was chic to have your children
    baptized at a home Mass where family and friends gathered around.
But soon that practice was dropped because it didn't reflect an adequate
    theology of baptism.
When we take our little band of seven today and anoint and baptize them,
    we don't incorporate them into our earthly family but into our
    heavenly family; we don't incorporate them only into our parish
    community of Holy Trinity but into the Body of Christ everywhere on
    earth and in heaven.

But as a celibate who has never known the joy and excitement of having my
    own children,
    I am thinking in a special way of the parents of these children today.
I am at that point in my life where I am simply in awe of parents today,
    how lovingly and hopefully they take on this charge.
How many parents I have known now in my life who have given their all to
    this charge, despite some awful challenges from children themselves
    because of human error, sickness, and disappointment.
And so I salute you young parents; I promise you the prayers and support
    of the church as you begin this wondrous, joyful, yet daunting task.

Years from now, dear parents and grandparents and godparents, tell the
    children that the day they were baptized,
    all the Scripture readings urged them not to give up.
Especially tell them that when they are tempted to give up on life, on
    church, even on God.

We meet Moses, whom we all remember as someone "whose boots were
    meant for walking"
    out of the land of slavery, into the mud of the Red Sea, and beyond to
    the Promised Land.
If you go to Rome, you see Michelangelo's mighty statue of Moses.
But if you look closely, there is a flaw in the dark marble that the artist used
    to construct his hero.
Art guides offer you two interpretations for the flaw:
    1. When Michelangelo was finished, he was disappointed in what he
    had created and so took a hammer and smashed the marble.
    2. The artist began with a flawed piece of marble to remind us that the
    great Moses was also a creature of God, capable of all the flaws that
    we are capable of.

I prefer the second interpretation and it certainly echoes the First Reading.
Moses' calling was always to represent not just God's Word to the people
    but the people's words to God.
Moses was a medium for this revelation.
He knew his mission, but he also never relied on his own talents—but
    always on God's word.
The book of Exodus calls him "the humblest man on earth," which is quite
    a tag for a hero, no?

In today's First Reading Moses stretches out his hands to protect his brood.
But, since he is a man, he soon grows weary,
    and so he has to be supported by rocks and others to continue his
    perseverance.

The apostle who writes to Timothy lives in a time of the church when
    persecution and defeat are everywhere.
He understands that Christians are getting weary, including Timothy.
But there is this bold charge to his protege:
    "Be persistent whether it is convenient or inconvenient; convince,
    reprimand, encourage through all patience and teaching."

And then the parable of the persistent widow!
What a model of persistence when we cannot find a bridge over
    troubled waters.
Luke Timothy Johnson, a biblical expert on Luke's Gospel, captures well
    who this widow is:
    "The parable makes its point so forcefully and humorously that little
    comment is required. Contemporary readers can easily imagine an
    enraged bag lady hitting the negligent magistrate over the head and
    literally 'giving him a black eye.' We are meant, I think, to laugh."*

Although the widow is a stock figure in a parable,
    there must have been widows like this in the early church.
Widows who had no clout in the community,
    who had to deal with arrogant court officials,
    who came back day after day after day demanding justice.
Each morning a widow like that would wake up and say,
    "Now what possibly could I do today to get his attention?"
She scratched her head, got an idea, and went back into town.

The parable makes it clear that the widow prayed always, but this does not
    mean that she was in perpetual prayer or some kind of novel method
    of mysticism.
That is not the kind of widow she was and not the kind of prayer
    she prayed.

---

*Luke Timothy Johnson, *The Gospel of Luke* (Collegeville, MN: The Liturgical
Press, 1991), 273.

Like Moses, she too most likely got weary and had to be propped up
>by others.

Her prayer was not perpetual, but it was consistent.

For the last three and a half years now, my name has been in the Prayer of
>the Faithful here,
>>mentioned among the sick.

Some might wonder when I'm getting off that list.

I wonder too.

But, for those of us who battle a chronic illness, we know that we need not
>the perpetual prayers,
>>but rather the consistent prayers of the faithful.

And I continue to be grateful that you prop me up when I grow weary.

So, let us, you and I, make a commitment to this little band of seven we
>baptize today.

Although we may often be a church that grows weary and frightened, we
>promise, despite this, to be consistent and persistent and loving in our
>support of the widow, the sick, the poor, the displaced, and the
>children in our midst.

Let us learn a lesson from the consistent widow.

RPW

Questions for Reflection

1. Who are the people who hold me up when I grow weary? How do they do this? What is the rock on which I rest when I can no longer stand on my own?

2. How do we make a meaningful connection between the comforting promises of these verses of Psalm 121:1–8 and the realities of war, disease, and poverty?

3. Paul exhorts us as people of God to correct, reprove, and appeal to one another. How do we do this in a way that enables us to hear without putting up our defenses?

Other Directions for Preaching

1. Some things never seem to change. Amalek attacks the Israelites, and in response Moses gives the order to counterattack. At the end of the day, "Joshua mowed down Amalek and his people with edge of the sword." Have our attitudes and responses to serious human conflict changed at all since the time of Amalek and Moses?

2. In our Judeo-Christian tradition, the poor, the widows, and orphans have a special claim upon God and upon us. As the gap between the rich and the poor widens, we are mandated to address the needs of the poor. Many groups, secular and religious, have come together around the world believing we are at a point where poverty can and must be eliminated.

The Problem with Religion
THIRTIETH SUNDAY IN ORDINARY TIME

READINGS:
Sirach 35:12–14, 16–18; 2 Timothy 4:6–8, 16–18;
Luke 18:9–14

During this season of the year it's not uncommon to spot a few pint-sized
mummies walking the neighborhood in search of treats.
But not long ago some scientists reported finding some real mummies.
They were mummies of three people who were sacrificed by the Incas five
hundred years ago.
The scientists speculate that the Incas worshiped gods who, they believed,
lived beyond the clouds high in the mountains in Peru.

Two things are strange here.
First, apparently two of the mummies were young virgins who voluntarily
went up into the mountains where they were strangled or bludgeoned
to death by Inca priests in order to appease the gods.
No one could say five hundred years ago that young Incas didn't have
religion!
Could they really have *voluntarily* gone up into the mountains?!
Perhaps they had too much religion!

The second feature of the story was the discovery of the mummy of a young
Inca man.
Now, what was he doing up there on the mountain?

Some think that the priests had tricked him.

They probably persuaded the young man to accompany the two young girls
   so that they would be protected from animals and thus arrive perfectly
   flawless for their sacrifice.

Once the girls arrived, the young man had served his purpose and was put
   to death by the priests.

I was haunted by this mummy story as I prayed over our parable for today.

At first glance, it seems that this parable also gives religion and religious
   leaders a bad name.

Till this day, we use the word *pharisaical* to describe religious people who
   are hypocrites.

Heaven forbid that we would be like them!

There is a story told of a Sunday School teacher who was teaching her class
   of boys and girls this parable of the Pharisee and tax collector.

She painted the Pharisee as a mean and hypocritical man and the tax
   collector as a good man.

And when she had finished the story, she said,
   "Now boys and girls, let us get down on our knees and thank God
   that we're nothing like that mean old Pharisee."

Once again, religion gets a bad name.

The irony, of course, is that the Sunday School teacher missed the meaning
   of the parable because she was so religious.

If we look closely at this parable, without all the prejudices that we have
   inherited over the years about Pharisees, we would have to ask
   ourselves, "What exactly did the Pharisee do wrong in his prayer?"

He prayed while standing up in the Temple, a normal religious practice.

Even his prayer was not unusual.

It was a prayer of thanksgiving similar to the one that rabbis were supposed
   to pray before entering and after leaving a house of study.

The Pharisee's prayer was similar to the one we find in the Talmud that goes
   something like this:

"I give thanks to Thee, O Lord my God, that Thou has set my portion with those who sit in your house and not with those who sit in the street corners. For I rise early for word of Torah and they rise early for frivolous talk. I run and they run. But I run to the life of the future world and they to the pit of destruction."

And no doubt the Pharisee was on target when he said that the tax collector was greedy and adulterous.
He probably was.
So why does the Pharisee get such a bum rap?
Wasn't he just following his religion and praying the way he was supposed to pray?
Wasn't he correct in describing the tax collector in the terms that he used?

Perhaps the tax collector was greedy and adulterous—we really don't know!
But he was also in the Temple at prayer.
His prayer pierced the clouds and reached the heart of God because it was the prayer of a powerless man who perceived the power of God.
The Pharisee couldn't see that.
His religion got in the way.

In fact, the only fault that some biblical scholars find with the Pharisee is that the story says he prayed to himself.
He prayed to himself rather than to God.
And while he was praying, he kept looking in disgust at the tax collector.
In other words, he allowed his religion to get in the way of his spirituality.
He allowed his religion to make him so arrogant that he simply could not go the extra mile.
He allowed his religion to keep him from looking with mercy on the tax collector,
    which, by the way, is how God had always looked on him.

It is sad how over the years this parable has been so misinterpreted.
There is an old Irish saying, "Never trust anyone in the front pew!"

Like the Sunday School teacher, we have missed the point of the parable if
we use it to put certain people down.
Some have even used this parable for their own purposes of anti-Semitism,
believing that the Jewish religion of the Pharisee was hypocritical and
self-righteous.
But we must remember that this parable is directed not just to the Pharisees
but everyone,
including the disciples,
including Catholics, Protestants, Muslims,
all who use their religion to trust themselves as being righteous while
scorning everyone else.

The mummies in Peru remind us that throughout history, religion can be a
dangerous thing.
In our own day, some religious radio and TV talk shows use religion to
strangle the human rights of others.
Today, as never before, religious reasons are given for the deadly sins of
nationalism, racism, and sexism.
A religion that leads to hatred, violence, or intolerance of others is not
worthy of the name.

That is why this parable is for all of us,
those in the front of the church and those in the back,
those who are leaders in the church and those who are just
holding on.
It is for all of us, especially if we come to church and pray to ourselves
rather than to a power outside our tiny selves.
The Good News that Jesus proclaims to us is that we have to have a whole
new way of looking at our religion so that it doesn't get in the way of
our relationship with God and with one another.
Then, we can leave here and, like the tax collector, go home changed.

RPW

Questions for Reflection

1. Who are "the lowly"? Does this designation have to do with economics, class, or self-perception?

2. Saint Paul likens the Christian life to a marathon or other sporting events. If this is so, what are some specific examples that fit Paul's categories?

3. Who are those who are held in contempt in our society?

Other Directions for Preaching

1. It is painful to sit in a courtroom as men and women come before a judge for sentencing. Often, as with Saint Paul, there is no one in the courtroom in support of the person being sentenced—except his or her attorney. No one is there to take the person's part, to smile encouragingly, to pray, simply to be there.

2. There is nothing wrong with piety, unless it is used as a substitute for living justly, loving tenderly, and walking humbly with our God (Mic 6:8). We must strive not to compartmentalize our lives so that, in one part, we are participating in daily devotion, while in the other part, we are living in opposition to the example of Christ.

A Graceful Descent
THIRTY-FIRST SUNDAY IN ORDINARY TIME

READINGS:
Wisdom 11:22—12:2; 2 Thessalonians 1:11—2:2;
Luke 19:1–10

Last Tuesday's *New York Times* op-ed page had a column by
　　Daniel Handler.*
You might not recognize that name, but if you know any ten- or twelve-
　　year-olds, ask them about Lemony Snicket.
This is Mr. Handler's pen name for a series of books about the Baudelaire
　　children.
The first book in the series starts this way: "If you are looking for happy
　　endings, you would be better off reading some other book."**
Within the first few pages the Baudelaire children lose their parents to a fire
　　and find themselves on the run from the evil Count Olaf.

In his column Mr. Handler wrote that, since 9/11, he is often asked if it is
　　appropriate to write such stories when there are so many real orphans
　　and villains to worry about these days.
His response was that it is more than appropriate, it is necessary, because
　　young readers are finding ways of contemplating our current troubles
　　through these stories.

---

　* Daniel Handler, "Frightening News," *The New York Times*, October 30, 2001, 17.
　** Daniel Handler, *The Bad Beginning* (New York: Harper Collins, 1999), 1.

Children ask him if Count Olaf is a terrorist, whether the Baudelaires were
    anywhere near the World Trade Center, if the unnamed country in the
    stories is in danger of being bombed.
All of which reveals that children are struggling with the same issues as the
    rest of us.
Furthermore, he writes:

> "Stories like these aren't cheerful, but they offer a truth: that real
> trouble cannot be erased, only endured. Certainly there are times when
> we want to escape to a trouble free imaginary world. But when the
> real world is so searing that it cannot be glossed over, we can find
> value in stories that admit the world is tumultuous, instead of
> reassuring us that it is not. It is unlikely that the story that began Sept.
> 11 will have a tidy resolution....Although it is understandable that
> some would like to turn away from this difficult fact, there is a kind of
> solace offered by stories that show us how endangered orphans go
> on living."

Mr. Handler's tribute to the power of stories, especially at times of stress,
    reminds me of why we keep going back to the story of Jesus and the
    stories he told and the stories told about him.
They help us to keep on going.
More than that, they give us hope.
The Zacchaeus story is a good example.
This chief tax collector is one of the most memorable characters in the
    Gospels.
He only appears in Luke: the little man who stands up to a sneering town,
    promises to make any amends he needs to make,
    and ends up taking Jesus home to dinner.
He starts off up a tree and ends up entertaining the Son of God.

Luke tells this story because of what it says about Jesus:
    "The Son of Man has come to seek and to save what was lost."
And what was lost?

Someone who was seeking something, someone not satisfied
   with all that he had.
The old translation from the Jerusalem Bible first describes Zacchaeus as
   "anxious to see what kind of man Jesus was" (Luke 19:4).
This is precisely what he found out, and in that discovery he was
   transformed.
Jesus must have looked up and saw this fellow in a tree and asked,
   "Who's that?"
Most likely one of the townspeople answered, with a sneer in his voice that
   matched his contempt, "Oh, that! That's Zacchaeus, the chief tax
   collector."

I remember Dr. Kenneth Bailey, a biblical scholar and expert in Middle
   Eastern culture, saying that being short was not the only thing that
   sent Zacchaeus up the sycamore.
Zacchaeus had to climb a tree because he could not trust a crowd.
He was a rich tax collector and would have been hated for two reasons:
   for collaborating with the Romans
   and for getting rich off his own people.
And Jesus certainly knew this.
But what is his reaction?
   "Zacchaeus, come down quickly, for today I must stay at your house."
And Zacchaeus, throwing all caution to the wind, jumps down into the
   middle of the crowd, faces down the sneerers and, before taking Jesus
   home to dinner, gives an eloquent little speech that captures his
   conversion: "Behold, half of my possessions, Lord, I shall give to the
   poor, and if I have extorted anything from anyone I shall repay it four
   times over."
Jesus' final words are the ones that reveal to Zacchaeus, the crowd, and us
   what kind of man Jesus was.
He was the bringer of salvation,
   "for the Son of Man came to seek out and to save the lost."

Such a story reassures us when we, too, are feeling "up a tree," lost, alone.

The Zacchaeus story reminds us that one has been sent to find us, to bring us out of our confined quarters where we can get used to living lives marked by loneliness and fear.

This story reminds us of the power at work in Jesus, the power of the Spirit of God.

From the beginning of his Gospel, Luke keeps pointing out that Jesus is full of the Spirit.

He was conceived by the Holy Spirit.

The Spirit comes upon him after his baptism while he is praying.

The Spirit leads him into the wilderness to be tempted.

And when this period was over, Luke writes that Jesus, filled with the power of the Spirit, returned to Galilee and began to teach and preach.

His first proclamation in his hometown synagogue was the words of Isaiah the prophet:

"The Spirit of the Lord is upon me, because he has anointed me to bring glad tidings to the poor...to proclaim liberty to captives."

After reading it, he simply said,

"Today this scripture passage is fulfilled in your hearing" (Luke 4:21).

Through Jesus the Spirit touched the lives of others.

Jesus does more than liberate Zacchaeus from a tree where he had to conceal himself.

In the Spirit, he frees him from the prison where he was trapped by his choices.

He restores him to himself, to his own humanity, and to his community:

Zacchaeus, hurry and come down. You've been out on a limb long enough.

I must stay at your house today.

Ever so gently, Jesus led Zacchaeus to a moment of decision.

When Zacchaeus makes that jump, you can see the Spirit as the wind beneath his wings.

You know it is the Spirit because we hear that he received Jesus with joy.

The first gift of the Spirit is freedom from fear; fear is replaced by joy.
"My spirit rejoices in God, my Savior," said Mary, herself once fearful
    before the angel.
Zacchaeus comes down to take Jesus home to dinner, but he also comes
    home to himself.
He is a changed person: giving to the poor, paying back anyone he defrauded
    fourfold (400 percent, whereas Torah only asked for 20 percent!).
The Spirit working through Jesus has come to renew and restore,
    and that is what happens to Zacchaeus, who is once more a true son
    of Abraham.

Wisdom reminds God in the first reading that
    "you love all things that are and loathe nothing that you have made;
    ...you spare all things, because they are yours, O LORD and lover of
    souls, for your imperishable spirit is in all things!"
This Spirit of God continues to come to us as gift from the Father and Son.

I was very moved by the words of Elie Wiesel in *Parade* magazine last
    weekend.
He wrote, addressing the horror of 9/11:

    "The American people did not bend. Never have they been more
    motivated, more generous. Instead of trying to save themselves, men
    and women, young and old, ran to Ground Zero to offer
    assistance...to donate blood, offering food and shelter, sandwiches and
    sodas....The terrorists achieved the opposite of what they wanted.
    They moved people to transcend themselves and choose that which is
    noble. For, in the end, it is always a matter of choice—to choose
    between escape and solidarity, shame and honor."

The Spirit at work in us enables us to choose service, to reach out to others,
    to give of ourselves.
True, sometimes we find ourselves hiding up a tree of our own making.
Fear, anger, hurt, depression can drive us there.

But Jesus comes a-calling: Hurry down—I must come home with you.
He waits for us to make the leap, holding out his arms to catch us.
And the Spirit helps to bring us down, gracefully, to earth.
May this meal of the Eucharist bring him into our hearts,
   so we can take him with us when we leave, into our lives and
   our world.

JAW

Questions for Reflection

1. Do you ever find yourself trapped in any way?

2. Have you come to know what kind of person Jesus is?

3. What is your response to Jesus? Do you bring him "home" with you from Mass?

Other Directions for Preaching

1. Wisdom calls attention to the wonder of creation and at the same time the way in which the universe is merely "a grain from a balance or a drop of morning dew" before its Creator. At a time when there is so much discussion of the theories of evolution and intelligent design, a homily might reflect on a sound faith vision of our world.

2. The reading from Wisdom also speaks of God rebuking those who sin "little by little," so that they may "abandon their wickedness and believe" in the Lord. The mercy of God is proclaimed both here and in the story of Zacchaeus.

3. The second reading begins to draw our attention to the Second Coming, a theme that will grow stronger these last weeks of the church year. Paul's prayer, that God may make the Thessalonians worthy of God's calling and bring to fulfillment every good purpose and effort of faith so that Christ is glorified in them, is the ongoing prayer of every pastor.

This Side of the Grave
THIRTY-SECOND SUNDAY IN ORDINARY TIME

READINGS:
2 Maccabees 7:1–2, 9–14; 2 Thessalonians 2:16—3:5;
Luke 20:27–38

I believe that this encounter between Jesus and the Sadducees is a defining
    moment in what is at stake in our notion of the resurrection.
Indeed, the attitude of the Sadducees concerning the resurrection has far
    from disappeared from our world.
The Sadducees are preoccupied with the fate of a single individual,
    and how that gets played out after the person is dead.
They get the true meaning of resurrection wrong.
Their focus, like that of so many, is on *immortality,* not on resurrection.
And we know anecdotally that most people today believe in some form of
    immortality, and yet the resurrection is quite another matter
    altogether.

We have our cultural narratives, our horror stories about those who come
    back from the dead—in a fog, usually sometime after midnight.
History and literature are riddled with restless ghosts, like Hamlet's father,
    who returns to tell his son of his ghastly murder.
Or the Headless Horseman, forever haunting Washington Irving's
    Sleepy Hollow.

Think of how many films Hollywood makes every year that deal with some
      grisly level of the supernatural to frighten us into belief.
Ghosts fascinate and scare us.
These stories indicate our belief that life goes on after death.
Yet, what kind of testimony are these to faith in a real resurrection?
      or to a belief in God's triumph over sin and death?
Even religious fanatics subscribe to a theory of immortality.
Tragically, they are often willing to die in a violent suicide mission in the
      knowledge that they shall live on blissfully and peacefully in paradise.

The resurrection described by Jesus and to which he himself will become the
      primary and ecstatic witness means more than just immortality.
We know that Jesus rose bodily from the dead in human history.
It happened.
No myth.
We know that he is alive and living among us.
Like Mary Magdalene, we have seen him and proclaimed him risen.
Far from a ghost story, the resuscitation of a corpse,
      the resurrection of Christ initiated a new world order,
      breaking a cycle of evil and beginning a new age, Resurrection Time.
As Paul tells us, Jesus was the firstfruits of those who have fallen asleep.

There are hints of this age to come already present with pious Jews,
      such as the seven brothers in the book of Maccabees.
They died not knowing the Lord but in the hope that there would be a new
      kingdom, a new order, a world unlike the unjust one of Antiochus
      that yoked them into religious slavery.
This new time would be God's reign of freedom and justice.
Thus, these seven brothers in the book of Maccabees stand in ironic
      counterpoint to the brothers imagined by the Sadducees.
The Maccabees yearn for an eschatology, an end time, when God will rule
      with justice and peace.
But the brothers dreamed up by the Sadducees in today's Gospel stumble
      around in the afterlife looking for their long-lost bride.

Which of these sounds like the world promised by Jesus,
    who taught us to pray, "thy kingdom come"?

The lives of the baptized, buried in Christ, are certainly testimony to this
    new, resurrected world order.
Our lives are a window into Jesus' resurrected horizon—not as angels,
    but as a Christian community filled with an endless future
    of faith, hope, and love.
That God's Son destroyed death forever is our greatest hope.
We need to image for ourselves the breakthrough that the power
    of God has in Christ to effect a new world order.
We can remind ourselves of God's love in our everyday lives.
Many of us are educators or teachers.
We know what it is like when suddenly a student or a parishioner has a
    kind of eternal, transcendent moment.
What was darkness has become illuminated.
We don't have to fear crossing over to the other side,
    where the world of immortality awaits us.
We don't need visitors from beyond the grave.
We are on the other side already, because that is where God's love is living
    and active.
Jesus is present among us to tell his people that we are on the other side of
    the empty tomb.
We only anticipate what awaits us when we love inside the fullness of the
    resurrection.

Nothing would ever be the same again after Jesus rose from the dead.
And so it is not by accident that we find ourselves a resurrected people,
    celebrating this eternal banquet, this Eucharist,
      this foretaste and promise of what is to come.
The Eucharist gives us one foot into the kingdom.
Here Christ is fully resurrected yet once more, as we carry on his memory.
Here we share in the fullness of God's reign on earth.

Having witnessed the risen One, we are called, like the early witnesses of
the resurrection, to go and tell the Good News to all the world.
There we can proclaim him risen, that injustice is at an end,
and that in a graced world, peace will come now.
The world of the resurrection is contagious and can only give life,
even to those who have fallen asleep.
What awaits us is beyond our imagining:
divine love here and now, resurrected love, given to us by God and
manifested in Christ.
God's love is the power that was unleashed at the sound of the opening of
that empty tomb two thousand years ago.
That love is where we put our trust now as we taste the bread of life
and the new wine of the kingdom.

GD

Questions for Reflection

1. How has the risen Lord changed my life? Do I behave differently
because I believe in Christ's victory over sin and death?

2. Do I fear death? What worries me about my life ending?

3. How can I make the Lord more fully alive to those I meet?

Other Directions in Preaching

1. Our culture is full of dead gods pretending to give life. If we can name
these empty illusions, we can find a wonderful new space—an empty tomb.

2. The Maccabees suffered torture and death for what they believed. Is
there anything worth dying for today?

3. God strengthens in faith all who call upon his name. We should cry
out to the Lord continually and boldly.

The Bottom Line
Thirty-Third Sunday in Ordinary Time

Readings:
Malachi 3:19–20a; 2 Thessalonians 3:7–12; Luke 21:5–19

Just when the generals are telling us that the dust is beginning to settle in
> Afghanistan and that we are close to bringing the terrorists to justice,

Just when the imminent threat of anthrax is beginning to get off the front
> burner to make way for the turkey and the cranberry sauce,

Just when we think we might get a reprieve from all this talk of evildoers,
> war, and how God could allow all these horrible events to happen,

Just at this moment, we hear a Gospel like this:
> the mighty Temple of Jerusalem destroyed,
> wars and insurrections, famines and plagues,
> and persecutions even by our families and our closest friends.

It's enough to make you change the Gospel of today and listen to something
> joyful and hopeful for a change.

But this is the church's season of what theologians call the last things or
> eschatology,
> a time when we crunch the brown leaves under our feet and consider
> the bottom line.

We cannot ignore the Gospel of the day, sugarcoat it, or explain it away.

But we can get a sense of both hope and thanksgiving by not running away
> from the bottom line.

In reading our terrifying times in light of the Gospel,

> we cannot fall into the temptation of some fundamentalist preachers who find all sorts of clues in it.

Jesus was not speaking about *our* times as much as his *own* time when he predicted the fall of the Temple in Jerusalem, which had not welcomed him.

In reading our terrifying times in light of the Gospel, we also do not glorify suffering as something we deserve, or need, or as part of God's will to test our strength.

God knows how strong *and* weak we are and, down in the pit of our stomachs, we know as well.

This does not mean that the Gospel of the day doesn't dovetail with our terrifying times.

It does.

As a cancer patient, for example, I was struck by the promise that "not a hair on your head will be destroyed."

It is true that when people are first diagnosed, the first two questions they ask the doctor are:

> "How long do I have to live?" and "Will I lose my hair?"

Strange, how we have ordered our lives, our priorities, our bottom line.

Yes, this Gospel, which tells a story about Jesus grappling with evil and power and destruction in his own times, certainly echoes our own.

But, once again, I think our Gospel of the day stretches us all to consider something even more important than our own sufferings and the horrors of war.

It stretches us to consider deeply and personally the bottom line of our lives:

> What is really important in my life right now?
>
> What am I struggling to achieve and am I sure it will bring me happiness?
>
> Whom or what would I be willing to shed my blood for, die for?

How can I continue to believe and trust God when the world has
gone mad?

I emphasize the words "consider deeply and personally" because, as Jesus
showed us,
religion can often become a sham, a soft cushion,
an escape from the messiness of people's lives.
Religion, like the beautiful stone temple, can fail us, defeat us, confuse us
if we do not "consider deeply and personally" what really matters
in life.

The day before Thanksgiving we will remember the terrible assassination of
President Kennedy,
who last celebrated Eucharist in this church of Holy Trinity.
His death eclipsed so much on November 22, 1963, including the death of
another famous person, the English author C. S. Lewis, who died the
same day.
In many of his writings this Oxford don focused on the problem of evil.
His was a conservative theology.
Had he preached today's homily, no doubt he would explain the problem of
evil as a result of fallen angels and that our pain leads us to a more
profound faith.
This is what C. S. Lewis taught from a purely theoretical stance in his book
The Problem of Pain.
But toward the end of his life, he wrote another book, *A Grief Observed.*
No grand theory here, simply his reflections on how he dealt with the tragic
loss of his wife, Joy.
His account of his grief and the search he endured is an elegant testimony of
a far more mature faith.
Lewis considered "deeply and personally" what really mattered in his life
and in his faith and left a classic testimony to that fact.

Of all the images and words following the attacks of 9/11, there is none
more eloquent than the testimony of ordinary people:

cops, policemen, nurses, volunteers, cooks, truck drivers,
ordinary people who taught us all the meaning of life and its
bottom line.
Jesus tells us tonight that this is what our battle with suffering and evil must
do for us:
help us to give testimony to others—
our neighbors, our children, our coworkers, our parishioners.
The Greek word for that testimony in today's Gospel is the same word
as martyr.

This Thanksgiving will be different.
People are fearful.
But let us hear loudly and clearly tonight Jesus' call for us not to be fearful
or deceived.
Let us be grateful this Thanksgiving for the living and dying testimony of so
many saints in our world.
And let us consider deeply and personally how we too can witness to our
God with the life God has given to us now.

RPW

Questions for Reflection

1. When we hear the word *judgment,* it doesn't sound like something to anticipate. But, especially in today's psalm, with its cosmic references, judgment refers to a proper ordering of life, in which life can thrive. What might this proper ordering look like?

2. Paul is expecting nothing from the Thessalonians that he himself did not model during his time among them. This can be a challenge to each of us. Is there any kind of behavior that we expect from others (spouse, children, friends) that we are not living out ourselves?

3. Jesus tells us that we can save our lives by patient endurance. How can this be?

Other Directions for Preaching

1. Fear of the Lord is the awe that we should feel when standing before God. When we live in this sense of awe, God promises us the healing rays of the sun of justice. The day of the proud and the evildoers is over. The psalm goes on to say that the rule of justice, brought by the Lord, will be cause for great celebration and joy.

2. The First Reading and the Gospel offer many signs that point to the coming of the Day of the Lord, which is that time when the Lord will come to set things right. The Day of the Lord is not a time of punishment but of purification and refinement. The Lord comes to bring salvation. If we live now in a way that transforms us, we will be ready for that day, whenever it arrives.

FEASTS

It's Raining, It's Pouring
THE SOLEMNITY OF THE MOST HOLY TRINITY

READINGS:
Proverbs 8:22–31; Romans 5:1–5; John 16:12–15

Many preachers dread the feast of the Most Holy Trinity.
Now you might react, "Dread it? Dread it? It's at the heart of our faith!"
True, but how do you talk about it?
It is daunting, the highest peak in the homiletic Himalayas!

My earliest memories of dedicated teachers trying to introduce me to this
great mystery include Sister Matthias drawing a triangle on the
blackboard.
Not too helpful.
I can remember another sister making use of the shamrock image à la
Saint Patrick.
Again, not too helpful.
Then, at some point, someone told the charming story of Saint Augustine
walking the beach, pondering this mystery, and coming upon a young
boy filling a hole he had dug in the sand with a bucket of ocean water.
When Augustine asked what he was doing, the boy said he was going to
pour the ocean into this hole.
The saint said, "Dear boy, that is impossible!"
And the boy responded, "No more impossible than you trying to
understand the Trinity."
Nice story, but it really doesn't help much either.

313

I remember in my college years reading an explanation of the mystery in a
    more logically coherent manner that went something like this:

God the Father has a thought about himself and, since the Father is God,
    that thought is a perfect thought and has fullness of being, which is
    the Son.

The Father and Son then exist in a relationship of perfect communion and
    love, and that relationship of love has fullness of being and we call it
    the Holy Spirit.

All of which leads to saying that the Son proceeds from the Father and the
    Holy Spirit proceeds from the Father and the Son—or in the Eastern
    church, it is said that the Holy Spirit proceeds from the Father through
    the Son.

This is the language of speculative theology, attempting to understand the
    Trinity from within and the relationships among Father, Son, and
    Holy Spirit.

It all does get a bit befuddling, which is why so often we end up shrugging
    and take refuge in that old comfortable believer's mantra, "It's a
    mystery."

The boy on the beach was right!

Well, true, it is a mystery, but one we are meant to ponder, not walk away
    from feeling befuddled.

This brings us to today's readings and how they can help us.

One image gives us something to meditate on.

It is the image of pouring, explicitly mentioned in the first two readings, and
    I would suggest it is being implied in the third.

When I think of pouring, I usually think of various park fountains in
    our city.

There is one in particular in Meridian Park on 16th Street here in
    Washington, DC.

It is one of the most beautiful I have ever seen,
        straight out of the gardens of an Italian palazzo in a Fellini film,
        with water pouring down level after level after level,

a luxurious pouring forth of pure, sparkling water (one hopes!) under
a clear blue sky.
Hold that in your mind for a moment.

The author of the book of Proverbs presents Wisdom speaking to us.
Wisdom is imagined as having a divine origin, as a being that existed before
all things, and is personified as a woman.
Wisdom's pedigree is set forth:
"The Lord possessed me, the beginning of his ways,
the forerunner of his prodigies of long ago."
Wisdom is presented as something belonging to God as a possession,
intimately related to the divine activities from the beginning.

Then we are given this lavish image:
"From of old, I was *poured forth,* at the first, before the earth."
"When there were no depths...
when there were no fountains or springs of water;
before the mountains were settled into place,
before the hills, I was brought forth;
while as yet the earth and fields were not made,
nor the first clods of the world."
Before all else, there is God pouring Wisdom into the abyss.
It is a breath-taking portrayal of what was first to come forth from God,
the first gift: Wisdom.

Wisdom was there when the heavens and the deep and the earth were
established and given their limits.
Wisdom was there as God's master worker, God's artist, God's darling and
delight, playing before God, and—listen to this—Wisdom concludes
by saying, "rejoicing in his inhabited world
and delighting in the human race" (Prov 8:31).
God's Wisdom took delight in humankind.
Wisdom goes on to speak to "my children,"
promising happiness to those who listen to her and keep her ways,

and promising that those who find her find life and obtain favor
from the Lord.
Let Wisdom be poured forth into our minds and hearts.

This image of pouring was heard again in the Second Reading
from Romans.
In this section of his letter, Paul reflects on what comes from having faith in
Jesus Christ.
First of all, we are at peace with God because through our faith we have
gained access to "this grace in which we stand," that is, to the favor of
God in which we now live.
This access makes us able to boast not only in the hope we have of sharing
God's glory, but we can rejoice even in our sorrows and afflictions,
sufferings and hardship.
And then Paul goes off on one of his rhetorical riffs, noting how affliction
can produce endurance, and endurance can produce character, and
character can produce hope.
And this hope does not disappoint us.
Why? (And here we come to the climax) Because the love of God has been
poured out into our hearts through the Holy Spirit that has been given
to us.
When? In baptism, of course.

You notice that all this pouring takes place at the beginning of things.
Wisdom poured out at the beginning of creation.
The Holy Spirit poured out at the new beginning that comes when we are
baptized into the saving death and resurrection of Christ.
So today we can think of the life of the Trinity as pouring over us and our
world, God pouring forth Wisdom in the person of Jesus Christ, the
Wisdom of God.
And then God, Father and Son, pouring the Holy Spirit, the bond of
communion between Father and Son, into our hearts, and drawing us
into that intimate union of love and life.

In the pouring of the water at baptism, we are immersed in the life
> of the Trinity.

In the Gospel we overhear Jesus speaking to his friends at the Last Supper.
He says that while he has much more to tell them, they can't bear to
> hear it now.
Their hearts are too heavy.
But the Holy Spirit will guide them to all truth,
> declaring all that the Father has given to Jesus.
I envision the work of the Holy Spirit not so much as pouring the truth into
> us, but as pouring us into the vast and unending truth of God as
> Father, Son, and Spirit, into the truth of the paschal mystery of Jesus
> Christ, and into the truth of the trinitarian life that was given to us
> in baptism.

When we celebrate this feast we are reminded of the great mystery that
> envelops us as a community.
We begin and end every Eucharist with the sign of the cross, made in the
> name of the Father, and of the Son, and of the Holy Spirit.
Let us do this with great care and with a renewed consciousness of what it
> means for us.
We are never alone, for we dwell in communion with this most Holy
> Trinity, which draws us into its life even now and gifts us with the
> promise of eternal life.
So, today let us join together singing the words of that wonderful old hymn:
> Praise God from whom all blessings flow,
> Praise God all creatures here below,
> Praise God above, ye heavenly host.
> Praise Father, Son, and Holy Ghost.
> Amen.

JAW

Questions for Reflection

1. How does the image of pouring draw you into the mystery of the Holy Trinity?

2. Can you think of times when you have felt the love of God being poured into your heart? Where did that lead?

3. Jesus promises that the Spirit of truth will guide us into the truth. Do you believe this? Do you pray for this?

Other Directions for Preaching

1. Consider the relevance of thinking about the artistry and craft of God's wisdom at work in creation and in the works of artists. How does the experience of beauty lead into the experience of the Triune God: Father, Word, Spirit?

2. Getting access to important people is very difficult in our day, yet we are told that we have access to God through Jesus Christ. What difference does that make?

3. The truth is a treasured and often rare commodity. The Holy Spirit guiding us to the truth is an ongoing reality, not a once-and-for-all accomplishment.

The Sign of the Kingdom
The Solemnity of the Most Holy Body and Blood of Christ

READINGS:
Genesis 14:18–20; 1 Corinthians 11:23–26;
Luke 9:11b–17

I have a friend named Denise who is a director of the child-welfare agency
in Chicago.
She spends countless hours taking care of problems too gruesome to
think about.
When she comes home, Denise, Jim, and her family always have room for
one more guest.

All of us probably know at least one story of a family who always has a
place at the dinner table for the unexpected person.
Young Willie has brought a friend home for something to eat after
the game.
Or Marilyn saw a neighbor at the grocery store whose husband has been
abusive and she needs a place to stay for a while.
Or Nick has a friend over who has not been eating because he recently lost
his wife.
I have to say that other people's generosity often makes me blush with
shame at my own failures in that department.

Setting the table for the guest, the poor, and the outcast is the call of
Christian mission, and reminds us of why we celebrate the feast of
Corpus Christi in the first place.

We are here because of an act of divine love and self-giving.

God has set the table for us and we are to do the same in loving service for
one another.

As it says in the alternative Opening Prayer for today's Eucharist,
"May we offer to our Father in heaven a solemn pledge of undivided
love. May we offer to our brothers and sisters a life poured out in
loving service of that kingdom where you live with the Father and the
Holy Spirit, one God, for ever and ever."

It is all about the table he set for us, isn't it?

And the bread and the wine that will be broken and poured out for the
People of God.

We are still consuming it and will do so until the end because he handed
himself over.

The Body of Christ has been distributed in love by the one who prepared
himself as the perfect meal.

There is always a place at his table for us at the hands of a merciful God.

Christ gave us his Body and Blood as the most complete act of service in
human history.

It was table service in which he would use an apron to serve us and even
surrender that little garment, at the last, to be crucified—naked on the
cross—for our redemption.

It was a handing over from sin to forgiveness.

It was a passover from death to life.

It was a deliverance from slavery into freedom.

Divine hospitality knows no limits but comes forth from an endless table.

The feeding story in Luke's Gospel clearly reflects the early church's
experience of the Eucharist, in which God's generosity pours forth in a
largess we can only imagine.

Not only did they all eat and were satisfied, but there were enough
  fragments to fill twelve wicker baskets—in other words, bread for the
  entire world.

Catherine of Siena has a marvelous meditation on divine hospitality in her
  mystical writings called *The Dialogue*.
Catherine writes of the Father who says that
  "the Holy Spirit, my loving charity, is the waiter who serves them my
  gifts and graces. This gentle waiter carries to me their tender loving
  desires, and carries back to them the reward for their labors, the
  sweetness of my charity for their enjoyment and nourishment. So you
  see, I am their table, my Son is their food, and the Holy Spirit, who
  proceeds from me the Father and from the Son, waits on them."*

It is all about the table he set for us and the one we make for one another.
The multiplication of the loaves in Luke's Gospel is the early church's
  reflection on the Eucharist event.
The feeding of the crowds is a sign of the kingdom of God that had come
  among them: Jesus was in their midst.
But our Lord was clearly charging the apostles to do the same with one of
  his most challenging commands in all of Luke's Gospel.
  "Give them some food yourselves."
He gave us something to eat, and now we must do the same for one
  another.

Paul describes the Eucharist as something that would be passed over from
  one group to the next, and which he himself gratefully inherited.
  "I received from the Lord what I also handed on to you," he tells the
  Corinthians.
We pass on the story of the One who set the table for his church.
  "This is my body that is for you. Do this in remembrance of me."

---

* Catherine of Siena, *The Dialogue*, in *Light from Light: An Anthology of Christian
Mysticism*, ed. Louis Dupré and James A. Wiseman, OSB (Mahwah, NJ: Paulist Press,
2001), 273.

The sign of the kingdom of God endures because the King himself broke his
body for us.

The feast of Corpus Christi never fails to remind us that the Lord Jesus has
come among us, has died, and has risen.

In a few moments we will proclaim just that, as once again God feeds us
with the Body and Blood of the Lord.

Let us also remember that the table that was set for us is meant to show us
the space we leave for another when we leave this church.

How do we feed one another after we have fed upon the Lamb of God?

We are called to become signs of change, transformed by the kingdom of
God, which has come upon us unexpectedly.

That reign of God is not ours to bring but has been already disclosed to us
in poverty:

simple bread and wine, the hidden God made manifest in our midst.

Let us proclaim the mystery of our faith when we eat this bread and drink
this cup to all those we encounter throughout our lives.

Let's set the table for them and give them something to eat.

GD

Questions for Reflection

1. How have I welcomed someone at my table in the last year or so? Am I stingy with the gifts God has provided for me?

2. Do I promote an atmosphere of thanksgiving and praise at the dinner table with my family? If not, why?

3. Do I share my experience of Christ in the Eucharist with others? Could I do more?

Other Directions for Preaching

1. We adore the real presence of the Body of Christ in bread and wine in this church and then show that love to the same Body when we respect one another after we leave Mass.

2. True poverty and humility recognize that God provides our very substance each and every day.

3. The Eucharist is the only meal in which we are changed into the food we consume—the Body of Christ.

God Does the Heavy Lifting
THE ASSUMPTION OF THE BLESSED VIRGIN MARY

READINGS:
Revelation 11:9a, 12:1–6a, 10ab; 1 Corinthians 15:20–27;
Luke 1:39–56

There is a phrase we hear again and again at every Mass:
> "Lift up your hearts," the presider says, as we begin the
> Eucharistic Prayer.

And the people respond,
> "We lift them up to the Lord."

It is a phrase that can become so routine that we stop hearing it or thinking
about what it means.

We all have days when it is not easy to lift up our hearts,
> times of sorrow, sadness, or depression.

When we think back over the past year, there have been many days when it
has been difficult to lift up our heads, much less our hearts.
The grief flowing from the terrorist attacks, the sorrow of child abuse in the
church, the disappointment many feel with our leaders, both civil
and church.
Then there are the losses that affect us personally, loss of loved ones in death,
loss of friends for one reason or another or no good reason at all.
Yet whenever we come here for Mass, we are called to lift up our hearts.
This feast tells us we have good reason to do so.

I remember a painting of the assumption I first saw as a child.

I think it was by an artist named Murillo.

Mary was being giving an angelic airlift by a number of angels,
  curly-headed faces carrying their precious cargo skyward.

The feast today proclaims that Mary was taken up body and soul into
  heaven to be with her Son, Jesus.

It is an ancient Marian feast, one of the first to be celebrated, going back to
  the church in Jerusalem.

While the Western church called it the assumption, the Eastern church
  called it the dormition, that is, the "falling asleep," of Mary.

There is a tender icon that pictures Mary on her deathbed, surrounded by
  the apostles.

Over her stands the risen Christ, holding in his hands a tiny depiction of her
  soul as a newborn, just as she once held the newborn Jesus in her arms.

This feast was always understood as closely connected to her being the
  mother of the Lord.

As she brought him into the world, giving him flesh and a human nature, so
  he brings her into eternal life and glory.

As he was raised from the dead, she also was raised, due to her special role
  in our salvation as the mother of the Son of God.

And so we gather on this day to remember the end of her earthly life, as
  blessed as the beginning when she was conceived in grace.

We come here to greet her and join with her cousin Elizabeth in saying:
  "Blessed are you among women, and blessed is the fruit of your
  womb....Blessed are you who believed that what was spoken to you
  by the Lord would be fulfilled."

But in remembering her, we look beyond her to the power of God at work
  for us all.

The readings today speak of the God who lifts up.

We have the image of the woman of Revelation, the woman who gives birth
  to the Messiah.

That woman has been understood in a number of ways:
  the heavenly Jerusalem giving birth to a new people,
  the church giving birth to the Messiah,
  Mary giving birth to Jesus.
All are true.
But at the heart of this reading is the threat to the child: the devouring
  dragon.
And it is God who *snatches* the child *up* to heaven,
  God who saves, who lifts up the child,
  God who does the heavy lifting of salvation.

This is the God we hear praised in the Magnificat.
  "My soul proclaims the greatness of the Lord; my spirit rejoices in
  God my Savior for he has looked upon his lowly servant....He has
  shown the strength of his arm....He has cast down the mighty...and
  has *lifted up* the lowly."
It is this God who has raised up Jesus Christ from the dead, as Paul
  proclaims,
  "the firstfruits of those who have fallen asleep."
The feast of the Assumption calls us to look to the God who lifts up,
  who has lifted us up to the new life of baptism and will raise us on
  the last day,
  as God has already lifted up Mary into the glory of eternal life.

Today's feast can be mistaken as separating Mary from us, increasing the
  distance, both spatially—if we think of Mary as going up, up and
  away—and emotionally—if we think of her as far removed from our
  worries and concerns.
To allow this to happen is to miss the point of the feast.
The preface for this Mass reminds us:
  "Mary was taken up into heaven to be the beginning and the pattern
  of the church in its perfection, and a sign of hope and comfort for
  your people on their pilgrim way."
What was done for her will be done for us.

At the moment of our baptism God came into the depths of our heart and
claimed us as children of the kingdom.

And at the moment of our death God will lift us into the embrace of divine
love, where we shall sleep until the resurrection on the last day.

We see in Mary on this feast our own future.

In the meantime we live in the hope we have because of Jesus, who was
raised and is the firstfruits of those who have fallen asleep.

We live despite the many faces of death that threaten our peace and
well-being.

We can look into the darkness of the tomb and never fear the terrors of
the night.

For we are always listening for the sound of those voices that continue to
speak to us in our dark nights as they spoke to those women at the
end of another dark night:

"He is not here; he has been raised."

We approach the table of the Lord, where we join with Mary and all angels
and saints, praising God as we lift up our hearts and say:

Holy, holy, holy, Lord God of hosts.

Blessed is he who comes in the name of the Lord.

Hosanna in the highest!

JAW

Questions for Reflection

1. How do you think about death? As something to be feared? As something that has been conquered? As a bridge? As Sister Death?

2. How do you presently need to be lifted up by God's grace?

3. Do I see this feast in the light of Jesus Christ, the risen Lord, the promise of eternal life for all who remain faithful?

Other Directions for Preaching

1. In a culture so obsessed with the body and yet so abusive of it, this feast speaks of the holiness of the body and God's pledge to raise us in Christ.

2. The image of God's protective hand can be found in the First Reading, protecting the woman, who stands for all humanity. Like her, we continue our sojourn in the desert.

3. The Magnificat, Mary's hymn of praise, reminds us of God's care and concern for the lowly, an agenda that is to be taken up and lived out now by the church as the people of God's promise sent to care for the poor.

In the Gutter Gazing at the Stars
THE SOLEMNITY OF ALL SAINTS

READINGS:
Revelation 7:2–4, 9–14; 1 John 3:1–3; Matthew 5:1–12a

If I were pope, on the first Sunday of Advent of my pontificate I would
   abolish forever the bureaucracy of the canonization of saints.
It is fitting on All Saints to explain why.

A simple head count would tell us that the process of canonization simply
   does not work; it is hardly representative of Jesus' recognition of the
   holiness of all types of people.
In the first eight decades of the twentieth century, for example, canonized
   saints numbered 75 percent men to 25 percent women.
Least represented among the canonized saints are married women.
This reflects the dualistic assessment that to be female is a handicap, and to
   be a sexually active woman renders one almost incapable of
   embodying the sacred.
The liturgical calendar perpetuates this bias;
   three-fourths of the annual feast days honor men and one-fourth
   honor women.

I agree with Elizabeth Johnson and other feminist authors that this disparity
   represents patriarchy at its worst, but I also believe that it represents
   an essential flaw in the determination of who is holy.*

---

*Elizabeth A. Johnson, *Friend of God and Prophets: A Feminist Theological
Reading of the Communion of Saints* (New York: Continuum, 1998), 27–29.

The pure that we hear mentioned in John's letter can be misunderstood to
    mean someone who never got angry, never was tempted, never sinned.
But that is not what pure means in the context of John's letter.
Pure is to enter into the same commitment of spirit that Jesus entered into
    so that we, mortal, sinful, with warts and all, are divinized by Christ.

Being a saint does not strip us of our gutsy, earthy, emotional life blood.
We stand with the great doctor of the church, Saint Teresa of Avila, who
    could often be quite infelicitous in her remarks.
She said once to the cardinals of the church in her time:
    "You are not sweet-smelling flowers but corruptions which cause the
    whole world to stink."

Jesus saw the crowds but he saw more than crowds.
He saw blessedness, holiness, saints in his midst.
And who where they?
Not "pure" people, at least not "pure" to other people.
He saw shepherds, fishermen, tax collectors, prostitutes, the sick, the
    maimed, the blind, the lepers, and the possessed.
These were people who would never get on the list for canonization.
Bad enough that they had terrible reputations,
    but they also suffered the humiliating religious belief that their
    suffering could be God's punishment for sin.
Jesus stripped away every last vestige of a religious faith that is permeated
    by fear, ignorance, and a sense of distance from the sacred by one
    word, one word;
    he called them blessed, *santos,* holy, all saints!

Try to imagine this:
It is toward the end of World War II.
You are a priest hearing confessions.
Into the confessional comes a man named Oscar Schindler, a German
    industrialist who during the war made a fortune on Jewish slave labor
    in Poland.

By all conventional standards, he was not a good man, not blessed, not one
    of the *santos,* holy, saints.
And so he confesses to you:
    "I really don't know when my last confession was.
    It was a long, long time ago.
    During that time, I drank too much, gambled too much, was arrogant
    in the way I lived.
    I slept with many women other than my wife.
    The only think I did good was that I managed to trick the Nazis and
    thus saved thousands of Jews from going to the gas chamber."
If you heard Herr Schindler's confession, what would you say to him?
What penance would you give?
And let's push the envelope:
    would he be ever worthy of canonization for his heroic acts?
Your answer depends upon your perspective of holiness and on the whole
    meaning of the Gospel.

Holiness, our mortal attempt to enter into the life of Christ, is lived out in
    our human weakness.
If we are blinded by patriarchal structures, we will not find the saints.
If we are insistent on using terms like *intrinsically evil* to describe our gay
    and lesbian brothers and sisters we will not appreciate their holiness.
If we don't believe in the ability for people to change we will never
    appreciate what Oscar Wilde once said,
      "We are all in the gutter, but some of us are looking at the stars."
Let us give thanks to God not just for the saints, but for *all* the saints!

RPW

Questions for Reflection

1. As God's children, do we feel a deep need from the core of our beings to give worship to God with the angels, the elders, and the saints of the book of Revelation?

2. The Beatitudes make connections between a way of being and the consequences connected to that way of being. Do we truly desire these consequences today?

3. Being holy seems like a very old-fashioned notion. How do we recognize holiness in others in our place and time?

Other Directions for Preaching

1. The Beatitudes come from a literary form found in the Jewish Wisdom tradition, not from a legal tradition. Explore how this origin of the Beatitudes might influence the way that we hear and appropriate them into our lives. Does it make a difference to see them as part of a long tradition of how to live wisely in order to be happy, as opposed to seeing them as laws or requirements laid down by Christ?

2. There are always natural and human-made disasters occurring around the world. As specifically as possible, address these crises in terms of the call of the Beatitudes. If we see ourselves as part of the Communion of Saints, we can do no less.

The Lady of the Harbor
THE IMMACULATE CONCEPTION

READINGS:
Genesis 3:9–15, 20; Ephesians 1:3–6, 11–12;
Luke 1:26–38

America has often envisioned itself as a capacious land,
    ripe with opportunity.
Captains of industry in the nineteenth century turned a frontier into iron-
    fisted railroads forging their way across the great plains and giant
    skyscrapers poking through the clouds.
The United States has also become the refuge for so many people of diverse
    origins and nationalities.
Where else on earth could claim such a mosaic of people?
Diversity, freedom, optimism.
Yet it must be said that this place of opportunity, this land of a vast array of
    colors and religion, has been bloody with prejudice and violence and
    racism as well.
Our nation has an ugly side.

Original sin is a citizen of every country, without exception.
There is no utopia on this planet, not even a democratic one.
Far from a melting pot, class systems and segregation still regularly rule the
    way many of us do business.
Sadly, the current immigration laws and their severe restrictions make
    hypocrites out of "the land of the free and the home of the brave."

Undoubtedly, many of our grandparents would have been refused a
   welcome from the Lady of the Harbor and her bright torch of
   welcome during these days of suspicion, surveillance, and mistrust.

We know our real refuge lies on far distant shores.
Thanks be to God that we have another Lady that never fails to welcome
   all who come under her protection, regardless of race, color, or
   nationality.
Countries and even poets who dream about nation-states and endless
   possibility will always be blinded by arrogance, ambition, and
   self-interest.
Only God is completely good and can provide a refuge for God's folk.
Only God could keep one free—immaculately so—from original sin.
And only she who was free from sin was capable of bearing the enormity of
   the infinite Word within her womb.
In her greatness, she took in multitudes:
      the New Eve who became the mother not of the living,
      but of the newly born and those baptized in her Son's name.

There is a good reason why we honor Mary as the patroness of the Americas.
Thousands of churches in this country have been dedicated to Mary, a sure
   sign of a people's devotion to the one who stands alone among all
   Christian disciples.
The Shrine of the Basilica of the Immaculate Conception in Washington,
   DC, is nothing less than gargantuan.
You can see the dome and spire from miles around.
Countless men and women from every walk of life file through the doors of
   the basilica each day.
To celebrate the eucharistic liturgy at the Shrine of the Immaculate
   Conception is to encounter what it means to be catholic—universal,
   global, endlessly diverse.

One morning, a tour group of Cherokee Indians from an Oklahoma high
   school spontaneously offered a chant in their native tongue,

while a group of Vietnamese pilgrims made their way through the
    various individual chapels scattered throughout the basilica.
A sense of extraordinary diversity inhabits the shrine.
Like the patron for whom it is named, the shrine refuses no one,
    an ongoing witness that there are no boundaries in God's house.
On the sides of the great upper church and in the crypt, there are numerous
    representations of Mary:
Our Lady of Guadalupe, Our Lady of Perpetual Help, Our Lady of China,
    and more.
All of these are encompassed by the Immaculate Conception itself,
    God's first loving and bountiful gift to the church.
It is a promise that would come full circle:
    the Spirit that came upon Mary at the annunciation of that good
    news would be the same Spirit that would encounter her at the
    Pentecost event.
She is twice mother:
    in Nazareth, mother of God
    and in the upper room at Pentecost she would again become mother—
    the mother of multitudes.
Mary was full of grace because God willed her to be mother of God and
    mother of the church.
As it says in the alternative Opening Prayer for today's feast,
    "Father, the image of the Virgin is found in the church."

This Advent season is a time to remember just how much our waiting for
    the coming of the Lord rests in the company of the mother of God.
We are all of us refugees within her safe borders,
    longing for the Word to come and save us.
No matter what our political affiliation or national sentiment,
    native citizen or immigrant, we must admit that any will to power
    must meet the same fate as Adam and Eve.
Humility and faith, not pride and aggression, are the marks of the true
    disciple, leaving footprints on the Promised Land and peace.
Until we get there, we put no trust in princes or politicians or spin doctors.

Language, even in Eden, is deceptive.

Rather, with the Psalmist, we say,

"Sing to the LORD a new song,

for he has done wondrous deeds" (98:1).

That wondrous, immaculate canticle of freedom began with Mary and continues in the church, which nurtures the baptized, those newly wrought, yes, unmistakably brought into salvation's bountiful oasis in Christ.

So it was done and accomplished by God in the work of Jesus, from the beginning of the ages until they are brought to an end.

And when that last day comes, the multitude will be there because of the woman who made true salvation possible by her faith, a shining Magnificat, lighting up the night harbor, through the God who still wills us into life even now.

GD

Questions for Reflection

1. Do I have Mary's courage to cooperate with God?

2. Original sin is manifested in our world in many ways. What are some of them?

3. What does the angel's message to Mary tell us about God?

Other Directions for Preaching

1. Far from being passive, Mary's cooperation with God was a deliberate choice, making her a woman who broke with social norms for the sake of the divine plan for redemption.

2. A human being was free from original sin and so broke the cycle of evil for us all.

3. We have been chosen by God from the beginning to share not in evil but in grace.

Christic Alone Is King
THE SOLEMNITY OF OUR LORD
JESUS CHRIST THE KING

READINGS:
2 Samuel 5:1–3; Colossians 1:12–20; Luke 23:35–43

Every November I ask my students in preaching class where this Solemnity
of Our Lord Jesus Christ the King comes from.
What are its origins? When was it first celebrated?
So far, not one student has given me a correct answer.
Curiously, most of them think that Christ the King originated in the
Middle Ages.
I tell them they would not do well on Liturgical Jeopardy!

No, Christ the King Sunday is not an ancient liturgical relic from the
Middle Ages; it is of our own times.
It is only about seventy-five years old.
That's a drop in the bucket of time in the tradition of a two-thousand-year-
old church.
Because it is a relatively new celebration in the church, it celebrates modern
concerns and questions that are still very much relevant to us today.

In 1925 Pope Pius XI understood that the old royal kingdoms of the world
were crumbling.
Instead of kings and queens dominating the world's quest for power,
there were new forces marshaling in Europe, like Nazism, socialism,
and communism.

Pius XI feared that these new "isms" could become a new terrifying royalty that could ravage peoples' freedom as sons and daughters of God.

The pope wanted to challenge these new emerging kingdoms.

He wanted to remind people that ultimate loyalty was due to the true throne in heaven.

And so he proclaimed the feast of the Solemnity of Our Lord Jesus Christ the King.

When the liturgists chose the Scripture readings for this new celebration they didn't have any difficulty finding passages from the Bible with royal themes.

When the Psalmist asked in Psalm 24,

"Who is this king of glory?"

the answer came,

"The LORD of hosts; he is the king of glory" (24:10).

Over and over again, ancient Israel was reminded by the prophets of this same lesson:

God alone was king of Israel;

God alone was to be feared, loved, and above all else was to be obeyed over anyone else.

But just like some people today, the people of Israel went "gaga" when they heard of the kings and queens of other nations.

They decided that they, too, wanted a king of flesh and blood like other nations.

They got their wish with their first king, Saul, but Samuel warned the people that there would be hell to pay because they would always be tempted to obey their king rather than the King of glory.

Today's First Reading is about Saul's successor, King David.

He was young and handsome and daring.

He captured Jerusalem as the royal city.

He who once shepherded sheep now shepherded—that is, protected—the people of Israel.

David was not a king with a stiff upper lip.

He was wild and crazy enough to strip down to his boxers and dance before
the Ark of the Covenant.

The people loved him.

But Solomon was right.

Kings and queens can be dangerous.

David was a marvelous king who restored God's people.

But he had feet of clay like the rest of us.

He was vain, deceitful, crooked, and lustful.

King David drank too much and had affairs with married women.

If he lived today, he would rival the antics of the British royal family and,
no doubt, appear on the cover of *People* magazine.

One thousand years later, when Jesus, the one who called himself the Good
Shepherd, rode into Jerusalem on a mule,
they greeted him as royalty by waving palms and crying out hosannas
and called him the Son of David.

They did so, not because Jesus reminded them of King David's sins,
but because of King David's covenant with the people.

Like David, Jesus was a shepherd king until the end.

That is what today's Gospel from Luke tells us about Christ the King.

He is the king who, even in the midst of humiliation, mockery,
abandonment, and the grisly dying of crucifixion with criminals, still
holds on to God's will.

Throughout his life Jesus resists every temptation to play up to the crowds,
to curry political favor, to get in good with the in groups.

Instead, he embraces God's will and remembers his covenant to be shepherd
even to those who reject him,
and especially to the sinner who is not only close to his cross
but close to his kingdom.

In the history of the bloody twentieth century we saw from time to time the
 practical relevancy of proclaiming Christ as our king.
In the mist of the madness of Hitler's holocaust, some German bishops
 declared that Christ alone is our king.
In the midst of the sinfulness of apartheid in South Africa, many religious
 leaders proclaimed that Christ alone is our king.
When the Soviet Union was trying to hold on to its domination of Eastern
 Europe, the shipyard workers in Gdansk grew in solidarity because
 they believed that Christ alone is our king.

We surrender our souls whenever we fail to speak to our rulers,
 whether senators and representatives or schoolboard members,
 parents or teachers,
 bosses or bishops or pastors.
We surrender our souls whenever we remain silent when those who rule
 over us forget they are not God.

Whether we declare it boldly and explicitly
 or whether we simply silently refuse to let others strip us and our
 world of our humanity,
 it is a great inheritance that Christ the King has left us:
 the power to bow to no person, no possession, no addiction,
 no demon.
Christ alone is king!

RPW

Questions for Reflection

1. The images of David as shepherd of the people and commander of the nation seem almost contradictory. Is this what God expects of those who govern?

2. What could be some of the ecological implications of Christ reconciling all of creation with God?

3. Jesus is crucified because he is seen as a threat to the religious authority of his time. As followers of Christ, are there times when we need to challenge the authorities of our time?

Other Directions for Preaching

1. What is it that drives us to abdicate our personal authority to others? We can then complain and criticize and, at the end of the day, sigh, "Well, what can I do about it? I'm only one person." Are we morally responsible for the actions of our nation? Of our church?

2. The use of power as God intends is at the heart of today's feast. We sometimes hear that power is never given; it can only be taken. The readings today make clear that the power given by God is to be used in service to others. This is not a triumphal feast, but one that celebrates the power of the crucified Christ to save all of humankind.